THOMAS JEFFERSON
AMONG THE ARTS

Fig. No. 1.

LIFE MASK OF THOMAS JEFFERSON, by *John H. I. Browere*

Courtesy of the Gallery of the New York State Historical Association,
Cooperstown, New York

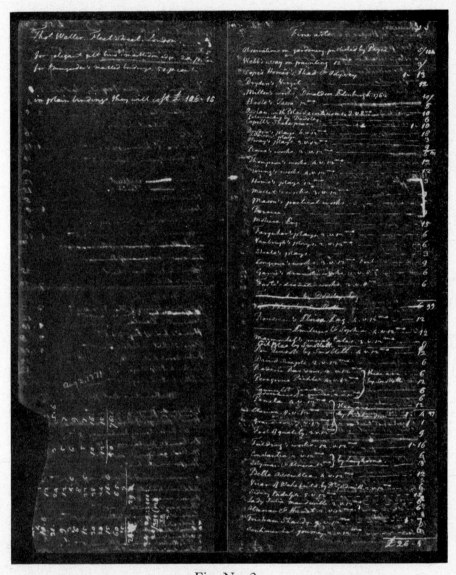

Fig. No. 2.
BOOKLIST RECOMMENDED FOR ROBERT SKIPWITH'S LIBRARY BY JEFFERSON
DATED AUGUST 3, 1771 (2 PAGES) IN HIS OWN HANDWRITING

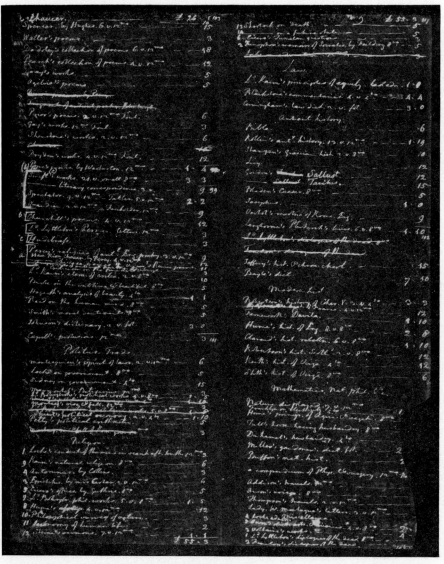

Fig. No. 2.

BOOKLIST RECOMMENDED FOR ROBERT SKIPWITH'S LIBRARY BY JEFFERSON
DATED AUGUST 3, 1771 (2 PAGES) IN HIS OWN HANDWRITING

OUTACITE,
Chief of the CHEROKEES

Fig. No. 3.

OUTACITE (ONTASSETÉ) CHIEF OF THE CHEROKEES, FOR WHOSE
ELOQUENCE AS AN ORATOR JEFFERSON HELD A LIFE-LONG ADMIRATION
From "Indians of North America" by Samuel G. Drake (1841).

THOMAS JEFFERSON AMONG THE ARTS

An Essay in Early American Esthetics

BY

ELEANOR DAVIDSON BERMAN, D.S.SC.

PHILOSOPHICAL LIBRARY

New York

To
DAVID AND PHILIP

CONTENTS

THOMAS JEFFERSON
AMONG THE ARTS

ILLUSTRATIONS

PREFACE

IT IS NOW more than two hundred years since Jefferson was born and one hundred and twenty-five years since he died. There has perhaps never been a time since his death when his life and career have received so much attention. It is true that the attention has largely centered around the celebrations of the two-hundredth anniversary of his birth, but the literary and scholarly undertakings that stem from it will go on for a generation.

My own study of Jefferson has developed as an aspect of my interest in the career of art in the United States. It became specific and directed when I decided that the thesis that I would prepare in partial fulfillment for the doctor's degree in the Graduate Faculty of Political and Social Science in the New School for Social Research would concern itself with Jefferson's relations to that career. In pursuing this study I have found it necessary, of course, not only to read through all the available writings of Jefferson, but I have also had to go into those eighteenth-century works, and others of earlier times, to which Jefferson makes reference. In addition I have consulted early and contemporary works on Jefferson. Out of these readings I have drawn the material on which the present essay is based. They have shown me that Jefferson's interest in many of the arts was as concrete, as intense and as precise as his interest in government; that in certain fields, especially architecture, he gave American taste and thought a new direction; that nevertheless his thinking rather digested and applied the esthetic teachings of writers such as Lord Kames, Edmund Burke and William Hogarth, and of architects such as Palladio.

In developing this study I have had of course the unfailing help and guidance of my teachers at the New School; and I am indebted for many helpful suggestions to Messrs. Gilbert Chinard, E. G. Swem, H. M. Sheffer, Archibald Shepperson, Leo Michelson, Mrs. Camilla Kenyon and Miss Belle da Costa Greene. I am especially indebted to Mr. Joseph Machlis for help with the manuscript. To all of them my deep thanks and appreciation.

Grateful acknowledgments are due also to Hannah and Roland Blenner-Hassett, Jean Rudd Bogaert, Richard Hickman, Addie Liveright, Babs Liveright, Dorothy Davidson Miller; to Mr. James L. Coger, Curator, Colonial Williamsburg, Inc.; to Miss Mary E. McWilliams, Assistant to the Director, Department of Research, Colonial Williamsburg, Inc.; Institut Français of Washington, D.C.; the New York Public Library; to Mr. Francis L. Berkeley, Jr., Curator of Manuscripts, Division of Rare Books and Manuscripts, Alderman Library, University of Virginia; to Miss Alice Lee Parker, Assistant Chief, Prints and Photographs Division, Library of Congress, Washington, D.C.; the Yale University Art Gallery at New Haven, Connecticut; to Dr. Bernard Mayo of the University of Virginia; to Mr. Stuart Mitchell of the Massachusetts Historical Society, Boston, Massachusetts, for permission to use photographs of original material in the archives of the Society; to Esther and Milton Lipson and to Janet R. McFarlane, Curator of the New York State Historical Association, Cooperstown, New

York, for suggestions and assistance with photographic material. I am indebted also to Mr. Samuel Herbert McVitty of Ridgewood Farm, Salem, Virginia, for permission to reproduce Jefferson's plans for the serpentine walls; to Mr. A. A. Ostrander for permission to reproduce Hogarth's serpentine line and to the New York Historical Society for making available to me their collections of books and pictures.

For permission to use quotations contained in this essay my thanks and appreciation go to Mr. Talbot Hamlin, author of *Greek Revival Architecture in America,* and the Oxford University Press; to Mr. I. T. Frary, author of *Thomas Jefferson—Architect and Builder* and *They Built the Capitol;* to Random House, Inc., publishers of *The Life and Selected Writings of Thomas Jefferson;* to Mr. Henry L. Mencken, author of *The American Language, Fourth Edition* and *The American Language, Supplement One,* published by Alfred A. Knopf, Inc.; to Mr. Fiske Kimball, author of *Thomas Jefferson, Architect* and "Jefferson and the Arts"; to Dr. Edwin E. Betts, editor of *Thomas Jefferson's Garden Book;* to Dr. Saul K. Padover, editor of *The Complete Jefferson,* published by Duell, Sloan and Pearce; and to Dr. Gilbert Chinard, author of the *Literary Bible of Thomas Jefferson* (The Johns Hopkins Press), and *Thomas Jefferson, The Apostle of Americanism* (Little Brown & Company).

ELEANOR DAVIDSON BERMAN

INTRODUCTION

"THAT JEFFERSON had no philosophy of art," Dr. Berman sums up her essay, "any more than he had a philosophy, in the professional sense, goes without saying. His writings do not contain a body of knowledge about art organized into a clearly constructed, formal system. His esthetic ideas express in effect a constellation of attitudes which are communicated via hundreds of observations occurring in all sorts of other connections throughout his voluminous writings. And these are heterogeneous. Their formal inconsistencies cannot be counted as they change from one decade to the next in the context of the experiences of that long and active life. Yet they give one the feeling of a certain vital unity, of a continuity. Yet they are condensable into certain principles which may be considered fundamental to their author's personality. To Jefferson art was an integral part of life. He looked upon life's daily round with the eye of a humanist and an empiricist. He believed in reason, in utility, in the reality and significance of matter, in a deistic God who set this matter to his laws, and in a human liberty ordained according to these laws, which are 'the laws of nature and of nature's God'."

Dr. Berman comes to her conclusions after assembling, classifying and collating in a series of somewhat unevenly styled chapters, each of which can stand by itself, all of Jefferson's available observations on painting, sculpture, architecture, gardening, music, oratory, rhetoric and poetry, fiction and letter-writing. There have been many studies of

Jefferson the architect. Long ago, there was a study of his versifyings. The bicentenary of his birth, which occurred in April 1943, evoked, together with diverse biographies, special essays such as that by Mr. Fiske Kimball, on Jefferson's predilections in painting and sculpture, and led to the undertaking of studies by others of Jefferson's musical interests, of his prose-style, and of his literary preferences. Even his predilections in drink and diet have been brought to public attention by Marie Kimball's assemblage of the Jeffersonian cookbook. But never heretofore has there been any attempt to bring together and collate our third president's remarks on each of the arts, to view them in their relation to each other, and to interpret them in the light of what Jefferson has had to say about the sense of beauty or other esthetic categories, such as the sublime; or about the role of fine art in the life and labors of a people. So far as I know, Dr. Berman's essay is the first undertaking of this kind.

The data she has gathered are drawn almost exclusively from Jefferson's letters. They are remarks *ad hoc,* made to specific persons, in response to specific occasions, under specific circumstances. That she should have been able to find them expressing a certain coherence and continuity of outlook and of attitude need be no more surprising than that they involve inconsistencies. For they are remarks made during a long and arduous life, often quite incidental to the writer's dominant interest at the time of writing. The ideas expressed cannot fail to vary with their occasions, nor yet to provide still another utterance of the writer's basic fighting faith. They show this writer—the author of the Declaration of Independence, of the Virginia Statute of Religious Liberty and the founder of the University of Virginia—to have been a practitioner of at least four skills acknowledged by his time to be arts. These were, in the order of Jefferson's conception of their importance, architecture, gardening, oratory, music. Dr. Berman adds letter-writing, since Jefferson was one of the most voluminous and self-conscious of letter writers. In addition, her data show him, on three occasions when he felt a familial matter very deeply, to have resorted to rhymed verse. They show him, incidentally, however, to have been one of the earliest, if not the earliest of Americans to concern himself with the relation of the art of housing to health; and with the layout of a city to the hazards of fire and other dangers. They show him, also incidentally, to be among the first to urge the advantages—at least the esthetic advantages of the gardener's art—of contour ploughing, as we call it today. They show him believing that, as we have an inborn moral sense, so we have also an inborn sense of beauty; yet making the measure of each and all of the arts their consequence to the freedom and happiness of mankind.

That is, in Dr. Berman's view, Jefferson esteems the arts less for what they are than for what they do. To him, hence, painting and sculpture are of secondary interest; they are valuable rather for their memorial and symbolic functions than for their intrinsic qualities. So, also, are the works of the poets and the novelists. In themselves, largely diversions for the idle or amusements for the rich, there accrues to them, when they "contribute to fix in the principles and practices of virtue" a utility such as would make Shakespeare's *King Lear* morally far more consequential than Jehovah's fourth commandment. Jefferson, Dr. Berman indicates, would judge the form of any communication first and last by its efficacy. As language must be viable, and appraised, not according to grammatical rule but according to functional role, so might every art be. She argues that Jefferson's preferences among the authors of classical antiquity, as among those of his own time, exemplify this precept.

In the general philosophy which Jefferson's taste and judgment expressed, Dr. Berman finds nothing new. She envisages him as a figure of the late eighteenth century transition from neo-classicism to romanticism, with the propensities of both in his esthetic disposition. She thinks that he derived such esthetic doctrines as he consciously held from Kames, Burke and Hogarth, and she follows Gilbert Chinard in stressing the very large influence of Kames on Jefferson's basic philosophy. She presents many parallels between observations by Jefferson and statements in Kames's *Elements of Criticism.* Nevertheless, she finds that what Jefferson had drawn from his readings—not only in Kames but in the ancients—is so compenetrated with the moods and methods of his native scene, that there is something identifiably American in his sentiment regarding the arts. Jefferson's role in this branch of the human enterprise, as in the political, economic and religious branches, was, certainly with respect to his own country, seminal and redirective. "With the vision of an artist and the faith of a lover of people, he saw freedom as first step toward happiness—and art as one of the first steps toward freedom."

Dr. Berman's essay makes a positive, an exciting addition to what we know and can understand about the mind and character of one of the greatest, if not the greatest, of the nation's Founding Fathers.

H. M. KALLEN

THOMAS JEFFERSON AND THE ARTS

GRADUALLY the judgment of history is reshaping itself to give Thomas Jefferson his due: a century and a quarter after the close of his life he stands revealed as one of the most spacious figures America has produced. The breadth and power of his intellect stamp him a key figure of the Age of Reason. His unwavering faith in people and in the illimitable potentialities of man makes him apostle of the type of democracy that bears his name. While the diversity of his interests—the Marquis de Chastellux, visiting at Monticello in 1782, described his host as "an American who, without having left his own country, is at once a musician, a draftsman, an astronomer, a geometer, a physicist, a jurist and a statesman"—reflects the same versatility, within the framework of the American scene, which so astonishes us in the French Encyclopedists.

Many influences came together in Jefferson, many opposites met. On his father's side he was an offspring of the early settlers in the Blue Ridge "wilderness," imbibing from earliest childhood the vigorous frontier democracy which informed his political thinking. But through his mother, one of the Virginia Randolphs, he was related to the tidewater aristocracy, whose broader culture he encountered at Williamsburg and Richmond. Himself a gentleman farmer, his

I

values were geared to the simpler virtues of agricultural life, engendering the characteristic mistrust of the ways of the city. Yet as American minister to France he was catapulted into the intellectual and artistic ferment of the most cosmopolitan of European capitals, in the exciting years immediately preceding the French Revolution, where he came in contact with the main current of European culture at its most sophisticated level. His social point of view stemmed from an era of small farmers and independent artisans; yet his prehensile mind turned eagerly to the scientific and technical discoveries which were ushering in the industrial age. He was proudly an American, conscious of our Revolution as the harbinger of a new society free from the crippling inequalities and feudal survivals of monarchical Europe; his most renowned composition, the Declaration of Independence, he described as "intended to be an expression of the American mind"; yet was he heir to the great European tradition, student of England's philosophers, intimate of the leaders of the French Enlightenment, and, in intellectual matters, wholly above insularity. When his foes denounced him as an enemy of his country because he looked abroad for the best possible teachers for the University of Virginia, he retorted that "science knows no country, but belongs to all mankind." The needs of the American Revolution thrust him, for over thirty years of his life, into constant political activity. Yet by instinct and inclination he was preeminently suited for the contemplative life, and considered the tranquil pursuits of the scholar infinitely preferable to the hectic triumphs of the politician. That he was able to harmonize these differences within himself, to marshal them into line for a continuous self-development, argues the inner strength of the man, his boundless capacity for growth, his irresistible vitality.

In the realm of art Jefferson's life spanned one of the momentous periods of change, in which the good order and rationality of the Enlightenment was giving way to the surge and thunder of the romantic period. The duality expresses itself in his predilection, on the one hand, for the Greek and Latin authors; on the other, for the un-Augustan exuberance of Sterne, Shakespeare and Ossian. In his admiration for the Roman temple at Nismes, the Maison Quarrée, he is a man of the eighteenth century; indeed, his design for the State Capitol at Richmond, based upon it, may be said to have started the classical revival in architecture in America. Yet his description of that admiration—"Here I am, Madam, gazing whole hours at the Maison Quarrée, like a lover at his mistress!"—bespeaks the man of sensibility of that transition hour from eighteenth century to nineteenth which heralded the dawn of romanticism. So too, his impassioned description of the Natural Bridge in Virginia, suffused as it is with deism, is couched in a language curiously reminiscent of his older contemporary Rousseau and his younger, Beethoven. Of the painters and sculptors of his time he revered most, perhaps, the two who proclaimed to revolutionary France, under the guise and symbols of classical antiquity, the stern virtues of the new republicanism: "I do not feel an interest in any pencil but that of David." And "He [Houdon] is among the foremost, or perhaps the foremost artist in the world." Yet his rapturous appreciation of the spurious poetry of Ossian, his interest in Percy's *Reliques* and Rousseau's *La Nouvelle Héloïse*, unmistakably link him with the nascent romantic spirit. The eighty-three years of his life witnessed the most comprehensive change in taste, in style, in manner and in esthetic known to modern times. They included Handel and Schubert, Dr. Johnson and Byron, Fragonard and Gericault, Gray and Shelley. Within his lifetime there occurred the passing of one great age in art, and the opening of another. Sensitive and aware, he gave himself to the burgeoning influences of both.

Jefferson's esthetic interests must be viewed against the background of colonial culture as a whole. Unquestionably he represented that culture at its highest; his pursuits were those of the advanced intellectuals of his time. His education, however, was fairly characteristic of that of the gentleman of the period. Learning was limited to the few; but those were well grounded. The training of the Virginian upper class followed the English tradition; Jefferson's early reading was not much different from that of a young man of similar circumstances abroad. Nor was the New World as far behind the Old as might at first blush be supposed. This was an age when a man's education depended largely upon his reading and his intellectual curiosity: life at William and Mary College, if less elaborate than at Oxford or Cambridge, definitely favored cultural pursuits. It is revealing to glance over the titles included in the library list that Jefferson drew up in 1771, when he was twenty-eight, for his friend and kinsman, Robert Skipwith.[1] Among the classics we find two best-sellers of the time, Pope's translation of Homer and Dryden's of the *Aeneid*; Antoninus, Epictetus, Xenophon and Plutarch; Terence, Cicero, Caesar and the Roman historians—Tacitus, Sallust, Livy, Josephus. English literature is represented by Shakespeare and Milton, Chaucer and Spenser. Jefferson is gen-

erous with the popular novelists—Richardson, Smollett,
Fielding and Sterne are well represented, as are the play-
wrights, with Congreve, Farquhar, Vanbrugh, Steele, Otway
and Addison, to mention only those on the list whose reputa-
tions have survived. Among the poets, besides Dryden and
Pope, are Waller, Prior, Gay, Thompson and the ubiquitous
Ossian. The inclusion of Molière, Rousseau, Marmontel
and Tasso bespeaks his interest in continental literature
even at this early date. Percy's *Reliques,* Swift, Lady Julia
Manderville and Lord Lyttelton's *Persian Letters* round
out the section listed as *Fine Arts.* Under *Criticism* we find
the three famous works which this study endeavors to show
exerted so powerful an influence on his philosophy of art—
Lord Kames' *Elements of Criticism,* Burke's *Essay On the
Sublime and Beautiful,* and Hogarth's *Analysis of Beauty.*
Here, too, are included Johnson's *Dictionary* and Reid's
On the Human Mind. Under *Politics and Trade* we en-
counter four of the most influential political thinkers of the
eighteenth century, Montesquieu—whose *Spirit of Laws*
Jefferson deems indispensable for the library of his friend—
Locke, Marmontel and Lord Bolingbroke; the *Trade* por-
tion of this section accounts for Shiert's *Political Economy*
and *Political Arithmetic.* Under *Religion* Jefferson includes
Locke's *Conduct of the Mind,* Kames' *Natural Religion,*
Bolingbroke's *Philosophical Works* in five volumes, Hume's
Apology, Sterne's *Sermons,* Sherlock's *On Death* and *On a
Future State,* Cicero's *Tusculan Questions* and Xenophon's
Memoirs of Socrates. *Law* includes Kames' *Principles of
Equity,* Blackstone's *Commentaries* and Cunningham's *Law
Dictionary.* The Bible is listed under *Ancient History,* along
with Livy and Tacitus—we may recall Jefferson's advice to

his nephew Peter Carr to read the Holy Book as he would the Roman historians. Under *Modern History* we find Hume's work on England, Robertson's on France and Stith's on Virginia. *Mathematics, Natural Philosophy*, etc., presents us with such items as Franklin's *On Electricity*, Home's (Lord Kames) *Principles of Agriculture and Vegetation*, Duhamel's *Husbandry*, Miller's *Gardener's Dictionary*, Buffon's *Natural History*, Tull's *Horse-Hoeing Husbandry*, and—somewhat irrelevantly—Lady Mary Montague's *Letters*. Under *Miscellaneous* we come upon Locke's *Education*, Fénelon's *Dialogues of the Dead*, and Voltaire.

But if the books Jefferson recommended to his friend were no different from those which appeared in any well-stocked library and were generally read by gentlemen of his station, the conclusions he drew from them were. From the first his sympathies and hopes transcended the interests of the majority of members of his class. They desired political freedom from the King mainly that they might have economic freedom for themselves. He desired freedom in its widest sense for all mankind—a breaking of the shackles that bound the human mind. They, once they had thrown off the yoke of English Toryism, became tories themselves, bent on regaining control over the plain people whose aid they had invoked in their own struggle. He saw this about-face as a betrayal of all for which he had fought. He realized that there was an irreconcilable clash between the interests of his own class and those of the mass of "producers"; he cast his lot with the latter, and never wavered. With his uncanny ability to penetrate to the heart of a matter, he discerned that beneath the rationalizations which men gave to their actions, beneath the banners under which they professed to fight, there was a fundamental cleavage which persisted, down through the ages, no matter what the labels, between those who allied themselves with the principle of change, with the dynamic element in society, their eyes on the future, and those who stood with the *status quo,* holding on to the past. In a letter to Henry Lee, written when Jefferson was already past eighty, he gave definitive expression to this cleavage: ". . . Men by their constitution are naturally divided into two parties: 1. Those who fear and distrust the people, and wish to draw all powers from them into the hands of the higher classes. 2ndly those who identify themselves with the people, have confidence in them, cherish and consider them as the most honest and safe, although not the most wise depository of the public interests. In every country these two parties exist, and in every one where they are free to think, speak, and write, they will declare themselves. Call them therefore liberals and serviles, Jacobins and Ultras, whigs and tories, republicans and federalists, aristocrats and democrats, or by whatever name you please, they are the same parties still and pursue the same object. The last appellation of aristocrats and democrats is the true one expressing the essence of all." [2]

Eleven years before Jefferson had written to John Adams in similar vein: ". . . Men have differed in opinion, and been divided into parties by these opinions, from the first origin of societies, and in all governments where they have been permitted freely to think and to speak. The same political parties which now agitate the United States, have existed through all time. Whether the power of the people or that of the *aristoi* should prevail, were questions which kept the

States of Greece and Rome in eternal convulsions, as they now schismatize every people whose minds and mouths are not shut up by the gag of a despot." [3]

What distinguished Jefferson from those of his early comrades who, led by his cousin John Marshall, became increasingly infected with Toryism after the success of the American Revolution, was that he had a vision—one from which he never wavered—the amelioration of the lot of man. True, he conceived of it in terms of an agrarian society; he lived too early to realize the enormous upheaval that large-scale industrial production would effect in society. But he did see that man could plan and control his destiny in a rational way, if only he could emancipate himself from those who blocked his forward path out of self-interest; and his faith in the ultimate triumph of the vision never faltered. The pamphleteers before the Revolution were in the habit of sloganizing in behalf of life, liberty and property. Jefferson, disciple of Locke though he was, changed the *property* to "pursuit of happiness" and turned from Locke to follow Bolingbroke. Freedom and happiness for man—these were his goals. Nor was the enthusiasm of the young radical ever exchanged, as so often happens, for the resignation or cynicism of the "tired liberal." Fifty years after he had made the phrase immortal in the Declaration of Independence—in the last letter he ever wrote, a week and a half before his death—the aged fighter stated his case to Roger Weightman with no diminution of eloquence: ". . . All eyes are opened, or opening, to the rights of man. The general spread of the light of science has already laid open to every view the palpable truth, that the mass of mankind has not been born with saddles on their backs, nor a

favored few booted and spurred, ready to ride them legiti-
mately, by the grace of God." [4]

The vision gave not only compassion to his thinking; it
also conferred upon it the comprehensiveness of a world-
view. Here was a system which unified every aspect of his
many-sidedness. Whether it was the invention of a violin
stand which could fold up to become a table, or the promul-
gation of the Virginia Statute for Religious Freedom; the
discussion of the principle of the catenary arch in Thomas
Paine's iron bridge or of a plan for universal education, Jefferson's goal was always the same—the advancement of
the freedom and happiness of mankind. Politics and tech-
nology, art, science, literature and ethics fell within a single
frame of reference. He could not separate the various fields
of human endeavor, as the specialists were beginning to do,
and did increasingly in the next century. He could not but
view them as so many manifestations of the same spirit—
better, as so many tools to the same end. In this catholicity
of outlook he was a worthy peer of the Encyclopedists; yet
in a sense he was even more rounded than they. Grimm was
cut off from reality by his esthetic preoccupations; Condorcet, d'Alembert, d'Holbach, Diderot—each in his way
became the victim of that separation of theory from practice which is the lot of the precursor of social change. But
Jefferson was not only of the stuff of the bookmen, the
philosophes; he also helped engineer a successful revolution,
and was called by a nation to direct its destinies during a
crucial period of its formative years. Rarely has the chief
power of the state fallen to one so truly a philosopher-statesman. When it is remembered that our third president was
also the author of an essay on English prosody and on

Anglo-Saxon; that he invented a copying-press, a plow with mold-board to reduce friction, a hemp-brake, and divers household appliances; that he designed a phaeton and cabriolet, as well as the Virginia State Capitol, the buildings for the University of Virginia, and that most eloquent embodiment of his artistic creativeness—Monticello; that his writings range from comments on Plato to paleontology, from a textual presentation of the philosophy of Jesus to theories of money, we begin to see the range of his quenchless curiosity. The comparison readily enough suggests itself with the Renaissance mind. Yet even in that period of titans, the trichotomy was not entirely bridged between statesman, philosopher and artist: Lorenzo, Machiavelli and Leonardo might look into each other's purlieu, but remained each within his own. That Jefferson was able to bridge the gap betwixt theory and action, to see life with a wholeness matched by few, was the result partly of historical circumstance, partly of his own encompassing temperament. It is that wholeness which makes him the avatar of a great age.

In such a matrix art can never exist for its own sake; we may expect to find in Jefferson's philosophy of art a handsome admixture of utilitarianism. Always the tool is viewed in relation to its purpose: art must not only further freedom and happiness but also inculcate virtue. Jefferson brought to his esthetic judgments not only the freshness of the frontier but also its moral sense; not only the sweet reasonableness of the Enlightenment but also the spontaneous emotion of the American "man of sensibility." Inevitably he revolted against the aristocratic idealism of Plato; he was far closer to Aristotle—and Hogarth. Art was to teach, even to preach; it must arouse the sympathetic "affections" and purify the emotion. Let us listen to the young moralist pronouncing upon the utility of art: "A little attention to the nature of the human mind evinces that the entertainments of fiction are useful as well as pleasant. That they are pleasant when well written, every person feels who reads. But wherein is its utility, asks the reverend sage, big with the notion that nothing can be useful but the learned lumber of Greek and Roman reading with which his head is stored? I answer everything is useful which contributes to fix in the principles and practices of virtue. . . . The field of imagination is thus laid open to our use and lessons may be formed to illustrate and carry home to the heart every moral rule of life. Thus a lively sense of filial duty is more effectually impressed on the mind of a son or daughter by reading King Lear, than by all the dry volumes of ethics and divinity that ever were written." [5]

In Jefferson's classic-romantic dualism he was a child of his time—a time which romanticized the classic, as Gibbon did, or like David, imposed an Hellenic chasteness upon the romantic. A soft glow bathes the last four decades of the eighteenth century, that gentle glimmer which belongs both to twilight and to dawn. Rousseau, Ossian, the compiler of the *Reliques*, Thompson, Cowper, Gray—these are harbingers of a new spirit in art. Perhaps we shall yet discover a late eighteenth-century romanticism more subtly distinctive than the full-blown variety of the nineteenth. We find here the buoyant freshness of an awakening: a great expectancy hung in the air—and revolution, in art as well as in government. The new art is truly the art of that unique moment in time when two ways of life met in mortal conflict, when the lusty young citizen snatched from the effete aristocrat dominion of the world. In one sense Jefferson was always a romantic: from the start he took his stand with the party of revolt, as every romantic does. Even to the classical heritage of the eighteenth-century gentleman he brought freedom from tradition, the ingenuousness and bold imagination of the frontiersman. His nature was too ardent, his impulses were too fresh, his vision of the future was too bright, for him to fit into the conventional classical mold. Perhaps we will do best to consider him an eighteenth-century romantic. Certainly his formative period and the years of his most intense preoccupation with artistic matters belonged to the old century. These were the decades of pre-romanticism; he came just too early for the lyric awakening which spoke to Europe through the winged words of Wordsworth and Coleridge, of Byron, Shelley, Keats. His presidency fell in the first eight years of the new century; public affairs claimed the major share of his attention through the crucial War of 1812, when, although he had relinquished the burden of office, he continued to act as elder statesman and adviser to his disciple and successor, Madison. By that time he was on the threshold of seventy. He surveyed the world with a sort of Olympian serenity, but he was passionately concerned with the world and the way it was going. But art no longer touched him as it had. What happened under stress of public office he confessed to John Burke: "In earlier life I was fond of it [poetry], and easily pleased. But as age and cares advanced, the powers of fancy have declined. Every year seems to have plucked a feather from her wings, till she can no longer waft one to those sublime heights to which it is necessary to accompany the poet. So

much has my relish for poetry deserted me that at present
I cannot read even Virgil with pleasure." [6]

It is impossible to separate the artist in Jefferson from
the philosopher-statesman or from the architect of human
freedom and happiness. One has but to go through Monticello, to view the rotunda of the University of Virginia, to
become aware of the profound sense of beauty, harmony
and proportion of their designer. No less impressive as
evidence of the creative impulse within him are the many
volumes of his correspondence, a respectable achievement
even for the great age of letter writing, and a prodigious
one when we remember the activities he was concurrently
engaged upon. Yet it is the profoundly intuitive quality of
the man, his insight, his ability to penetrate instantaneously
beneath the surface of things, that proclaim his creative
spirit. It has often been pointed out that the scientist's
ability to leap to a new hypothesis, long before there are
the data at hand to support it, is akin to the intuitions of
the artist. As we read Jefferson's conjectures on natural
phenomena, some of which, like those on the climate of
Virginia or the origins of the Indians, anticipated later discoveries, we are reminded of the notes of Leonardo. Jefferson was neither artist nor esthetician in the professional
sense; yet one comes away from his writings with an in-
escapable awareness that he had at times all the clairvoy-
ance, the visionary sense of the artist—and the sensitivity.
It was this that enabled him to gather up in himself the
main impulses of his time, to give them more eloquent expression than they had received hitherto.

He was able to believe that life in the young republic he
had helped to create should be joyous, and that art should

be a means of making it so. In this, as in so many other
things, he voiced the American dream at its best, distilled
from the worthiest ingredients of the Old World, yet transmuted to the needs and values of the New.

CHAPTER ONE

1. Unpublished MSS. from Massachusetts Historical Society. See Appendix I.

2. To Henry Lee: Monticello, Aug. 10, 1824: Ford, Fed. Ed. XII, p. 375.

3. To John Adams: Monticello, June 27, 1813, ME, XIII, pp 279–284.

4. To Roger O. Weightman: Monticello, June 24, 1826: Ford, Fed. Ed.
XII, p. 477.

5. To Robert Skipwith: Monticello, Aug. 3, 1771, ME, IV, pp. 237–240

6. To John D. Burke: Washington, June 21, 1801, Ford, Fed. Ed. IX
p. 267.

JEFFERSON'S PHILOSOPHY OF ART: SOME SOURCES—I.

THE ESTHETIC of the eighteenth century was firmly rooted in its residual philosophy. Consequently, we cannot achieve a rounded view of Jefferson's esthetic without examining his position in regard to the main currents in the philosophy of his time.

As a philosopher of revolution, Jefferson was oriented to a "utilitarian intuitionalism" which is encountered again and again in eighteenth-century English and French thought. "Wollaston expressed one version of it, Hume another, Bentham gave it 'scientific' statement, and the French sensationalist philosophers Helvetius, d'Holbach and Cabanis . . . made an attempt at a logical system founded upon these very ideas." [1] Gilbert Chinard has pointed out that, contrary to the generally accepted view, Jefferson was influenced far more profoundly by English philosophy than by the French. [2] The Frenchmen carried their materialism too far for his taste; and the atheism of the French, as we shall see, was less congenial to his bent of mind than the deism of the British. In any case, from the intellectual ferment of his time—a time of revolution in thought, be it remembered, as well as in political and social life—Jefferson selected what he needed with a sure hand. Locke's empiricism and humanism, Shaftesbury's altruism, Kames' doctrine of the innate moral sense, Burke's "social passion" and "sympathy," Reid's "common sense" each in varying degree entered into the many-colored web of his philosophy and became an essential part of his intellectual equipment. Yet, as in a chemical process whose familiar elements combine to form a new compound, the sum total of what emerged was neither Locke nor Shaftesbury nor Kames nor Burke nor Reid—it was Jefferson. In absorbing the materials for his own ends, he had transmuted them into something different and new.

Of the intellectual giants of his century, Jefferson's deepest reverence went to Locke. Did he not tell Alexander Hamilton that Bacon, Newton and Locke were his "trinity of the three greatest men the world had ever produced"?[3] Locke's "faith in the senses" reinforced the empiricist in Jefferson. And the British philosopher's conception of the human mind as a "tabula rasa" upon which the senses inscribe their impressions and perceptions was a view most congenial to the American democrat, implying as it did that environment is a more powerful determinant factor than heredity, and that men may rise to undreamt-of heights or sink to the depths of depravity, not because of their innate dispositions, but because of the social conditions under which their lives are passed. Locke's stressing of the "inner sense" approached the problem of human existence through maximum emphasis of the rights of the individual. The doctrine which regarded pleasure and pain as the fundamental determinants of human conduct also elevated the pursuit of happiness as the strongest force in social life. The Lockian philosophy may be described as a defense of the dignity of the individual, justification of intellectual, religious and social freedom. As such, it may be said to involve an attack upon dogma, tradition, clericalism and royalism. Jefferson included Locke's *Treatise on Government* in the list to Skipwith, as well as two basic treatises of the sensationalist philosophy, Locke's *Conduct of the Mind* and his *Education*. Many hold that the American wrote the English thinker's idea of natural rights into the Declaration of Independence; in a letter to James Madison Jefferson remarked that "Richard Henry Lee charged it [the Declaration of Independence] as copied from Locke's treatise on Government." [4] In this connection Prof. Chinard writes: "The Declaration of Independence is essentially of Lockian origin, but it does not ensue that Jefferson had memorized Locke, nor even that he was conscious, when he wrote the document, that he was using a Lockian phraseology." [5]

Locke's thorough-going empiricism eschewed all speculation that could not be based upon the evidence of the senses. Jefferson's sympathy with this idea may be gathered from what he wrote to the Rev. Isaac Story on the transmigration of souls: "The laws of nature have withheld from us the means of physical knowledge of the country of spirits, and revelation has, for reasons unknown to us, chosen to leave us in the dark as we were. When I was young I was fond of the speculations which seemed to promise some insight into that hidden country, but observing at length that they left me in the same ignorance in which they had found me, I have for very many years ceased to read or to think concerning them, and have reposed my head on that pillow of ignorance which a benevolent Creator has made so soft for us, knowing how much we should be forced to use it." [6]

Locke's humanism represented a monumental attempt to

supersede the "egoistic morality" of Hobbes which had found such widespread acceptance in the preceding century. Lord Shaftesbury inherited and continued this Lockian enterprise. His philosophy became a fertilizing current in the swelling stream of democratic thought. Shaftesbury kept esthetics classically coincident with ethics; he identified the Beautiful with the Good and the True in eighteenth-century manner. His views influenced Jefferson as well as other thinkers of the revolutionary age. Shaftesbury taught that there is a specific sense of beauty born in man, that man's sense of beauty is like his sense of goodness or his sympathy for his kind. Thereby the preoccupation with beauty took on the seriousness of an ethical goal. The ideal citizen of the new dispensation—Shaftesbury's "virtuoso"—was the man of consummate taste;[7] he perfected his own nature and realized his own potentialities; he harmonized the contradictions within himself through identification with his fellows. As a social reformer, Shaftesbury had boundless faith in the innate goodness of man, his teachableness, his perfectibility. As a utilitarian, he viewed beauty as a necessary concomitant of man's happiness. The artist was hence one with the teacher, the healer, the priest. It is superfluous to point out how strongly Jefferson's views on the utility of art concurred with this doctrine.

The direct link between Locke and Shaftesbury on the one hand, and Jefferson on the other, was Lord Kames, who taught that "a taste in the fine arts goes hand in hand with the moral sense, to which indeed it is nearly allied."[8] The impression that Kames' doctrines made upon young Jefferson was so deep that he was able to quote the Scottish thinker in his old age, although "it being fifty years since I read his book." [9] Kames was one of the most prominent spokesmen for the "inner sense" school of thought: "Every feeling, pleasant or painful, must be in the mind." [10] A staunch utilitarian, Kames gave careful consideration to the specific benefits that could be derived from the cultivation of the arts. They could "revive the spirits when sunk by sensual gratification" as well as "relax them when overstrained in any violent pursuit." [11] There is a real obligation, as well as interest, "to second the purposes of nature by cultivating the pleasures of the eye and ear, those especially that require extraordinary culture, such as arise from poetry, painting, sculpture, music, gardening and architecture. This especially is the duty of the opulent, who have leisure to improve their minds and their feelings." [12]

Jefferson comes quite close to this view when, accepting honorary membership in and offering his good wishes to the Society of Artists of the United States, he hopes that while "embellishing with taste a country already overflowing with the useful productions, it may be able to give an innocent and pleasing direction to accumulations of wealth, which would otherwise be employed in the nourishment of coarse and vicious habits." [13]

In the same spirit Kames lists the manifold "advantages of criticism, when thus studied as a rational science." After enumerating the increased pleasure which the art-lover will feel as a result of a thorough knowledge of the why and wherefore of beauty, he remarks that the arts, which in the prime of life are delightful, "being supported by the force of novelty and the heat of imagination," tend to lose their relish with time, and "are generally neglected in the maturity of life, which disposes to more serious and more important occupations." By giving scope to "judgment as well as to fancy, the fine arts are a favorite entertainment, and in old age maintain that relish which they produce in the morning of life." [14]

Similarly, Jefferson recurs again and again to the role which the arts may play in warding off the ennui of old age, and in retaining the keenness of the mind after the body has begun to lose its powers: "In place of this [letter-writing] has come on a canine appetite for reading. And I indulge it, because I see in it a relief against the *taedium senectutis*; a lamp to lighten my path through the dreary wilderness of time before me, whose bourne I see not. Losing daily all interest in the things around us, something else is necessary to fill the void. With me it is reading." [15]

Finally, Kames adduces one of the preferred arguments of the Age of Reason in favor of abstract speculation: a philosophic inquiry into the principles of the fine arts strengthens the reasoning faculties and tends to a habit which "prepares the mind for entering into subjects more intricate and abstract." [16] There is a direct echo of this view of the advantages of the practice of criticism, which is interchangeable with the modern term "esthetic," in the letter sent by Jefferson to his friend Bernard Moore: "The faculties of the mind, like the members of the body, are strengthened and improved by exercise." [17]

Kames, man of sensibility that he is, does not content himself with enumerating only the intellectual advantages of esthetic speculation; the science of rational criticism tended to "improve the heart no less than the understanding." It not only sweetened the temper and softened the turbulence of passion, but also procured to a man so much mental enjoyment that he was not "tempted to deliver up his youth to hunting, gaming, drinking; nor his middle age to ambition; nor his old age to avarice." [18] In similar vein Jefferson writes to his daughter Martha to pursue music, drawing and books as so many resources against ennui: "A mind always employed is always happy. This is the true secret, the grand recipe for felicity. The idle are only the wretched. In a world which furnishes so many employments which are so useful, so many which are amusing, it is our own fault if we ever know what ennui is, or if we are ever driven to the miserable resources of gaming, which corrupts our dispositions, and teaching us a habit of hostility against all mankind." [19]

Kames, carrying on the Shaftesburian doctrine of altruism, taught that delicacy of taste tended "to invigorate the social affections" and heightened our sympathy. Jefferson makes the point in the "Dialogue between my Heart and my Head": "When languishing then under disease, how grateful is the solace of our friends! how are we penetrated with their assiduities and attentions! how much are we supported by their encouragements and kind offices! When heaven has taken from us some object of our love, how sweet is it to have a bosom whereon to recline our heads, and into which we may pour the torrent of our tears! Grief, with such a comfort, is almost a luxury!" [20]

This train of thought fitted in well with that glorification of friendship which was one of the outstanding impulses of the *grand siècle*. Indeed, has it not been said that the men of the eighteenth century conferred upon friendship some of the romantic idealization which the nineteenth gave to love? Burke, in whose writings the older "altruism" becomes "sympathy," remarks in his *Essay* that "good company, lively conversations and the endearments of friendship fill the mind with pleasure." In like fashion Jefferson writes to Dr. Rush: "I find friendship to be like wine, raw when new, ripened with age, the true old man's milk and restorative cordial." [21] While to Mrs. Cosway he writes: "Friendship is precious, not only in the shade, but in the sunshine of life; and thanks to a benevolent arrangement of things, the greater part of life is sunshine." [22]

The relating of our feeling for beauty to our feeling for virtue, important as it was in itself, rested upon a deeper-lying tenet—the innate moral sense of man. This, accordingly, was the foundation upon which Kames, and Jefferson after him, reared the imposing facade of their esthetic. Kames believed the fundamental principles of the fine arts are drawn from "human nature, the true source of criticism." [23] Kames taught that *the sympathetic emotion of virtue,* resembles, in one respect, the well-known appetites that lead to the propagation and preservation of the species" besides disposing the reader of histories of conquerors and heroes to feel himself moved to great or noble actions accompanied by an unusual dignity of character.[24] It prompts us to imitate what we admire. "When we contemplate a virtuous action," he writes, "our propensity at the same time to such actions is so much enlivened, as to become for a time an actual emotion." [25] Further, he declares, "every exercise of virtue, internal and external, leads to habit; for a disposition or propensity of the mind, like a limb of the body, becomes stronger by exercise." [26] Jefferson echoes this doctrine almost word for word in his letter to Skipwith: "When any original act of charity or of gratitude for instance, is presented either to our sight or imagination, we are deeply impressed with its beauty and feel a strong desire in ourselves of doing charitable and grateful acts also. On the contrary, when we see or read of any atrocious deed, we are disgusted with its deformity, and conceive an abhorrence of vice. Now every emotion of this kind is an exercise of our virtuous dispositions, and dispositions of the mind, like limbs of the body, acquire strength by practice. But exercise produces habit, and in the instance of which we speak, the exercise being of the moral feelings, produces a habit of thinking and acting virtuously." [27]

Jefferson recurs to the innate goodness of man with noteworthy persistence. To Peter Carr he writes that "the moral sense of conscience is as much a part of a man as his leg or arm." [28] To Thomas Law: "I sincerely . . . believe with you in the general existence of a moral instinct." [29] The moral sense, to him, was an integral part of the social sense, as he averred to Peter Carr: "Man was destined for society. His morality, therefore, was to be formed to this object." [30] And to John Adams, twenty-nine years later, he states: "I believe . . . that the moral sense is as much a part of our constitution as that of feeling, seeing or hearing; as a wise creator must have seen to be necessary in an animal destined to live in society." [31]

In his impressive letter to Thomas Law on the existence of a moral sense—it is there that Jefferson stated that "nature has constituted *utility* to man the standard and test of virtue"—he examines one after another the possible foundations of morality in man. Of all the theories on this question he observes "the most whimsical seems to have been that of Wollaston, who considers *truth* as the foundation of morality." He continues: "Truth is certainly a branch of morality . . . but presented as its foundation, it is as if a tree taken up by the roots, had its stem reversed in the air, and one of its branches planted in the ground." He next considers *love of God* as the foundation of morality. But if we did a good act merely from the love of God, "whence arises the morality of the Atheist?" In dissociating himself from the extreme materialism of the French philosophers, Jefferson makes a telling observation on moral philosophy in Catholic and Protestant countries: "I have observed, indeed, generally, that while in Protestant countries the defections from the Platonic Christianity of the priests is to Deism, in Catholic countries they are to Atheism. Diderot, d'Alembert, d'Holbach, Condorcet, are known to have been among the most virtuous of men. Their virtue, then, must have had some other foundation than the love of God." [32]

Perhaps the most significant passage in this discussion is the one in which Jefferson posits the existence of an innate sense of the beautiful as distinct from—although, as we shall see later, not unrelated to—the moral sense: "The TO KALON of others is founded in a different faculty, that of taste, which is not even a branch of morality. We have indeed an innate sense of what we call beautiful, but that is exercised chiefly on subjects addressed to the fancy, whether through the eye in visible forms, as landscape, animal figure, dress, drapery, architecture, the composition of colors, etc., or to the imagination directly, as imagery, style or measure in prose or poetry, or whatever else constitutes the domain of criticism or taste, a faculty entirely distinct from the moral one." [33]

Like Kames, Jefferson comes out strongly against Hobbes'

"egoistic" morality in this communication to Law: "Self-love, therefore, is no part of morality. . . . It is the sole antagonist of virtue, leading us constantly by our propensities to self-gratification in violation of our moral duties to others. Accordingly, it is against this enemy that are erected the batteries of moralists and religionists, as the only obstacle to the practice of morality. Take from man his selfish propensities, and he can have nothing to seduce him from the practice of virtue. Or subdue those propensities by education, instruction or restraint, and virtue remains without a competitor." [34]

Interesting is his alienation from the French materialist-atheist school led by Helvetius. This bears out the assertion of Prof. Chinard previously alluded to that Jefferson was much more under English than French influence: "So Helvetius, one of the best men on earth . . . after defining 'interest' to mean not merely that which is pecuniary, but whatever may procure us pleasure or withdraw us from pain (*de l'esprit* 2, I,) says (*ibid.* 2, 2,) 'the humane man is he to whom the sight of misfortune is insupportable, and who to rescue himself from this spectacle, is forced to succor the unfortunate object.' This indeed is true. But it is one step short of the ultimate question. These good acts give us pleasure, but how happens it that they give us pleasure? Because nature hath implanted in our breasts a love of others, a sense of duty to them, a moral instinct, in short, which prompts us irresistibly to feel and to succor their distresses." [35]

As against all egoists, Jefferson adopts the contention of the "altruists" in his letter to Miles King: "He [God] has formed us moral agents . . . that we may promote the happiness of those with whom He has placed us in society, by acting honestly towards all, benevolently to those who fall within our way, respecting sacredly their rights, bodily and mental, and cherishing especially their freedom of conscience, as we value our own." [36]

The establishment of pleasure and pain as a dominant motivation of human behavior was an integral achievement of Lockian sensationalism. Its historical significance was that it led the eighteenth-century mind to acknowledge the pursuit of happiness as a valid human goal. Locke propounded the view that the removal or lessening of a pain operates as a pleasure, and the loss or diminishing of a pleasure operates as a pain. Burke, in opposition to this, advanced the opinion that pleasure and pain "are each of a positive nature, and by no means necessarily depend on each other for their existence." [37] Jefferson's conception draws upon elements of both views to achieve a synthesis of his own. He considered pain as a necessary counterpart of pleasure; but, with Burke, made no attempt to predicate the emotional value of the one upon the other: "We have no rose without its thorn; no pleasure without alloy. It is the law of our existence; and we must acquiesce." [38] Thirty years later, in a letter to John Adams, he makes a typically "common sense" observation on this favorite problem of eighteenth-century speculation: "I do not agree that an age of pleasure is no compensation for a moment of pain. I think, with you, that life is a fair matter of account, and the balance often, nay generally, in its favor. It is not indeed easy, by calculation of intensity and time, to apply a common measure, or to fix the par between pleasure and pain; yet it exists, and is measurable." [39] Of course, too much is known of Jefferson's attitude towards life to infer from this a facile hedonism. Prof. Chinard, in his Introduction to Jefferson's *Literary Bible,* mentions the strain of pessimism in his make-up.[40] Yet this emotional bent existed side by side with an unwavering faith in the possibility of achieving at least a fair measure of happiness for mankind. This faith—the mainstay of revolutionary activity—is what linked Jefferson most intimately with the leading members of the British materialist-humanist school. The seeds of his belief, which reached their full flowering of expression in the Declaration of Independence, may be traced back to his early life. In a letter to John Page, at the age of twenty, he writes: "Perfect happiness, I believe was never intended by the Deity to be the lot of one of his creatures in this world; but that he has very much put in our power the nearness of our approaches to it, is what I have steadfastly believed." [41]

Burke's dictum that "pity is a passion accompanied with pleasure, because it arises from love and social affections"— an enunciation of the principle of sympathy that lies at the root of social behavior—is found in another form in Kames. Not only does Kames think affection social which prompts an action solely for the advancement of another's happiness but "the action is justly denominated *social.*" He thinks since pity tends to soften the temper, such social affections as sympathy and humanity represent the finest temper of mind, and have an advantage not only with regard to pleasure and pain, but because the social pains of sympathy are voluntary. The culmination of this line of reasoning comes in Kames' statement: "To perceive the social principle in its triumphant state, a man must forget himself, and turn his thoughts upon the character and conduct of his fellow creatures: he will feel a secret charm in every passion that tends to the good of others, and a secret aversion against every unfeeling heart that is indifferent to the happiness and distress of others." [42]

In the extracts from the "Dialogue between my Head and Heart" already quoted, as well as in his many tributes to friendship, Jefferson brings this "social feeling" into the realm of personal relationships.

It must be remembered that the primary purpose of writers on the arts like Kames and Burke was to formulate a philosophy of art by means of a study of human nature which they termed "criticism" or "taste." If they entered into subtle disquisitions concerning the social feelings as distinct from the egoistic, the nature of pleasure and pain, emotions and passions, perceptions and sensations, that was primarily to establish in a logical way a psychological basis for their esthetic theories. In so doing, they naturally drew upon the entire body of eighteenth-century thought for support of their doctrine of the beautiful and the sublime. Their line of reasoning was in keeping with the encyclopedic character of eighteenth-century thought which saw life whole and drew freely upon one area of human experience to facilitate its understanding of another. Such a habit of mind allowed for the most varied material, bringing about an all-encompassing point of view which enabled men like Kames, Burke, Jefferson or the French Encyclopedists to shift from one subject to another yet treat them in terms of the same underlying principles. By Addison's time, "It was the fashion already in England to connect the esthetic ideas of sublimity and grandeur with the political ideal of liberty." [43]

As a good example of the process, take the handling of the concept of self-preservation. This, in line with the temper of the Enlightenment, was coming to be taken as a fundamental factor in the new psychology. Burke, attempting to analyze the passions which turn on pain and danger, remarks that "the passions belonging to self-preservation are the strongest of all the passions." Kames, in similar fashion, concludes that "self-preservation is a matter of too great importance to be left entirely to the conduct of reason. . . . Fear provides for self-preservation by flying from harm; anger, by repelling it." Jefferson, in a purely political context, similarly uses the concepts of the psychologist-esthetician. Writing on the French treaties in 1793, he remarks, "The law of self-preservation over-rules the laws of obligation to others." So, too, he applies the principles of social feeling, which the English and Scottish thinkers had examined abstractly, to a specific issue in the building of the state: "A strict observance of the written laws is doubtless *one* of the high duties of a good citizen, but it is not *the highest*. The laws of necessity, of self-preservation, of saving our country when in danger, are of higher obligation. . . . The unwritten laws of necessity, of self-preservation, and of the public safety, control the written laws of *meum* and *tuum*." [44]

We have seen how Jefferson postulated the existence of a sense of beauty distinct from a sense of morality. That the two were not separated in his mind is quite clear from his views on literature, painting and sculpture—but especially the first. It must be remembered that one of the reasons which prompted the estheticians of the eighteenth century to devote so much attention to the nature of sympathy, identification and social feeling, was that it helped them to explain the effect of tragedy upon the mind. Shaftesbury's teaching on the moral implications of art is projected with singular felicity in a passage in which Kames states that "fiction, by means of language, has the command of our sympathy for the good of others." [45] Imaginary examples of virtue and vice raise virtuous emotions which "becoming stronger by exercise, tend to make us virtuous by habit, as well as by principle." The reader will recall that Jefferson made the same point about the "strengthening" of virtue through exercise in his letter to Skipwith. The power that fiction exercises over the mind, according to Kames, "affords an endless variety of refined amusements, always at hand to employ a vacant hour; such amusements are a fine resource in solitude; and, by cheering and sweetening the mind, contribute mightily to social happiness." [46]

In his letter to Robert Skipwith, parts of which have already been quoted, Jefferson, almost echoing Kames, says: "A little attention to the nature of the human mind evinces that the entertainments of fiction are useful as well as pleasant . . . I appeal to every reader of feeling and sentiment whether the fictitious murder of Duncan by Macbeth, in Shakespeare, does not excite in him as great a horror of villainy, as the real one of Henry IV by Ravaillac, as related by Davila? And whether the fidelity of Nelson and generosity of Blandford in Marmontel, do not dilate his breast and elevate his sentiments as much as any similar incident which real history can furnish? Does he not in fact feel himself a better man while reading them, and privately covenant to copy the fair example? We neither know nor care whether Laurence Sterne really went to France, whether he was

there accosted by the Franciscan, at first rebuked him un-
kindly, and then gave him a peace offering: or whether the
whole be not fiction. In either case we equally are sorrowful
at the rebuke, and secretly resolve we will never do so: we
are pleased with the subsequent atonement, and view with
emulation a soul candidly acknowledging its fault and making a just reparation." [47]

Kames remarks that "It therefore shows great wisdom
to form us in such a manner as to be susceptible to the same
improvement from fable that we receive from genuine history." [48] In the same vein Jefferson writes Skipwith: "Considering history as a moral exercise, her lessons would be
too infrequent if confined to real life . . . we are, therefore, wisely framed to be as warmly interested for a fictitious
as for a real personage." [49]

Since so much has been made by Jefferson's enemies of his
supposed atheism, we should not leave this examination of
the relations between his ideas and those of Kames without
remarking that, while he was outspokenly unsympathetic to
the French atheists Helvetius, d'Holbach and Cabanis, he
endorsed the beliefs of such a writer as Kames who taught
that "Nature hath a wonderful power of connecting systems
with each other, and of propagating that connection through
all her works. . . . All space is filled with the works of
God, which are conducted by one plan, to answer unerringly
one great end." [50] It is fairly apparent, from some of Jefferson's remarks quoted in this chapter that he was far closer
to English deism than to French atheism. A nice indication
of his feelings in this matter is to remember that in his
letter to Thomas Law he states "God has made us moral
agents."

Towards Burke, Jefferson's attitude was far more ambivalent. As we have seen, he included Burke's *Essay on the Sublime and the Beautiful* in his list of recommended readings to Skipwith. Burke's grounding of the sense of beauty in the social instincts of sympathy and emulation, his positing of an innate moral sense and his pervading deism were matters that Jefferson could agree with. Burke broadened the eighteenth-century conception of the sublime to include many varieties of emotional experience, especially those of terror. "Whatever is fitted in any sort to excite the ideas of pain and danger, that is to say, whatever is in any sort terrible, or is conversant about terrible objects, or operates in a manner analogous to terror, is a source of the *sublime*; that is, it is productive of the strongest emotion which the mind is capable of feeling." [51] This was an original conception which could not but exert a profound influence upon those to whom it was advanced. In addition, Burke had been instrumental in propagating Jefferson's early pamphlets on the wrongs of the Colonies throughout England, and had taken an admirable stand throughout the American Revolution.

Despite these points of agreement, however, Burke stood on the other side of the bar from Jefferson. He was the most frankly mystical of the thinkers of the Enlightenment. He was anti-rational, anti-sceptical; and, as time wore on, increasingly for the *status quo*. Despite his "sympathy" as a social passion, he entertained a static view of human nature; he conceived of it as an immutable entity, thus justifying his fundamentally aristocratic world-view. He was anti-utilitarian and anti-progressive; he rejected Hogarth's identification of beauty with fitness and use. He took the "inner sense" rather metaphysically: "In beauty, the effect is previous to any knowledge of the use." [52] And Burke held that "beauty demands no assistance from our reasoning; even the will is unconcerned; the appearance of beauty as effectually causes some degree of love in us as the application of ice or fire produces the ideas of heat or cold." [53] He believed "beauty is no idea belonging to mensuration; nor has it anything to do with calculation and geometry." [54] Very adroitly he separated beauty from goodness—thus challenging the basic tenets of the latest school of esthetics then current—and he separated it even from reason: "Beauty is a thing much too affecting not to depend upon some positive qualities. And since it is no creature of our reason, since it strikes us without any reference to use, and even where no use at all can be discerned . . . we must conclude that beauty is, for the greater part, some quality in bodies acting mechanically upon the human mind by the intervention of the senses." [55]

More, the whole atmosphere of the linkage of the sublime with terror was a "Gothic" concept rather than a "Hellenic" one. It was far closer to the "terror" school in English literature at the turn of the century—Horace Walpole's *Castle of Otranto* which first appeared anonymously in 1765 comes readily to mind as an example. The general tenor of the early nineteenth-century attitude falls in with it more readily than with the sunnier vistas of the Age of Reason. Although Jefferson, in his appreciation of the poetry of Ossian and of the Natural Bridge of Virginia amply demonstrated that he understood the "sublime" in Burke's terms, the author of the Declaration of Independence could not but feel the most violent antipathy towards the official spokesman of British Toryism; particularly after the issues were clearly drawn with the outbreak of the Revolution in France. He could not accept what he termed the "rotten-ness" of Burke's mind in a letter to Benjamin Vaughan in 1791 in which he wrote: "The Revolution of France does not astonish me so much, as the Revolution of Mr. Burke. I wish I could believe the latter proceeded from as pure motives as the former." [56] So, too, he attacked Burke's sentimental defense of Marie Antoinette: "This angel, as gaudily painted in the rhapsodies of the Rhetor Burke, with some smartness of fancy, but no sound sense, was proud, disdainful of restraint, indignant at all obstacles to her will, eager in the pursuit of pleasure, and firm enough to hold to her desires, or perish in their wreck." [57] For the final re-buttal of the "Rhetor," Jefferson appealed to the author of *Common Sense:* "Mr. Paine's answer to Burke will be a refreshing shower to their minds [the English]. It would bring England itself to reason and revolution if it was per-mitted to be read there." [58]

Of the thinkers who provided the climate of intellectual opinion within which Jefferson's own views took shape, one more should be mentioned: Thomas Reid, the Scottish vindicator of "common sense" whose *On the Human Mind* Jefferson included in his list to Skipwith. Reid attempted to lead esthetic speculation back to safely materialist grounds, to make the widest possible distinction between esthetic sub-ject and object, to uphold the primacy of the external world and to drive out all mysticism that might creep into sensa-tionalist investigation by the clean breath of his "common sense" practicality. Such an approach could not but be con-genial to the Virginian's practical, scientific mind. His admiration for "plain common sense" is expressed not only in relation to the daily conduct of affairs, but also within the larger framework of his ultimate faith in the reasoning powers of mankind. To John Adams he writes: "I can never fear that things will go far wrong where common sense has fair play." [59] The same year similarly to Ezra Stiles: "Let common sense and common honesty have fair play and they will soon set things to right." [60] And fourteen years later to Jeremiah Moor: "I have great confidence in the common sense of mankind in general: but it requires a great deal to get the better of notions which our tutors have instilled in our minds while incapable of questioning them, and to rise superior to antipathies strongly rooted." [61] Twelve more years went by and Jefferson elevates the homespun logic glorified by the Scottish philosopher into a general principle of government: "Common sense is the foundation of all authorities, of the laws themselves, and of their construction." [62]

We thus see that Jefferson, in his general philosophy, as well as his philosophy of art, was an eclectic who drew whatever suited his needs from a variety of sources, recombining them, however, into something subtly distinctive and individual—a whole in a real sense quite different if not greater than the sum of its parts. This was in line with what we have noticed was one of his most important cultural functions—to be a link, intellectually, between Europe and America; and to adapt the most fruitful tenets of a mature, at times overripe, culture to the needs of the pioneer civilization which had been brought into being by—and was now to point the way for—the old.

CHAPTER TWO

1. Adrienne Koch: *The Philosophy of Thomas Jefferson,* pp. 20–21, New York (1943).

2. Gilbert Chinard: "Jefferson Among the Philosophers," p. 258, *Ethics,* Vol. LIII, No. 4 (1943).

3. To Dr. Benjamin Rush: Monticello, January 16, 1811, Ford, Fed. Ed. XI, p. 168.

4. To James Madison: Monticello, Aug. 3, 1823, ME, XV, p. 462.

5. Gilbert Chinard: *Thomas Jefferson, Apostle of Americanism,* p. 72, Boston (1939).

6. To Rev. Isaac Story: Washington, Dec. 5, 1801, Ford, Fed. Ed., IX, pp. 310–320.

7. *Note:* Interesting in this connection is that on May 14, 1743, Benjamin Franklin published his *Proposal for Promoting Useful Knowledge among the British Plantations in America,* saying, among other things: "That One Society be formed by Virtuosi or ingenious Men residing in the several colonies, to be called The American Philosophical Society who are to maintain a constant correspondence." This is reproduced in photostat from the Mason collection of Frankliniana at Yale University as Plate III in Vol. 87, No. 3, of the *Proceedings of the American Philosophical Society,* July (1943).

8. Lord Kames: *Elements of Criticism,* p. 26, Edited by James R. Boyd, New York (1883).

9. To Thomas Law: Poplar Forest, June 13, 1814, ME, XIV, p. 144.

10. Lord Kames: *Elements of Criticism,* p. 24 (Edition 1883).

11. *Ibid.,* p. 25.

12. *Ibid.,* p. 25.

13. To Thomas Sully: Monticello, January 8, 1812, ME, XIII, p. 120.

14. Lord Kames: *Elements of Criticism,* p. 27, Edited by James R. Boyd, New York (1883).

15. To John Adams: Monticello, May 17, 1818, ME, XV, pp. 169–170.

16. Lord Kames: *Ibid.,* p. 27.

17. To Bernard Moore: circa 1764, Ford, Fed. Ed., XI, pp. 420–421.

18. Lord Kames: *Elements of Criticism,* p. 28, Edited by James R. Boyd, New York (1883).

19. To Martha Jefferson: nearing Toulouse, May 21, 1787, Ford, Fed. Ed., V, p. 283.

20. To Maria Cosway: Paris, Oct. 10, 1786, ME, V, pp. 440–441.

21. To Dr. Benjamin Rush: Poplar Forest, Aug. 17, 1811, Ford, Fed. Ed., XI, p. 213.

22. To Maria Cosway: Paris, Oct. 10, 1786, ME, V, p. 445.

23. Lord Kames: *Elements of Criticism,* p. 50 (Edition 1883).

24. *Ibid.*, p. 50.

25. *Ibid.*, p. 51.

26. *Ibid.*, p. 51.

27. To Robert Skipwith: Monticello, August 3, 1771, ME, IV, pp. 237–240.

28. To Peter Carr: Paris, Aug. 10, 1787, ME, VI, p. 257.

29. To Thomas Law: Poplar Forest, June 13, 1814, ME, XIV, p. 143.

30. To Peter Carr: Paris, August 10, 1787, ME, VI, p. 257.

31. To John Adams: Monticello, Oct. 14, 1816, ME, XV, p. 76.

32. To Thomas Law: Poplar Forest, June 13, 1814, ME, XIV, pp. 139–149.

33. *Ibid.*, p. 141.

34. *Ibid.*

35. *Ibid.*

36. To Miles King: Monticello, Sept. 26, 1814, ME, XIV, pp. 196–197.

37. Edmund Burke: *Essay on the Sublime and Beautiful*, p. 84, London (1925).

38. To Maria Cosway: Paris, Oct. 10, 1786, ME, V, p. 445.

39. To John Adams: Monticello, Aug. 1, 1816, ME, XV, p. 57.

40. Gilbert Chinard: *The Literary Bible of Thomas Jefferson*, p. 9, Baltimore (1928).

41. To John Page: Shadwell, July 15, 1763, Ford, Fed. Ed., I, pp. 442–443.

42. Lord Kames: *Elements of Criticism*, p. 104 (Edition 1883).

43. Katherine Gilbert and Helmut Kuhn: *A History of Esthetics*, p. 302, New York (1939).

44. To J. B. Colvin: Monticello, Sept. 20, 1810, Ford, Fed. Ed., XI, pp. 146–147.

45. Lord Kames: *Elements of Criticism*, I, pp. 88–104, Edinburgh (Edition 1774).

46. *Ibid.*

47. To Robert Skipwith: Monticello, Aug. 3, 1771, ME, IV, pp. 237–240.

48. Lord Kames: *Elements of Criticism*, I, pp. 88–104, Edinburgh (Edition 1774).

49. To Robert Skipwith: *Ibid.*

50. Lord Kames: *Elements of Criticism*, p. 182, New York (Edition 1883).

51. Edmund Burke: *Essay on the Sublime and Beautiful*, p. 91.

52. *Ibid.*, p. 155.

53. *Ibid.*, p. 139.

54. *Ibid.*, p. 140.

55. *Ibid.*, p. 160.

56. To Benjamin Vaughan: Philadelphia, May 11, 1791, Ford, Fed. Ed., VI, pp. 260–261.

57. *Autobiography:* Ford, Fed. Ed., I, p. 149.

58. To Benjamin Vaughan: *Ibid.*

59. To John Adams: Paris, 1786.
60. To Ezra Stiles: Paris, 1786.
61. To Jeremiah Moor: Monticello, Aug. 14, 1800, Ford, Fed. Ed., IX, pp. 142–143.
62. *The Batture at New Orleans*, ME, XVIII, pp. 1–132.

JEFFERSON'S PHILOSOPHY OF ART:
SOME SOURCES—II.

WE HAVE SEEN that Jefferson stood at the confluence of several important streams of thought. His esthetic views were colored, like his intellectual and political attitudes, by the many-sided character of this cultural heritage.

He was not an esthetician in the narrow sense of the term. He somewhat antedated the modern development of esthetics as a separate division of philosophy which was signalized by the publication in 1750 of Baumgarten's *Aesthetica*. The German inaugurated "an *ars pulchra cogitandi*" as a branch of knowledge separate and distinct "from those branches which converse of the True and the Good." [1] Jefferson's concern, rather, was that of the eighteenth-century gentleman who made things with his hands, who studded his writings with observations and value judgments on the fine and useful arts, and whose interest in matters of taste and criticism was, in the finest sense, an extension of his interest in people and the world. This was an age when taste had become a matter for debate among the lettered and privileged "which ran obbligato across the more momentous undertakings and disputations . . . of the Enlightenment." [2] Here Jefferson followed in the path laid down by the Earl of Shaftesbury. A firm believer in progress and in mankind's ability to solve its problems through ra-

tional means, Jefferson was primarily concerned with the
freedom and happiness of man. Art held an inviolate place
in this scheme: beauty walked hand in hand with the useful.

His categories were fundamentally Baconian. In a letter
to his favorite granddaughter Ellen Randolph he writes: "I
must observe that neither the number of the fine arts nor the
particular arts entitled to that appelation have been fixed
by general consent. many reckon but five Painting, sculpture,
architecture, music & poetry. to these some have added
Oratory, including within that Rhetoric which is the art
of style & compositions. others again, add Gardening as a
7th fine art. not horticulture but the art of embellishing
grounds by fancy. I think L'Kaims has justly proved this to
be entitled to the appellation of a fine art. it is nearly allied
to landscape painting, & accordingly we generally find the
landscape painter the best designer of a garden. no perfect
definition of what is a fine art has ever yet been given, some
say that as those are mechanical arts, which consist in
manual operation unconnected with the understanding, those
are fine arts which to manual operation join the exercise of
the imagination or genius. this would comprehend sculpture,
painting, architecture & gardening, but neither music, poetry
nor oratory. others say that the sciences are objects of the
understanding, the fine arts of the senses. this would add
gardening, but neither poetry nor oratory. a definition which
should include Poetry & Oratory & no more would be very
difficult to form. . . ." [3]

There is nothing to indicate that Jefferson ever read
Alexander Gottlieb Baumgarten. Nor had the German
esthetician then exerted an immediate influence upon English thought. Bernard Bosanquet, who follows in the tradi-

tion of Baumgarten, holds that British writers on beauty and art within the decade following the publication of the *Aesthetica,* such as Edmund Burke, Lord Kames, William Hogarth and Sir Joshua Reynolds, were to be distinguished from philosophers in the strict sense. Although Bosanquet concedes that Burke, Kames and Hogarth "exercised a traceable influence on the German movement," [4] he withholds from them the accolade of professional esthetician. None the less, these men expressed the dominant currents in critical thinking at the beginning of the rococo phase of eighteenth-century art. The *Elements of Criticism* by Lord Kames, the Scottish jurist who was a friend and correspondent of Benjamin Franklin; the *Essay on the Sublime and Beautiful* by Burke, the Irishman with the fiery tongue who became one of England's great ministers of state; and the *Analysis of Beauty* by Hogarth, the Englishman who was also a correspondent of Benjamin Franklin and one of the most original painters of his or any other time, not only had wide circulation in England but were known on this side of the Atlantic. We may recall again that Jefferson at the age of twenty-eight included all three titles in the list of books which he sent to Robert Skipwith.[5]

Jefferson read Burke, Kames and Hogarth shortly after their books appeared. He refers to Kames' *Elements of Criticism* in a letter to Bernard Moore written between 1764 and 1766; [6] the book was published in 1761. Gilbert Chinard traces the pervasive influence of Kames on Jefferson's political thinking in his authoritative *Thomas Jefferson, the Apostle of Americanism.*[7] Adrienne Koch tells us that Jefferson "had an extravagantly high opinion of Kames; he owned nearly all his books." [8] Although he later turned with

disgust from Burke's Toryism and defense of Marie Antoinette—"how mortifying that this evidence of the rotten-
ness of his [Burke's] mind must oblige us now to ascribe
to wicked motives those actions of his life which wore the
mark of virtue and patriotism" [9]—Jefferson's esteem for
the esthetician belonged to a quarter century before, when
he was in his late twenties. As for Hogarth, consideration
of the painter's influence on Jefferson is reserved for a later
chapter. Suffice it for the moment to point out that the
Analysis of Beauty was published in 1753; Burke's *Essay
on the Beautiful and Sublime* stems from it. Hogarth was
the original mind amongst the three men who expressed the
dominant way of thinking about the arts and criticism that
characterized the beginning rococo phase of eighteenth-century art. Kames and Burke were the variants leading into
rococo. "In many ways it [*Analysis of Beauty*] formulated
the esthetic rules characteristic of rococo, and the new version of the classic tradition reshaped in the rococo style." [10]

Hogarth's linking of the beautiful and the useful—"In
nature's machines how wonderfully do we see beauty and
use go hand in hand," he wrote in the *Analysis of Beauty* [11]
—was extended by Jefferson into the moral sphere when,
at seventy-seven, he wrote: "Nature has constituted utility
to man the standard and test of virtue." [12]

In the *Elements of Criticism* Lord Kames pointed out
that the principles of the fine arts opened up "a direct avenue to the heart of man." [13] Influenced as he was by Locke,
his analysis of esthetic perceptions led him to an orientation
that was unmistakably psychological in its bent. Kames, together with Addison, Burke, Bishop Lowth, Fielding and
Pope—all of whom Jefferson read and quoted—were, of

course, influenced by the critical writers of antiquity.
Longinus' *On the Sublime*, Demetrius Phalereus' treatise
On Elocution, the discussion *On Composition* by Dionysius
of Halicarnassus and Quintilian's *De Institutiones* formed
an integral part of Kames' intellectual equipment, as they
did of that of other intellectuals of the eighteenth century.[14]

Through Henry Home, Lord Kames, then, the young
Jefferson came in contact with the main currents of criticism
of his own, as well as of an earlier time; and it is significant
that his esthetic categories deal with most, if not all, of the
matters touched on by Longinus' treatise. For Longinus,
who was primarily a worker with words, the factors which
contributed to a sublime or lofty style were a grasp of great
conceptions, strong and impetuous passion, proper handling
of figures of thought and diction, noble phraseology, and
lastly, dignified and spirited composition.[15] Longinus' use
of "sublime"—the word comes from *sublimis,* meaning
height—is distinctive; there is no reason to suppose that
the term was used before him in any specific literary sense.[16]
In the Treatise, written for men in public life, he made
sublimity almost equivalent to greatness. He used the word
in both a concrete and abstract sense, as noun and adjective,
in the singular and the plural; and drew heavily on images
from the craft of the mason, as well as the phenomena of
the sea, for illustrations.[17]

It is revealing to turn from Longinus' conceptions to
Jefferson's own characteristic use of such a term as *sublime*
—a use so broad that it was well-nigh reduced to the level
of the present-day colloquial *wonderful.* Jefferson found the
Natural Bridge of Virginia sublime; the gallery containing
Wanderwerff's paintings at Düsseldorf was sublime; so

was the triumphal arch of Marius at Orange. "Nothing is more moral, more sublime than David's description of the good man in his 15th Psalm." [18] Homer's measures were sublime, so was the poetry of Ossian and the *Hymn to Zeus* of Cleanthes. There were also "the sublime delights of riding in the storm." Or take Jefferson's uses of *beautiful*. The French Revolution was "a beautiful revolution"; Harvey's discovery of the circulation of the blood was "a beautiful addition to our knowledge"; the Ohio "is the most beautiful river in the world"; "Lake George is without comparison the most beautiful water." He recorded his admiration for the beauty of Arabian horses. Nor is it surprising to find an indissoluble linking of beauty with utility. In a letter to Charles Willson Peale there is a truly bucolic conception of beauty, together with a real perception of the Hogarthian serpentine: "The plough is to the farmer what the wand is to the sorcerer . . . We now plough horizontally, following the curvatures of the hills and hollows . . . In point of beauty nothing can exceed that of the waving lines and rows winding along the face of the hills and valleys." [19]

In the same vein he wrote Peale that Dr. Allison had made "a beautiful improvement [in the spinning jenny] by a very simple addition for the preparatory operation of roving." This was the man who wrote to Maria Cosway: "How sublime to look down into the workhouse of nature, to see her clouds, hail, snow, rain, thunder, all fabricated at our feet! and the glorious sun, when rising as if out of a distant water, just gilding the tops of the mountains, and giving life to all nature! . . . And what more sublime delight than to mingle tears with one whom the hand of heaven hath smitten! to watch over the bed of sickness, and to beguile its tedious and its painful moments! to share our bread with one to whom misfortune has left none!" [20]

It is understandable enough how Jefferson could find the poetry of Burns "beautiful." Nor need it be pointed out how close to the romantic spirit all his "sublimities" were.

Kames' *Elements of Criticism* contained a detailed consideration of beauty and grandeur in their relation to the sublime. Kames appropriated beauty to objects of sight which aroused emotions possessing the common character of sweetness and gaiety. Like Burke, Kames was primarily concerned with visual beauty, and tended to equate beauty with that which was eminently agreeable. According to Kames, the beauty of visible objects was either intrinsic or relative. An object without intrinsic beauty might be made to appear beautiful because of its utility; in fine, utility transferred the quality of the effect to that of the cause. This doctrine found a powerful echo in Jefferson's esthetic attitudes. To Benjamin Hawkins, for example, he wrote that "the most beautiful bean in the world is the Carcacalla bean." [21] Unlike Kames and Hogarth, who paid no attention to the concept of the ugly, Jefferson found almost as many phenomena ugly as he did beautiful. Burke mentions ugliness as the opposite of beauty, yet consistent with an idea of the sublime. He does not insinuate ugliness of itself was a sublime idea unless united with qualities that excite strong terror.[22] Jefferson applied the term ugly to visible objects as well as to emotions and concepts. He found "gewgaws" ugly, as well as distress, vassalage, the "rotten machine of English government," London architecture, German gardens, physical and moral oppression.

For Kames, grandeur and sublimity signified not only that quality in objects which produced these emotions, they were sometimes also identified with the emotions themselves. The distinction between grandeur and beauty was one of degree or magnitude: he thought that grandeur needed less regularity than beauty, but that order and regularity applied to it as well as to sublimity. In this he followed Longinus, who had declared that "in works of art we have regard to exact proportion; in those of nature to grandeur and magnificence." [23] Kames carefully discussed the impression made by elevated objects and the pleasant emotions aroused by large ones. So, too, he called attention to the agreeableness of ascent and descent. He came to the conclusion that part of the pleasure of elevation derived from looking down on objects. Even if the object was so far below as to cause dizziness, there would be a kind of pleasure mixed with the pain. There is a striking parallelism to these doctrines in Jefferson's description of the Natural Bridge of Virginia: "The Natural Bridge, the most sublime of nature's works . . . is on the ascent of a hill . . . Though the sides of this bridge are provided in some parts with a parapet of fixed rocks, yet few men have resolution to walk to them, and look over into the abyss. You involuntarily fall on your hands and feet, creep to the parapet, and peep over it. Looking down from this height about a minute, gave me a violent head-ache. If the view from the top be painful and intolerable, that from below is delightful in an equal extreme. It is impossible for the emotions arising from the sublime to be felt beyond what they are here; so beautiful an arch, so elevated, so light, and springing as it were up

Fig. No. 4.

VIEW OF THE NATURAL BRIDGE, VIRGINIA

Fig. No. 5.

John Trumbull: SIGNING OF THE DECLARATION OF INDEPENDENCE

Courtesy of Yale University Art Gallery

to heaven! The rapture of the spectator is really in-
describable!" [24]

Kames taught that "an expression or sentiment that raises
the mind is denominated great or elevated . . . hence the
SUBLIME in poetry." [25] In this connection Jefferson's letter to Charles McPherson, a cousin of the poet, may be
recalled: "Ossian's poems . . . have been and will, I think,
during my life, continue to be to me the sources of daily
pleasures. The tender and the sublime emotions of the mind
were never before so wrought up by the human hand. I am
not ashamed to own that I think this rude bard of the North
the greatest poet that has ever existed. Merely for the
pleasure of reading his works I am become desirous of learning the language [Gaelic] in which he sung, and of possessing his songs in their original form." [26] For Kames, the
grandest emotion raised by a visible object was when it
could be taken in at one view; he regarded Ossian's description of the battle from *Fingal* "remarkably sublime." He
believed that too much detail, with no grand or total view
and with no feeling of elevation, could be very fatiguing.
Furthermore, this rule of comprehension in one view could
be applied to fine arts other than poetry, such as gardening
or painting. Jefferson seems to have followed a similar line
of reasoning in his choice of a hilltop for Monticello, for to
him, anything was sublime that gave him a sense of power
and elevation. In the words of De Chastellux, "it seems as
if, from his youth up, he had set his mind like his house on
heights from which he could contemplate the entire universe." Kames further believed, with Addison,[27] that
grandeur of manner depended on a judicious selection of

capital circumstances. Straining an elevated object beyond
its due bounds constituted, for Kames, the "false sublime"
or bombast—an offense against taste of which he held both
Ben Jonson and Dryden guilty. It is melancholy to reflect
that the poems of Ossian which both he and Jefferson so
revered have been relegated by posterity to the same
category.

As we have seen in the first chapter, it is impossible to
separate the esthetic of Jefferson the art-lover from the
"intuitional utilitarianism" of Jefferson, the social philosopher. Given his world-view, he could not but gravitate towards the functional approach to art. Of paramount importance is Jefferson's distinction between the arts "which
arouse the best feelings of man, which call him into action,
which substantiate his freedom and conduct him to happiness" and the "subordinate" arts which "serve to amuse him
only." For Jefferson was concerned with what the arts were
saying and doing and not merely with their techniques.

The kernel of the matter lies in the fact that essentially
Jefferson's esthetic was one with "his vision of the order
of the world and of the nature and destiny of man. . . .
The order of nature, the institutions of society, the conduct
of the individual, have but one end and one means: Freedom." [28] The self-reliance of the frontiersman, the in-
transigence of the revolutionary, met with the passionate
individualism and hatred of restraint of the artist. In his
unwavering attachment to the ideal of personal freedom
Jefferson came closest, perhaps, to the artist nature, that
element in society which most consistently opposes conformity to convention, submission to fiat and the deadening
sameness which men seek to impose upon their fellows. The

democrat in him knew that the individual must be free; the artist in him knew that the individual must have the "right to be different"; and the romantic in him knew that this right has to be constantly fought for. In his biography Nock makes the shrewd observation that Jefferson's interest in art was mostly that "of a participant." [29] In his championing of the right of man not to conform, Jefferson is truly one with the artists whose works he read, whose friendship he valued and whose pursuits he encouraged. Consider the inclination of his mind when writing of variety and uniformity. Let us remember that Hogarth maintained that "All the senses delight in it [variety] and equally are averse to sameness." [30] Burke, too, felt that "change of surface, continual and yet hardly perceptible at any point . . . forms one of the great constituents of beauty." [31] Kames held that while uniformity is pleasant when a few objects are compared "one tires of a scene that is not diversified." [32] Further, he believed "It is indeed admirable that the human visage, in which uniformity is so prevalent, should yet be so marked, as to leave no room among millions, for mistaking one person for another." [33] Thus wrote Jefferson to his very dear and ancient friend Charles Thomson: "It is a singular anxiety which some people have that we should all think alike. Would the world be more beautiful were all our faces alike? were our tempers, our talents, our tastes, our forms, our wishes, aversions and pursuits cast exactly in the same mould? If no varieties existed in the animal, vegetable or mineral creation, but all move strictly uniform, catholic & orthodox, what a world of physical and moral monotony it would be!" [34]

Here are the slogans of the democratic system of the next

century and a half. In politics, states' rights assiduously defended against the encroachments of the central government. In economics, laissez-faire and free enterprise. In intellectual matters, "eternal hostility against every form of
tyranny over the mind of man." In the domain of art, freedom from the cramping effects of rigid dogmas. To William
Wirt Jefferson wrote: "I have always very much despised
the artificial canons of criticism. When I have read a work
in prose or poetry or seen a painting, etc., I have only asked
myself whether it gives me pleasure, whether it is animating,
interesting, attracting? If it is, it is good for these reasons." [35]

So too, to Noah Webster, who had disagreed with him,
Jefferson commented: "No republic is more real than that
of letters, and I am the last in principles, as I am the least in
pretensions, to any dictatorship in it. Had I other dispositions, the philosophical and dispassionate spirit with which
you have expressed your own opinions in opposition to
mine, would still have commended my approbation." [36]

In another connection, Jefferson's dictum "Utility to man
is the standard and test of virtue" has been quoted. Apropos
of this statement Dr. Kallen asks: "And if of virtue, can
utility fail, when all is said and done, to be the test of
beauty too?" [37] Nock, in discussing Jefferson's interest in
landscape-gardening and architecture, whose principle "was
as practical as that of all his interests, whether in the realm
of the flesh or of the spirit," quotes Jefferson's remark that
"it is desirable to introduce taste into an art which shows
so much" and presents a summation of Jefferson's view of
the art of building: "Houses, grounds and towns should be
planned with an eye to the effect made upon the human spirit

by being continually surrounded by a maximum of beauty. Mean and hideous surroundings, in other words—surroundings that reflect a low, commonplace or eccentric taste—have a debasing and dehumanizing effect upon the spirit. Cultivation of the instinct of beauty, therefore, is a primary practical concern, not only of the moralist but of the statesman and especially so under a form of government which makes no place for the tutelage of an aristocracy." [38]

Yet nowhere did this man who so closely identified himself with the America of his time, who so proudly sought to give expression to the American spirit, feel more apart from his countrymen than when it came to matters of art. Was this the eternal sense of apartness of the artist, or the equally compelling loneliness which all men feel who stand ahead of their age? Nock asserts of Jefferson's artistic preoccupations in Paris: "He found, however, that he was in these respects rather out of the current of popular sentiment in America. He was well aware that 'the first object of young societies is bread and covering,' and made allowances accordingly; but beyond that lay the great preoccupation with turning the immense resources of the country into money as quickly as possible—and these factors of necessity and greed together put a heavy discount on any devotion to the arts, no matter how practical its purpose. An interest in art marked one as alien, a dawdler and effeminate, and not quite to be trusted in the serious businesses of life. Mr. Jefferson felt the force of this discriminative sentiment, and once at least, attempted to vindicate himself against it in the eyes of an old friend. His enthusiasm for the arts, he wrote Madison in 1785, was one 'of which I am not ashamed, as its object is to improve the taste of my countrymen, to increase their reputation, to reconcile to them the respect of the world and procure them its praise.' " [39]

But because he was a revolutionary thinker, the alienation from the majority of his fellows produced in Jefferson nothing of melancholy self-pity. A vision that embraced all mankind could not but lead to optimism. Give America the freedom to grow and develop; strike down all the agencies that might enslave the human spirit; establish religious liberty and freedom of conscience and free universities dedicated to the "illimitable freedom of the human mind to explore and expose every subject susceptible of its contemplation"; introduce a spirit of noble beauty and purity into the institutions and the buildings of the commonwealth—and men would slowly, inevitably find their way to the good, the true, the beautiful.

Because Jefferson was a revolutionary thinker, too, his was a dynamic view of life. He saw society in continual flux, and inveighed against those who "look at constitutions with sanctimonious reverence, and deem them like the ark of the covenant, too sacred to be touched." It was unnecessary to ascribe "to the men of the preceding age a wisdom more than human"; or to suppose that what they had done was "beyond amendment." He viewed the social process in all its manifestations—economic, political, cultural—as a continuous forward movement: "Laws and institutions must go hand in hand with the progress of the human mind. As that becomes more developed, more enlightened, as new discoveries are made, new truths disclosed, and manners and opinions change with the change of circumstances, institutions must advance also, and keep pace with the times. We might as well require a man to wear still the coat which fitted him when a boy, as civilized society to remain ever under the regimen of their barbarous ancestors." [40]

To shake off the shackles of the past, to dare to be different, to espouse the new and the untried—this was in every age the creed of the free and creative spirit. Jefferson realized that it was precisely the reluctance to strike out in new paths which had prevented so many generations of men from realizing their full potentialities. His espousal of freedoom on an emotional, cultural and personal level—as a necessary counterpart of freedom on the political level—clearly marks his affinity with the essential spirit of the artist.

CHAPTER THREE

1. H. M. Kallen: *Art and Freedom,* I, pp. 193–195, New York (1942).
2. *Ibid.*
3. To Ellen Randolph: Washington, July 10, 1805, from Edwin Morris Betts: *Thomas Jefferson's Garden Book,* pp. 303–304, Philadelphia (1944).
4. Bernard Bosanquet: *History of Aesthetic,* pp. 206–227, London (1910).
5. See Appendix I.
6. To Bernard Moore: approx, 1764, Ford, Fed. Ed., XI, pp. 490–496.
7. Gilbert Chinard: *Thomas Jefferson, Apostle of Americanism,* pp. 29, 30, 45, 84, 85, Boston (1939).
8. Adrienne Koch: *The Philosophy of Thomas Jefferson,* Footnote, p. 17.
9. To Benjamin Vaughan: Philadelphia, May 11, 1791, Ford, Fed. Ed., VI, p. 260.
10. H. M. Kallen: "Jefferson's Garden Wall," p. 80, *The American Bookman,* Vol. I, No. 1 (1944).
11. William Hogarth: *Analysis of Beauty,* p. 133, Pittsfield (1909).
12. To Thomas Law: Poplar Forest, July 13, 1814, ME, XIV, p. 143.
13. Lord Kames: *Elements of Criticism,* I, p. 33–34, Edinburgh (1774).
14. Alexander Fraser Tytler (Lord Woodhouselee): *Memoirs of the Life and Writings of the Hon. Henry Home of Kames,* 2 Vol. (1807).
15. A. O. Prickard: *Longinus on the Sublime,* Appendix, p. 112, Oxford (1930).
16. *Ibid.,* Introd. p. xiii-xiv.
17. *Ibid.,* pp. 26, 74.
18. To Isaac Engelbrecht: Monticello, Feb. 25, 1824, ME, XVI, p. 16.

19. To Charles W. Peale: Monticello, April 17, 1813, ME, XVIII, pp. 276-279.

20. To Maria Cosway: Paris, Oct. 10, 1786, ME, V, pp. 436-437, 440.

21. To Benjamin Hawkins: Philadelphia, April 1, 1792, ME, XIX, pp. 93-94.

22. Edmund Burke: *Essay on the Sublime and Beautiful,* p. 167.

23. A. O. Prickard: *Longinus on the Sublime,* Chap. 30.

24. *Notes on Virginia:* ME, II, pp. 30-32.

25. Lord Kames: *The Elements of Criticism,* I, pp. 210-249, Edinburgh (1774).

26. To Charles McPherson: Albemarle, Feb. 25, 1773, Ford, Fed. Ed., II, p. 36.

27. Joseph Addison: *The Spectator,* Vol. V, No. 415, New York (1854).

28. H. M. Kallen: "The Arts and Thomas Jefferson," *Ethics,* Vol. LIII, No. 4, pp. 277-278 (1943).

29. Albert Jay Nock: *Jefferson,* p. 282, New York (1926).

30. William Hogarth: *Analysis of Beauty,* p. 31.

31. Edmund Burke: *Essay on the Sublime and the Beautiful,* p. 168.

32. Lord Kames: *Elements of Criticism,* p. 175 (Edition 1883).

33. *Ibid.,* p. 183.

34. To Charles Thomson: Monticello, Jan. 29, 1817, Ford, Fed. Ed., XII, p. 52.

35. To William Wirt: Poplar Forest, Nov. 12, 1816, Ford, Fed. Ed., XII, p. 35.

36. To Noah Webster: Philadelphia, Dec. 4, 1790, Ford, Fed. Ed., VI, pp. 158-159.

37. H. M. Kallen: "The Arts and Thomas Jefferson," *ibid.,* p. 281.

38. Albert Jay Nock: *Jefferson,* p. 282.

39. *Ibid.,* p. 283.

40. To Samuel Kercheval: Monticello, July 12, 1816, Ford, Fed. Ed., XII, pp. 11-12.

ROCOCO AND THE PRE-ROMANTIC: THE HOGARTHIAN INFLUENCE

I

IN EXAMINING the artistic preoccupations of Jefferson, the conclusion inescapably forces itself upon one that he was perhaps America's first esthetician—and certainly one of the earliest links between the New World and the classical esthetic tradition as it flourished in eighteenth-century England. But the character of this linkage may be understood only if the frame of reference is remembered within which Jefferson's loyalties functioned. His Americanism was not insular. He took over the best that the old culture and tradition had to offer. But he carefully sifted the European heritage, reserving for his America what he believed could be advantageously adapted to the needs of the young republic, rigorously excluding the rest. The grand manner in the art and literature of Europe was strongly tinged with the seductive colors of a monarchical culture. To salvage the culture but keep out the monarchy was a goal which Jefferson followed with unremitting zeal.

His perception of what must be taken over from Europe and what dropped was immediate and sure; his patriotism was based upon a keen awareness of the fundamental differences between the Old World and the New. Again and again he gave expression to this awareness, deriving from the comparison a reassuring picture of the way of life he so passionately preferred. To Charles Bellini Jefferson observed: "But you are, perhaps, curious to know how this new scene (Europe) has struck a savage of the mountains of America. Not advantageously, I assure you. I find the general fate of humanity here most deplorable. The truth of Voltaire's observation offers itself perpetually, that every man here must be either the hammer or the anvil." [1] Even more glaring is the contrast he draws in a letter to Joseph Jones: "With all the defects of our constitutions, whether general or particular, the comparison of our governments with those of Europe are like a comparison of heaven and hell. England, like the earth, may be allowed to take an intermediate station." [2]

As Jefferson inveighs against life in decadent Paris the voice of the frontiersman, extolling the simple life, is heard. It may be pointed out that his strictures would apply to the behavior of the society woman in New York or Philadelphia no less than to that of the Parisienne. To the fashionable Mrs. Bingham he writes: "At eleven o'clock, it is day, *chez madame*. The curtains are drawn. Propped on bolsters and pillows, and her head scratched into a little order, the bulletins of the sick are read, and the billets of the well." [3] He goes on to describe the day of the lady of leisure—visits, the coiffeur, supper, cards—then comments: "Thus the days of life are consumed, one by one, without an object beyond the present moment; ever flying from the ennui of that, yet carrying it with us; eternally in pursuit of happiness, which keeps eternally before us." [4] Now the lesson is brought home: "In America, on the other hand, the society of your husband, the fond cares for the children, the arrangements of the house, the improvements of the grounds, fill every moment with a healthy and an useful activity." [5]

The contrast is no less compelling when it comes to the crucial matter of education. He notes with stern disapproval to young Bannister the disposition of the aristocratic families of Virginia to send their sons abroad for education: "Let us view the disadvantages of sending a youth to Europe. To enumerate them all, would require a volume. I will select a few. If he goes to England, he learns drinking, horse racing, and boxing . . . He acquires a fondness for European luxury and dissipation, and a contempt for the simplicity of his own country; he is fascinated with the privileges of the European aristocrats, and sees, with abhorrence, the lovely equality which the poor enjoy with the rich, in his own country; . . . he recollects the voluptuary dress and arts of the European women and pities and despises the chaste affections and simplicity of those of his own country . . . It appears to me, then, that an American, coming to Europe for education, loses in his knowledge, in his morals, in his health, in his habits, and in his happiness. I had entertained only doubts on this head before I came to Europe: what I see and hear, since I came here, proves more than I had even suspected." [6]

And to Baron Geismer he wrote: "I am savage enough to prefer the woods, the wilds and the independence of Monticello, to all the brilliant pleasures of this gay Capital." [7] Jefferson's fervent love of America and his longing to return is expressed in his letter to Dr. Gilmer: "I am as happy nowhere else, and in no other society, and all my

wishes end, where I hope my days will end, at Monticello." [8]

There is, then, in Jefferson, hand in hand with a most
fervent appreciation of the values of European culture, a
condign rejection of many of these values. This selectiveness
could not but engender nice distinctions and subtle adaptations. It provides the keynote to an understanding of his
characteristic two-sidedness I have already referred to.
Perhaps, in disentangling the strands of the frontiersman—
aristocrat—democrat—philosopher—man of action—utilitarian—visionary—rationalist—deist, within the intricate
pattern, it would be more accurate to speak of a many-
sidedness. His esthetic creed was an American attitude,
created by adapting his materials, after reading, dissecting,
sifting, re-combining, to the conditions and demands of the
American scene and the American point of view.

In the following chapters, I will have occasion to examine
the contours of this adaptation. Now, I propose to go on
with the tracing of the effect on Jefferson of the then current
school of esthetics, through one of its most memorable figures: William Hogarth, prophet of the "serpentine."

2

The age of the Enlightenment, roughly the eighteenth
century, was an age of paradox, as is every age in which the
old order is dying and the new is struggling to be born. It
encompassed both the splendors of Versailles and the "Terror" of the guillotine; the high-water mark of the rule of a
hereditary aristocracy, and the final destruction of that
aristocracy by the rise of democracy. In such a time men

turn to different symbols, or to the same symbols for different reasons. From the irrationality of a world full of luxury for the few and misery for the many, they took refuge in "reason." The eighteenth century is also called "the age of reason." The apologists for the *status quo*, seeking a rational defense for the existing order, came up with the clichés of a spurious optimism: Leibnitz vindicated with arguments this "best of all possible worlds"; while Pope, who had placed his genius at the disposal of the tory nobility, affirmed "Whatever is, is right." On the opposite side, Voltaire, Diderot and the other harbingers of change invoked reason no less pertinently to arraign that which they so passionately hated. So, too, Rousseau held up the "return to nature" and the ideal of the "noble savage" in protest against the refinements of a corrupt, artificial, decadent society which debased its pampered darlings no less than its wretched victims. Man—Rousseau believed, along with most social reformers—was innately good, and would recover his pristine virtue as soon as he was liberated from the corruption of social institutions. On the feminine side, Mme. de Pompadour's favorite retreat was her "dairy" at Fontainebleau; the ladies of Mme. d'Houdetot's circle "herbalized" several hours daily; and the peeresses of Marie Antoinette's entourage played at being shepherdesses amidst the glitter of Trianon. It must be remembered that from the reign of the Grand Monarque, when absolutism reached its apogee, throughout that of his frivolous successor, the vital power of the absolute state underwent a slow but steady decline. The old order was indeed tottering when Bishop Bossuet, under the fifteenth Louis, in his celebrated treatise on the divine right of kings, undertook to defend what, only a half century before, no one would have dreamed of questioning.

In similar fashion, the symbols of classical antiquity appealed to both camps. For the intellectual spokesmen of the eighteenth-century aristocracy, Hellenic art and culture became the embodiment of a rationalistic urbanity. The preferred qualities in that culture—balance, restraint, logic, serenity—became also those most preferred by the entire eighteenth century. They are the qualities of its classicism. With the mutterings of an enraged jacquerie—the rumble of impending doom—in their ears, the grand seigneurs found it of crucial importance to remain detached, objective, serene. The isles of Greece became the distant, never-never land of the ideal. From the passion of Homer and the dark splendor of the masters of tragedy to the lyrical self-indulgence of Anacreon or Sappho, from the austerity of Epictetus and the Stoics to the self-mastery of the Epicureans, Greek poetry, drama and philosophy provided whatever could be used of counsel, solace or escape.

Now also the *idéologues* of the Revolution were nurtured on the same symbols and adapted them to their own purpose. The city-state of Hellas became the embodiment of a rational and wise democracy; the stern virtue of republican Rome offered eloquent testimony against despots. Where the aristocrat found a detached and chivalric idealism, a sense of the tragic that was serene because it was purged of its revolt, the republican discovered the rationale for his violent hatred of tyrants, an atmosphere of passionate devotion to liberty, and a clear-eyed, vigorously hopeful materialism. Nor should it be forgotten that the distinction between aristocrat and republican was neither fixed nor rigid. Bolingbroke, Lafayette and Jefferson himself were only three among the scores of well-born gentlemen who, when it came to basic issues, sided with the plain people against their own caste.

The dominant values in eighteenth-century classicism were those, naturally, acceptable to the aristocracy; through the system of patronage they were able to exert decisive pressure upon the artist. Perhaps never before or since have artists created for so highly selected, so discriminating and sophisticated an audience as that of the closing decades of the old regime. But the accent, throughout, was on form rather than content, on the exquisite manner, the chiseled style; on refinement of workmanship and limpidity of texture. To the eighteenth-century mind, the Newtonian conception of the universe revealed the orderly, spacious patterns of a logical and harmonious architecture. "For these liberated minds 'classic' had come to symbolize scientific knowledge, social order, power and loving kindness, 'Gothic' to symbolize ignorance, confusion, weakness, superstition and cruelty. 'Classic' stood for the vitality of commonsense, the inner light which must burn of itself and cannot take fire from without. In that light, to that generation, form is the consequence of function, and function follows the laws of a Newtonian Nature." [9] In poetry, the polished heroic couplet of Pope, the facile maxims of his *Moral Essays*. In music, the spatial design and carefully laid out key relationships of sonata form. In painting, the balanced design of Watteau and Chardin, of Reynolds and Gainsborough. In landscape architecture, the stately gardens of Le Nôtre, surrounding the no less stately mansions which followed the current revival of interest in Palladio's classic style. All of these, in the realm of art, served to affirm the stability of a world of well-ordered, static relationships in which whatever is, is morally as well as mechanically right.

No less did the republicans claim this heritage of the past. Jefferson admired Palladio as much as the Earl of Burlington did, but for another reason. Thus the paradox came about that the same style which infused the great country houses of the English lords was adopted by Jefferson for the public buildings which commemorated the successful revolt against those lords. There, Palladian classicism upheld the past against the future; here it celebrated the triumph of the future over the past.

The "deluge" that broke over the muddled heads of Louis XVI and his spouse spread like a cleansing stream through Europe, ushering in a revolution not only in the conduct of the state but in the manner of thinking and feeling, in the arts and sciences, in the method of production and the social organization—in fine, in the total way of life. Once that upheaval was consummated, new currents and new themes in European art are dealt with. The "Gothic" replaces the Hellenic as the land of dreams; Ossian points the way for Walter Scott and Victor Hugo; passion, ecstasy and abandon have their definitive triumph over the "good sense" that Pope loved to hymn.

But transformations are no more abrupt in art than in any other domain: each change is adumbrated and prepared in a thousand ways. Thus, the romantic spirit by no means flashes upon European culture with the storming of the Bastille. The breakdown of the grand style begins decades earlier, through a series of changes that mark the transition from the world of Louis XV to that of Bonaparte in most

subtle gradation. This is the essence of the period called
"pre-romantic"; of that paradoxical, controversial mid-
eighteenth century which became a focus of conflicting influences, a borderland between two opposing ways of life.
It is precisely these decades which coincide with the formative years of Jefferson, exposing him to all the diverse
tendencies which have been assembled under the duality
"classic-romantic." Basically, it was during these decades
that the rigid structure of Louis XIV's world order began
to crumble, so that the Jacobins, at the end of the century,
had merely to administer the coup de grace. In the realm of
ideas, Voltaire, Rousseau, Diderot and the social forces
which centered about the *Encyclopédie* constituted the leaven
of revolt. In literature, the serene detachment of the classical outlook was being replaced, throughout the middle
decades of the century, by the new world view which found
expression in the extraordinary flowering of the bourgeois
novel, by the emergence of *sensibilité,* and—prophetically—
by the first outcroppings of the "Gothic." In painting, the
static rigidity of the classic tradition was making way for a
dynamic conception: Nature, ceasing to be a clock-work
mechanism which had reached its final, immutable shape,
was seen to be a movement, a continual becoming, a flowing
process of change and growth. The Newtonian conception
was loosened, humanized; the logical, four-square outlines
of Le Nôtre were exchanged for the soft, wavy contours
of the rococo; the straight line of the classic style was superseded by the serpentine of Hogarth—"the line of grace and
beauty."

The change has been explained in various ways. To begin
with, the grand manner of Louis XIV's court was gauged

to the exigencies of an expanding imperialism. The efforts of Louis XIII and Richelieu to consolidate the monarchy had come to success in a centralized state, focussed about the glamorized person of the Roi Soleil whose France was emerging as the dominant power in Europe; a pure and elevated classicism well suited the temper of the time, finding its durable expression in the august alexandrine of Racine and Corneille, in the stately measures of Lully and the spacious design of Poussin. But under the reign of his great-grandson, France was on the defensive; her empire was steadily contracting before the inroads of the British; the grandeur of the great age weighed like a burden upon this lesser generation. "The time inevitably came when the . . . grand manner [of Louis XIV's court] bored his courtiers. Their fatigue announced itself by a relaxation of form whose equivalent in the arts was the Rococo [which] came as the after-image of the harsh classicism of Louis XIV. The word rococo derives from "rocaille." Rocaille was the name given to rockwork, a popular art of putting together stones and shells with analogies to Pallisy's 'Style rustique.' The patterns thus composed were often comically gothic or baroque, but not less often they fell into smooth, free-moving, well-ordered, curving lines, charming, gracious, subtle." [10]

The transformation brought home the rebellion of the human heart against the artificially imposed shackles of the haughtiest of the Bourbon monarchs. In vain the Academy of the Sun-King sought to imprison life within the confines of a fixed pattern. Life burgeoned and burst its bonds, change could not be warded off, the rigid line ordered by fashion crumpled and wavered before the subtle, unfixable promptings of the new sensibility.

The esthetic of rococo naturalism was given definitive formulation by Hogarth in his *Analysis of Beauty*. This, as has been seen, was published in 1753 and enormously influenced Burke's *Essay on the Sublime and the Beautiful* which appeared three years later. The central point of Hogarth's work is its advocacy of the serpentine; this is his special contribution to English esthetics. He was, indeed, the first of the English writers to use the term: "The eye has . . . enjoyment in winding walks, and serpentine rivers, and all sorts of objects, whose forms, as we shall see hereafter, are composed principally of what I call the *waving* and *serpentine lines*. Intricacy in form, therefore, I shall define to be that peculiarity in the lines, which compose it, that *leads the eye a wanton kind of chase,* and from the pleasure that gives the mind, entitles it to the name of beautiful . . ." [11]

One may compare this with its counterpart in Jefferson— his remarks on the unpleasing effect of straight walks in the gardens of England: "*Caversham.* . . . A straight, broad gravel walk passes before the front and parallel to it . . . This straight walk has an ill effect . . . Stowe. . . . The straight approach is very ill." [12] So, too, in his tour through France and Italy, he notes: "Between Maison-neuve and Vitteaux the road leads through an avenue of trees, eight American miles long, in a right line. It is impossible to paint the ennui of this avenue." [13]

Hogarth's treatise is an extended exposition of the esthetic of the serpentine. "For as among the vast variety of waving-lines that may be conceived, there is but one that truly deserves the name of *the line of beauty,* so there is only one precise serpentine-line that I call *the line of grace.*" [14] In 1745 Hogarth had used, as a frontispiece to a collection of his engraved works, the symbol of a serpentine line lying on a painter's pallet with the motto "The Line of Beauty." In response to the many requests for an explanation he brought out the *Analysis,* in which he promulgated his theory that the greatest grace and spirit is imparted by large flowing lines, and that no forms express motion so well as those of the flame, and the gliding wavy lines of the serpent.

Like Jefferson after him, Hogarth was interested in a dynamic view of Nature, in a rationalistic, utilitarian interpretation according to which "beauty and use go hand in hand." He saw nature as a continuous process, a movement. Form was functional, arising from fitness for movement. "The greater the variety movements have, the more beautiful are the parts that cause them." [15] It has already been seen how well this esthetic of movement could express a society in flux. So, too, the contradictory nature of the age found expression in Hogarth's insistence upon the element of pleasing variety which later displaced the geometric uniformity and oversimplification of the older style. He pointed out the pleasing variety in Nature: "The shapes and colors of plants, flowers, leaves, the paintings in butterflies' wings, shells, etc., seem of little other intended use than that of entertaining the eye with the pleasure of variety. All the senses delight in it, and equally are averse to sameness." [16] Hogarth sums up the artist's endeavor: "In a word, it may be said, the art of composing well is the art of varying well." [17] In similar fashion he describes the serpentine line, the line of grace and beauty, as "constantly flowing and delicately varying over every part."

The *Analysis of Beauty* won wide popularity. Laurence Sterne, whom Jefferson read avidly, and for whose *Tristram*

Shandy Hogarth made the frontispiece, advised his readers to acquaint themselves with the book. Through Burke's *Essay*, the new doctrine reached an ever-increasing circle of readers. Kames' *Elements of Criticism* mentioned the constrained posture of a French dancing master in one of Hogarth's pieces.[18] Jefferson, careful student of Kames that he was, could hardly be assumed to have overlooked this item, nor Kames' use of several Hogarthian terms, especially the "serpentine" in his discussions on gardening. The general public, naturally, already knew Hogarth as a painter; "sets of Hogarth prints served the cause of virtue in almost every English home of any consequence . . ." [19]

In France the Hogarthian esthetic made its way with Diderot, who knew the painter personally, as the middleman. In his *Salon de 1765* Diderot refuted the statement made in the *Analysis of Beauty* that France "hath not produced one remarkable good colorist": "You've lied about it, Mons. Hogarth. It's either ignorance on your part, or platitude . . . Paint, paint better, if you can; learn to draw, and don't write." [20] The admonition was a little late, as Hogarth had been dead for some months. A few pages further on, in speaking of Loutherbourg, Diderot seems to be remembering something else from the *Analysis:* "The pyramid is more beautiful than the cone, which is simple, but without variety. The equestrian statue pleases more than the pedestrian, the broken line more than the circular line, and the serpentine more than the oval." [21]

Hogarth's reputation spread fairly early to America, where he was known both in his capacity as painter and as esthetician. Benjamin Franklin was in London in 1725 when Hogarth "had set up on his own account and had published his first engraving." [22] When Hogarth was seized with his fatal attack in 1764 he was about to draft a reply to an "agreeable letter" recently received from Franklin.

It is impossible to ascertain whether the *Analysis of Beauty* was in the library of William and Mary College in 1760 when Jefferson was a student there, since the library was destroyed by fire in 1859. However, the book, as has been seen, was included by Jefferson in the list of titles he sent to Skipwith in 1771; as was the *Hudibras* and *Don Quixote,* for both of which Hogarth had drawn the illustrations, and *Tristram Shandy,* in which the *Analysis* was mentioned. By 1775 Trusler's *Hogarth Moralized* was advertised for sale in Williamsburg.[23] As for the pictures, Richard Altick asserts that "as late as the second decade of the next century no wealthy Boston merchant could even pretend to culture without his set of framed Hogarths, prominently displayed." [24]

Of the American painters who went to England to make their names—a group that included Benjamin West, Gilbert Stuart, Washington Allston, John Singleton Copley, John Trumbull, Charles Leslie, Charles Willson Peale— only Leslie seems to have paid any attention to Hogarth. Soon after he returned from America to England in 1811, he copied Hogarth's *Gate of Calais* and sent it to this country, where Thomas Sully made a copy.[25]

However, the influence of the *Analysis of Beauty* on Jefferson, with which there is primary concern in this study, was quite independent of Hogarth's influence upon American painting. The impact of his ideas of necessity was profound, because while Hogarth was the first in England to systematize and articulate them, those ideas were "in the air," they were in line with the dynamic conception of nature and society expressive of the changing age. Above all, they harmonized the neo-classic esthetic of rococo naturalism with the groping, slowly gathering impulse of the two great revolutions.

3

The link between Jefferson and the Hogarthian esthetic is established primarily through the inclusion of the *Analysis of Beauty* in the book list he sent to Robert Skipwith in 1771. Jefferson, then, knew this work at least from his twenty-eighth year. It could thus have exerted an influence upon his thinking at the very time of his life when he was most given to speculation upon esthetic problems.

"Serpentine," the term which might be called Hogarth's signature, occurs in two places in Jefferson's available writings. The first is in his account of his travels in Italy: "From the summit of the first hill, after leaving Pont St. Esprit there is a beautiful view of the bridge at about two miles distance and a fine landscape of the country both ways. From thence, an excellent road, judiciously conducted, through very romantic scenes. In one part, descending the face of a hill, it is laid out in *serpentine* [italics mine], and not zig-zag, to ease the descent." [26]

It is to be noticed that Jefferson here uses the term in a utilitarian rather than an esthetic context, despite the fact that zig-zag is derived from frontier usage; the "serpentine" is to "ease the descent." All the same, the association is with "very romantic scenes." Furthermore, in this connection "serpentine" did not come into general usage until Hogarth.

The second place is in Jefferson's letter to Dr. Emmett with directions for the construction of a wall to enclose a botanical garden on the grounds of the University of Virginia: ". . . 2. Operation. Enclose the ground with a *serpentine* [italics mine] wall seven feet high. This would take about 80,000 bricks and cost $800., and it must depend on our finances whether they will afford that immediately or allow us, for awhile, but enclosure of posts and rails." [27]

Although Archibald Shepperson, in his description of the plantation at Green Spring, Virginia, mentions "two serpentine walls, each leading to a brick pavilion," [28] and Dr. E. G. Swem, Librarian of William and Mary College, mentions a serpentine wall at Green Plains, an old estate in Gloucester County, Virginia,[29] there is little evidence to indicate that Jefferson had any precedent for the wall he wanted built at the University of Virginia. The poet William Shenstone's works are known to have been purchased by Jefferson in 1765.[30] Dodsley's description of "The Leasowes," Shenstone's country estate so much admired by Jefferson, is in the second volume of the poet's collected works, and contains the phrase "serpentine" no less than seven times.[31] Shenstone himself, in his "Unconnected Thoughts on Gardening" refers also to Burke's *Essay on the Sublime and Beautiful*,[32] which, as has already been indicated, stems from the Hogarthian esthetic. Paul Wilstach says in the ruins of "Barboursville," James Barbour's splendid estate in Virginia, reportedly designed by Jefferson, which burned on Christmas Day, 1884, "the garden walls remain and they are of the same graceful sinuous patterns as the Serpentine

Walls which he [Jefferson] designed for the University." [33] Actually, as Dr. Edwin M. Betts, the annotator of *Thomas Jefferson's Garden Book* has pointed out, the serpentine wall referred to in Jefferson's letter to Dr. Emmett was never built, nor was the botanical garden laid out; the Legislature of Virginia failed to give Jefferson the necessary appropriations.[34]

What is known today as the serpentine wall of the University of Virginia was put up in 1823, at Jefferson's instigation, around the professors' gardens. Here we have a tangible adaptation of Hogarth's serpentine line; yet most Jefferson scholars agree that this adaptation was prompted by utilitarian rather than esthetic considerations. Philip Bruce suggests that Jefferson "might have drawn the idea of the wall from the gardens of England, but the available letters giving Jefferson's opinions of English gardens do not mention such walls." [35] Prof. Chinard is of the opinion that the recesses in such a wall "can be used most advantageously as places in which the rays of the sun are concentrated, and also as wind breakers. In these recesses the vegetation is about two weeks ahead of the rest of the garden. . . . Finally trees can be trained against these walls as is done in northern and central France, and in that way, early peaches, and even figs, are obtainable. . . . Whether Mr. Jefferson intended to do so is rather uncertain since after all he died before he could push very far his projects of development." [36] Fiske Kimball has stated that he is "confident that Jefferson's serpentine wall was an original and logical inference from his purely practical and economical problem of building a wall, which, though only one brick thick, would not fall down, in spite of being built by the most unskilful labor." [37] Similarly, I. T. Frary speaks of Jefferson's having "demonstrated the possibility of building a substantial brick wall four inches thick by making it serpentine in plan, thus introducing the constructional principle of the arch." [38]

Despite these opinions, Jefferson's predilection for a serpentine wall cannot be completely dissociated from his response to "wavy and wandering lines and masses." Functional considerations do not necessarily preclude esthetic ones. For Hogarth they implied each other. Indeed, it is the highest achievement of the functional approach to art to attempt to unite the two. Jefferson, understood as the "man of sensibility" in the eighteenth-century meaning of the term; above all, as a reason-loving pre-romantic could not but be congenial to the spirit of the rococo which symbolized a softening of the great classical style. As I have pointed out, Jefferson drew from the heritage of European culture only what could be advantageously adapted to the needs of the young republic. In this transformation the pillars of the Greek city states, the domes of the Roman republic, rose afresh in what Jefferson and his associates envisaged as the new home of man's freedom, their severity tempered by the graciousness of that specifically eighteenth-century scenic sinuosity which we have come to know as serpentine.

CHAPTER FOUR

1. To Charles Bellini: Paris, Sept. 30, 1785, ME, V, pp. 152–153.
2. To Joseph Jones: Paris, Aug. 14, 1787, Ford, Fed. Ed., V, p. 332.
3. To Mrs. William Bingham: Paris, Feb. 7, 1787, ME, VI, pp. 81–82.
4. *Ibid.*
5. *Ibid.*
6. To John Bannister, Jr.: Paris, Oct. 15, 1785, ME, V, pp. 186–188.

7. To Baron Geismer: Paris, Sept. 6, 1785, ME, V, pp. 128–129.

8. To Dr. George Gilmer: Paris, Aug. 11, 1787, ME, VI, p. 265.

9. H. M. Kallen: "Jefferson's Garden Wall," p. 79.

10. H. M. Kallen: *Art and Freedom*, I, p. 166.

11. William Hogarth: *Analysis of Beauty*, p. 50.

12. *A Tour to Some Gardens of England:* ME, XVII, pp. 236–244.

13. "Memoranda taken on a Journey from Paris into the Southern Parts of France, and Northern of Italy, in the year 1787": ME, XVII, p. 153.

14. William Hogarth: *Analysis of Beauty*, p. 102.

15. *Ibid.,* p. 30.

16. *Ibid.,* p. 30.

17. *Ibid.,* p. 78.

18. Lord Kames: *Elements of Criticism*, p. 101 (Edition 1883).

19. Richard Altick: "Humorous Hogarth—his Literary Associations," pp. 255–267, Vol. 18, *Sewanee Review*, April, 1939.

20. Austin Dobson: *William Hogarth*, p. 123, London (1902).

21. Denis Diderot: *Oeuvres*, x. p. 368 (1876).

22. Carl Van Doren: *Benjamin Franklin*, p. 51, New York (1941).

23. Letter from Dr. E. G. Swem to Eleanor Davidson Berman: Williamsburg, Feb. 12, 1943.

24. Richard Altick: "Humorous Hogarth—his Literary Associations," pp. 255–267, Vol. 18, *Sewanee Review*, April, 1939.

25. William Dunlap: *History of the Rise and Progress of the Arts of Design in the United States*, II, p. 137, New York (1834).

26. *Memoranda of Travels in Europe*, 1787: ME, XVII, p. 169.

27. To Dr. John P. Emmett: Monticello, April 27, 1826, ME, XVI, p. 166.

28. Archibald Shepperson: *John Paradise and Lucy Ludwell*, pp. 13–15, Richmond (1942).

29. Letter from Dr. E. G. Swem to Eleanor Davidson Berman: Williamsburg, Feb. 23, 1943.

30. Marie Kimball: *Road to Glory*, p. 148, New York (1943).

31. William Shenstone: *Works*, II, pp. 285–320, London (1775).

32. William Shenstone: *Ibid.,* p. 111.

33. Paul Wilstach: *Jefferson and Monticello*, p. 229, New York (1925).

34. Letter to H. M. Kallen from Prof. Edwin Betts: Charlottesville, June 14, 1944.

35. Philip Bruce: *History of the University of Virginia*, I, p. 273.

36. Gilbert Chinard: quoted by H. M. Kallen in "Jefferson's Garden Wall," pp. 81–82.

37. Fiske Kimball: quoted by H. M. Kallen in "Jefferson's Garden Wall," pp. 81–82.

38. I. T. Frary: *Thomas Jefferson, Architect and Builder*, p. 55, Richmond (1939).

JEFFERSON'S IDEAS ABOUT PAINTING

JEFFERSON's attitude towards the plastic arts may be gauged from his remarks on fiction. This attitude was allied to the social or functional view of art. For Jefferson there was no "pure" art, any more than there was a "pure" science: the most sacred function of both was to promote the freedom and happiness of man. Each art had a specific role to play in terms of its own medium. Just as literature could inculcate virtue, so painting could foster patriotism, devotion to duty, reverence for those who had guided the nation through its trials and dangers; it could lift man's thoughts to its heroes, just as the painting of the Renaissance and the Baroque had lifted his thoughts to his God.

Apart, therefore, from the joy he took in the lines and liquid surfaces of the great masters, Jefferson was concerned with the "message," the purpose, the subject matter of the work of art. Problems of form did not exist for him apart from problems of content. He may have differed occasionally in his esthetic judgments from the experts: thus, he considered the gallery at Düsseldorf "sublime," "particularly the room of Wanderwerff"—while the painter Trumbull considered the Wanderwerffs, of all the pictures he had seen, "the very worst—mere monuments of labor, patience, and want of genius." But he had a sure feeling for the social function of painting. He counted it, along with literature, as one of the glories of man's cultural heritage. Its function had been to preserve the visages of kings; now it would hand down to posterity the lineaments of the leaders of the American Revolution. Its function had been to promulgate the symbols of the Church. Now, it would, with equal eloquence, promulgate the symbols of democracy. Jefferson wanted painting to become an essential part of the life of the nation. In his Bill for a System of Public Education he included provision for a public art gallery, and a Department of Fine Arts with a school which would offer instruction in architecture, painting, sculpture, and the theory of music. To this school would go the gentleman, the architect, the pleasure gardener, the painter, sculptor and musician. At eighty-three, he was looking for a "drawing master in the Military or landscape line for the University. It is a branch of male education most highly and justly valued on the continent of Europe."

Jefferson's interest in painting dates from a comparatively early period of his life. According to the evidence presented by Fiske Kimball, the young Virginian, travelling to Philadelphia in 1766 to be inoculated against smallpox, made the acquaintance of Dr. John Morgan, "foremost of the Philadelphia Collectors." [1] Jefferson is presumed to have seen the art collections at that time in the city. These included the *Venus* of Titian, owned by Judge William Allen; the *Concert* of Giorgione and a *Holy Family* by Correggio; John Penn's "very great and elegant collection" and former Governor James Bush's purported Murillo, a *St. Ignatius* taken from a Spanish ship, copies of classics by West, as well as "seven statues of fine Italian marble curiously wrought."

In his recommendations for a library to Robert Skipwith in 1771 were included, besides the books by Kames, Burke and Hogarth—each of these contains specific observations upon painting and taste in the fine arts—Webb's *Essay on Painting, An Inquiry into the Beauties of Painting* (1760) and the *Elements of Antiquity*, published at Edinburgh. In Jefferson's *Library Catalogue of 1815*, Chapter 31 is titled "Gardening, Painting, Sculpture" and lists the following books together with architecture, as Fine Arts, under the Faculty of Imagination: Felibien's *Lives of Painters and Architects*, Michael Angelo's *La Gemme Antiche Figurate*, Vasari's *Lives of Painters, Sculptors and Architects*, Winckelmann's *History of Art*, Spence's *Polymetis* and Perrier's *The Perfect Painter*. Also included are Da Vinci *On Painting; Annales de Musée Beaux Arts, Le Manuel du Muséum Français*, Guerini's *Description de l'Académie de Peinture et de Sculpture*, and Atkinson & Walker's *Picturesque Representation of the Russians*. Chapter 30 of this catalogue includes, under Fine Arts "Architecture," Leoni's *Palladio* with Inigo Jones' notes, as well as an Italian, French and English version of Palladio together with Chambray's edition of Palladio's four books on architecture.[2] Fiske Kimball, in addition, is of the opinion that Jefferson, before he went abroad, had read Jonathan Richardson's *Theory of Painting and Essays on a Connoisseur*, Da Vinci *On Painting*, William Gilpin's *Essay on Prints* and the *Aedes Walpoliana*.[3] These are all listed in the 1815 catalogue of Jefferson's library.

From these books he compiled independently lists of

paintings not only in his building notebooks, but in his
library catalogue. Fiske Kimball reaches the conclusion from
a meticulous examination of those documents that Jefferson
did not follow any one writer's but made his own list on
the strength of his reading.[4] In 1782, when Charles Bellini
told him where historical canvasses made by a good hand
at £15 could be obtained, he noted this as well as the
paintings and prints he wished to secure for himself—
some by subject and some by name. The list of that year
included: "Belisarius from Salvator Rosa; Jeptha meeting
his daughter—Zocchi; St. Ignatius at Prayer; The Prodigal
Son from Salvator Rosa; Susanna and the two Elders—
Rubens; Curtius leaping into the gulph—from Mola; Paul
preaching at Athens; The sacrifice of Iphigenia; Seleucus
giving his wife Stratonice to his son; Prints by Hogarth;
Twelve prints 'from dramatic and humorous painting by
Hayman' (of Falstaff for the most part)."[5]

During his five years as American minister in Paris Jefferson frequented soirées and salons, where he came in
contact with the leading figures of the world of taste. He
was a friend of Comte d'Angiviller, of Mme. d'Houdetot,
the intimate of Rousseau; Mme. de Tesse, Mme. de Staël,
Baron Grimm, whom he described to John Adams as "a
man of genius, of taste, of point"; Duchesse d'Anville,
Baron de Grignon, whose opinion on painting "was decisive"; of the painter Maria Cosway for whom he appears to have formed a real attachment. It is known that in
Paris he bought a copy of a *Holy Family* by Raphael, a
Weeping Virgin by Carlo Muratti, a *St. Peter* of Guido Reni,
*A Daughter of Herodias with the head of St. John the
Baptist* attributed to Simon Vouet, and a *Prodigal Son* by

an unknown master. These took their place among the many
other paintings which later adorned Monticello. A visitor
to Monticello in the summer of 1816 summarized its contents in a piece reproduced in *Niles' Register* of the following January, and stated that the collection of paintings "is
considered by connoisseurs to be of the first rate; among
them is the *Ascension,* by Poussin; the Holy Family by
Raphael; *Scourging of Christ* by Rubens; *Crucifixion* by
Guido; and a great many other scriptural and historical
pieces, by the first masters . . . of celebrated characters
and events." [6]

In Europe it had for centuries been accepted that statesmen, philosophers and princes, both temporal and churchly,
should evince the liveliest interest in the arts. The Colonies,
obviously, had not yet reached that condition. For, as we
may remember Albert Nock remarked, Jefferson felt it in-
cumbent upon himself to defend his esthetic predilections.
The argument he advances is characteristic. He is not
ashamed of his enthusiasm for art, "as its object is to improve the taste of my countrymen" and to procure them the
respect and praise of the world.

Painting, in Jefferson's estimation, had two things to contribute to the happiness of man. First—a typically Kamesian
notion—"to give a pleasing and innocent direction to accumulations of wealth which would otherwise be employed
in the nourishing of coarse and vicious habits." [7] The other
also has already been alluded to. Dr. Kallen describes it as
the presenting to posterity "by means of their representative and symbolic creations, the great men and the great
events in the history of the race." [8] The symbolico-historical
function combined happily with the utilitarian in the com-

Fig. No. 6.
John Trumbull: SIGNING OF THE DECLARATION OF INDEPENDENCE
Detail: JEFFERSON

DESK ON WHICH THE DECLARATION OF INDEPENDENCE WAS WRITTEN.
FROM A DRAWING BY THOMAS JEFFERSON.

Fig. No. 7.
"DESK ON WHICH THE DECLARATION OF INDEPENDENCE
WAS WRITTEN"
From a drawing by Thomas Jefferson

Culver Service

Fig. No. 8.
FIREPLACE AND DUMB WAITER AT MONTICELLO
Designed by Thomas Jefferson

Culver Service

memorative canvases and statues by which the new-born republic sought to immortalize the memory of its founders.

Of the second function, Monticello offered numerous
examples. Jefferson surrounded himself with portraits of
the men he revered most—his "trinity of the three greatest"—Newton, Bacon and Locke; of Columbus, Raleigh
and Vespucci, of Adams, Washington, Lafayette and
Franklin, as well as busts of the last three. Another contemporary, William Wirt, describes the drawing room at
Monticello as "a noble salon . . . hung thick with the
finest reproductions of the pencil—historical paintings of
the most striking subjects from all countries and all ages;
the portraits of distinguished men and patriots, both of
Europe and America and medallions and engravings in endless profusion." [9] Jefferson's papers contain the memorandum: "46 portraits in oil; 11 portraits in crayon; 14 pictures, prints and engravings with frames more than 12
inches; 39 pictures under 12 inches with gilt frames." [10]

As one of the leaders of the American Revolution, Jefferson was most sympathetic with the painter John Trumbull's decision to record in a picture the signing of the Declaration of Independence. Trumbull tells how Jefferson,
with whom he became friendly in Paris, encouraged him in
his intention, and how he began the composition of the
signing of the Declaration "with the assistance of his [Jef-
ferson's] information and advice." [11] Both Jefferson and
Adams "particularly recommended that . . . absolute authenticity should be attempted, as far as it could be obtained." [12] Trumbull was urged to obtain his portrait, wherever possible, from the living person. Where the person was
dead, his mentors advised copying the finest portrait that

could be secured. He was by no means to admit "any ideal representation, lest, it being known that some such were to be found in the painting, a doubt of the truth of others should be excited in the minds of posterity." [13] These preoccupations, it need hardly be pointed out, are those of the statesman, the revolutionary and the historian. They lie well within Jefferson's frame of reference and the tenor of his time. In this connection, it is interesting to remember that Trumbull not always followed this advice, and Jefferson took occasion when writing to Samuel Adams Wells in 1819 to observe: "The painting lately executed by Colo. Trumbull I have never seen, but as far back as the days of Horace at least we are told that *pictoribus atque poetis; Quidlibet audendi semper fuit aequa potestas.* He has exercised this licentia pictoris in like manner in the surrender of York, where he has placed Ld. Cornwallis at the head of the surrender altho' it is well known that he was excused by General Washington from appearing." [14]

Fully aware of the interest that future generations of Americans would have in the epic of the founding of their Republic, Jefferson remarked, concerning the writing-box on which he had drafted the Declaration of Independence: "Its imaginary value will increase with years, and if he [Joseph Coolidge, Jr.] lives to my age, or another half-century, he may see it carried in the procession of our nation's birthday, as the relics of the saints are in those of the Church." [15] In this connection, it is worth while glancing at Kames' remarks on the relations which connect things: "Veneration for relics has the same natural foundation," he holds, as "pride, of which self is the object, expands itself upon a house, a garden, servants, equipage, and every ac-

cessory." That foundation, teaches the Scottish moralist,
"with the superstructure of superstition, has occasioned
much blind devotion to the most ridiculous objects—to the
supposed milk, for example, of the Virgin Mary, or the
supposed blood of St. Januarius." And he concludes: "Thus
it is, that the respect and esteem which the great, the powerful, the opulent naturally command, are in some measure
communicated to their dress, to their manners, and to all
their connections: and it is this communication of properties,
which, prevailing even over the natural taste of beauty, helps
to give currency to what is called *the fashion*." [16] Jefferson
had not forgotten Kamesian insights reflected in criticism.

Jefferson accepted the chore of posing for painters as part
of his duty as a public figure. He was painted by many of
them—Stuart, West, Otis and Sully among others. In ac-
ceding to the request of Sully, the Sage of Monticello writes
charmingly to Jared Mansfield: "Mr. Sully, I fear, however, will consider the trouble of his journey, and the employment of his fine pencil, as illy bestowed on an ottamy
of 78. Voltaire, when requested by a female friend to sit
for his bust by the sculptor Pigalle, answered, 'I'm seventy-
six years old; and M. Pigalle, I am told, has come to model
my face. But, Madame, it would be necessary that I have a
face. One will hardly find its place: my eyes are buried in
three pouches, my jaws are of old parchment badly stretched
over bones which hold on to nothing; the few teeth I had
are gone.' I will conclude, however, with him, that what
remains is at your service, and that of the pencil of Mr.
Sully." [17]

Concerning Stuart's and Otis' portraits of himself he
wrote to William Thornton: "Stuart's original takes as

much room on the walls as the thing is worth. With respect
to the merit of Otis' painting I am not qualified to say anything, for this is a case where the precept of 'know thy-
self' does not apply. The ladies from the studies of their
looking glasses may be good judges of their own faces; but
we see ours only under a mask of soap suds and the scrap-
ings of the razor." [18]

It was in line with this social viewpoint that Jefferson declared to Dr. Priestley that the arts must not place themselves at the "service of superstition and despotism." He
observed "The Gothic idea that we are to look backwards
instead of forwards for the improvement of the human
mind . . . is worthy of those bigots in religion and government, by whom it has been recommended, and whose purposes it would answer." [19]

Jefferson's deep-rooted aversion to everything in art that
smacked of the Gothic—the term which eighteenth-century
writers used as a symbol of "ignorance, confusion, weakness, superstition and cruelty" [20]—gave a definite slant to
his artistic predilections. In his monumental *History of the
Warfare of Science with Theology in Christendom*, Andrew
D. White, one-time President of Cornell University and
American Ambassador to Russia, comments on the esthetic
reaction at the beginning of the nineteenth century which
put an end to the classical taste and found new beauties in
medieval architecture and ritual. This reaction was represented by such figures as Chateaubriand, Manzoni, Victor
Hugo and Walter Scott, and Mr. White draws particular
attention to the indifference with which the intellectuals of
the Enlightenment regarded the very relics which elicited
such enthusiasm among the romantics of a later age: "A

very curious example of this insensibility among persons of really high culture is to be found in American literature toward the end of the 18th century. Mrs. Adams, wife of John Adams . . . one of the most gifted women of her time . . . in her very interesting letters from England . . . refers to Canterbury Cathedral, seen from her carriage windows, and which she evidently did not take the trouble to enter, as 'looking like a vast prison.' So, too, about the same time, Thomas Jefferson, the American plenipotentiary in France, a devoted lover of classical and Renaissance architecture, giving an account of his journey to Paris, never refers to any of the beautiful cathedrals or churches upon his route." [21]

Jefferson's interest in painting was intensified by warm personal relationships with the artists of his time. He had a lifelong friendship with Charles Willson Peale, who painted over sixty portraits of George Washington and who was largely responsible for the successful establishment of the Pennsylvania Academy of Fine Arts in 1805. There was his romantic attachment to the painter Maria Cosway, whom he regarded as an "inimitable painter of landscape." It was through Trumbull that he met her and her husband, Richard Cosway, one of the most successful miniature painters of the time. For Jacques Louis David, who "ennobled the contemporary countenance with the classical quality of ancient republican virtue" [22] he had the most fervent admiration. He called his pencil the finest in France; and to Mme. de Brehan he wrote: "We have nothing new and excellent in your charming art of painting. In fact, I do not feel an interest in any pencil but that of David." [23] This admiration, naturally, was in line with his strong apprecia-

tion of the social role of painting: "The inference is reasonable that Jefferson appreciated painting and sculpture for
what they communicated more than for what they were in
themselves. When they combine verisimilitude with sym-
bolism, they provide not only remembrance of times past
but models for the new generations to emulate as well as
to reverence." [24] Utterly sympathetic with the struggles of
the French against their tyrants, he could not but feel the
liveliest esthetic satisfaction with the great hortatory canvases, steeped in the virtues of republican Rome, through
which the painter of the French Revolution gave expression
to the egalitarian aspirations of the age.

As to the actual use of the accoutrements and garb of
ancient Greece and Rome to glorify the heroes of the eighteenth century, Jefferson seems to have been of two minds.
Asking General Washington's approval of modern dress in
Houdon's statue of the First President, he writes: "I found
it strongly the sentiment of West, Copley, Trumbull and
Brown in London; after which, it would be ridiculous to
add, that it was my own. I think a modern in an antique
dress as just an object of ridicule as a Hercules or Marius
with a periwig and a chapeau bras." [25] Yet this opinion
seems to have been adopted out of deference to the pro-
fessionals in art. Nineteen years later his deep classic bent
comes to the fore. Writing about the projected statue of
George Washington by Canova, he says: "As to style or
costume, I am sure the artist and every person of taste in
Europe would be for the Roman, the effect of which is undoubtedly of a different order. Our boots and regimentals
have a very puny effect." [26]

With John Trumbull, the one-eyed historical painter who

studied under West in London, Jefferson's relationship was even closer. Their acquaintance, begun in London in 1785, flowered into a charming companionship in Paris in the summer of 1786 when they moved in the Cosway circle and went on trips together to various museums and art collections. In Trumbull's journal from August 5th through the 19th, 1786, there is a record of several trips with Jefferson and others of their friends, with a detailed listing of various collections, including those of Versailles, the Louvre and the Royal Collection, as well as the precious accumulations of Count d'Angervilliers and Sir John Lambert. Since Jefferson participated in these excursions almost daily, it is known what paintings he saw. It may be that the lavishness and cost of these collections prompted him to advise young Rutledge and Shippen that painting and statuary were "too expensive for the state of wealth of our country. It would be useless, therefore, and preposterous, for us to make ourselves connoisseurs in those arts." He reaches a practical conclusion: "They are worth seeing, but not studying." [27]

In 1787 Trumbull painted Jefferson's portrait for his original *Declaration of Independence*; this was the smaller version, and he regarded the portrait of Jefferson as among his best. The friendship between the two reached its peak in 1789, when Jefferson invited Trumbull to become his private secretary at three hundred pounds a year, plus board and lodging. A few days later he repeated his offer to aid Trumbull's "great pursuit . . . and further his improvement." [28] This was perhaps the first time that an American statesman was taking over the European practice of offering a distinguished national artist a political sinecure so that he might be able to continue with his work. Trumbull declined, on the ground that he wished to go on with his painting "depending upon subscriptions" [29] from his countrymen.

When both men met again in America, after the outbreak of the French Revolution, the friendship rapidly deteriorated. Trumbull aligned himself with Hamilton, became a member of the reactionary Order of Cincinnati, and turned against Jefferson, whom he considered an apologist for the French Revolution and the incarnation of everything he abhorred. The break between them, described in great detail in Trumbull's *Autobiography*, came at a dinner party given by Jefferson, then Secretary of State. The issue, curiously, was an attack upon New England Puritanism made by Senator Giles from Virginia. Trumbull relates that when Giles proceeded "to ridicule the character, conduct and doctrines of the divine founder of our religion" Jefferson smiled and nodded approbation—a strange accusation, when we remember Jefferson's repeated references to the "most sublime morality of Jesus" and the "pure and sublime morality of the Four Evangelists." Trumbull very adroitly lets it appear that the issue between them was Christianity, and not the opposition of the Hamiltonian Federalist to the arch-democrat.[30] Nowhere in Jefferson's available correspondence is there a word of disparagement about Trumbull.

Although Jefferson, according to Dr. Kallen, "seems to have been indifferent to the materials, the tools, and skills of the painter," [31] Fiske Kimball tells us that he bought engraving utensils in Paris in 1786,[32] even though there is no evidence that he attempted to practice this art, as did so many famous amateurs of the period. Nor is there any evidence that he himself ever tried to paint, although he was pleased to have his daughters and granddaughters learn to draw, and considered it a desirable accomplishment for a young lady. He wrote of it, in this context, in terms curiously unlike those of the connoisseur: "The ornaments too, and the amusements of life, are entitled to their portion of attention. These, for a female, are dancing, drawing, and music. . . . Drawing is thought less of in this country than in Europe. It is an innocent and engaging amusement, often useful, and a qualification not to be neglected in one who is to become a mother and an instructor." [33]

Whether or not Jefferson tried to do engraving, he was greatly interested in the problems of that art. Again, the utilitarian reason was joined with the esthetic; he wrote John Page that he had inquired in Philadelphia about getting his seal done, and had found not only an excellent drawer but an engraver who had executed the great seals for Jamaica, Barbados and the Philosophical Society. In criticizing the work of the engraver he showed his usual common-sense discernment: "I like the device of the first side of the seal much. The second I think is too much crowded, nor is the design so striking. But for God's sake what is the *'Deus nobis haec otia facit'*? It puzzles everybody here; if my country really enjoys that otium, it is singular, as every other colony seems to be hard struggling. . . . This device is too enigmatical, since it puzzles now, it will be absolutely insoluble fifty years hence." [34]

Ten years later he evidenced his acquaintance with the techniques of the art in an observation to Benjamin Franklin that "Hoffman's method of engraving with ink was, I believe, known to you." [35] Actually, Jefferson's greatest concern with engraving was that of the statesman and historiographer. His capacity for infinite care, in all matters that concerned the culture and history of America, comes out in his meticulous research regarding the print of Columbus which appeared "in the book of Munoz," [36] requested by Joseph Delaplaine. He translates the remarks of Munoz concerning the print, then enters upon a detailed explanatory note concerning the history and authenticity of the print. To Delaplaine, too, he describes his efforts, during his stay in Paris, to obtain for the young republic the portraits of its first discoverers: "I considered it as even of some public concern that our country should not be without the portraits of its first discoverers. . . . I wish them to be multiplied for safe preservation, and consider them as worthy a place in every collection." [37]

In subscribing to Trumbull's print of the *Declaration of Independence*, the social reformer in Jefferson deplores the taste of his countrymen, while the democrat hopes for a mass distribution of the print among them: "what discourages our citizens in the purchase of prints is the tawdry taste prevailing for gew-gaw gilt frames. these flaring things injure greatly the effect of the print. a narrow fillet of gilt on the inner and outer edge, merely to relieve the black of the main breadth, permits the eye to rest in composure on the field of the print, undisturbed by the glare of a massive, refulgent border, frames of the prevailing style cost as much, and often more than the print itself. while it is right to indulge the luxury of the rich with copies of exquisite and perfect execution, would it not be worth your while to have one of mere outline engraved which could be sold for a dollar apiece? were such to be had, scarcely a hovel in the U.S. would be without one, and 50. of them would be sold for one of the superior." [38]

Jefferson, the gentleman who worked with his hands, saw art in anything made by others who worked with their hands, and he appreciated the dynamic relation of free possession of tools to the life and destiny of the artist. This intensely human approach comes out in his discussion of the Bankrupt Bill: "The British courts adjudge that any artists may be bankrupts if the material of their art are bought, such as shoemakers, blacksmiths, carpenters, etc. Will the body of our artists desire to be brought within the vortex of this law? It will follow as a consequence that the master who has an artist of this kind in his family, whether hired, indentured, or a slave, to serve the purposes of his farm or family, but who may at leisure times do something for his neighbors also, may be a bankrupt." [39]

So too, in his *Notes on Virginia*, he remarks on the ability of the Indians as painters: "The Indians . . . will crayon out an animal, a plant, or a country, so as to prove the existence of a germ in their minds which only wants cultivation." [40]

It goes without saying that the estheticians whom Jefferson read in his youth played a definitive part in forming his taste in painting. Kames' dictum that "a good historical picture makes a deeper impression than words can" was not lost upon the future lawgiver. Kames ranked painting between reading and acting—more effective than words, although not equal to the immediacy of theatrical representation. "A picture is confined to a single instant of time and cannot take in a succession of incidents" he taught. The impression of painting was the deepest that could be made instantaneously.

Hogarth, in his discussion of painting, attempted to achieve some sort of reconciliation between the classic style of the Renaissance and the new rococo. The principle of composition in nature and art most pleasant and entertaining to the eye was, according to him, derived from the "serpentine" or *S* line. What Hogarth displayed was the "lability of rococo petrified into a rigid geometric line. The *S* line may be discerned in the canvases of Rubens . . . Raphael . . . Peter of Costona and Correggio." [41] These were among the artists whose paintings Jefferson viewed at the "sublime" gallery in Düsseldorf. Annibal Caracci's *Murder of the Innocents* was in the third apartment of the Gallery. Caracci was the painter whose *Samaritan Woman* Hogarth used to illustrate the effect of serpentine lines.[42]

Burke, in regard to historical painting, leaned somewhat to the classical side: he maintained that gay or gaudy drapery could never have a happy effect in this genre, and that "much of gilding, mosaics, painting or statues contribute but little to the sublime." Like Kames, he posited well-defined limits beyond which the art of painting must not venture: "When painters have attempted to give us clear representations of these very fanciful and terrible ideas, they have, I think, almost always failed; insomuch that I have been at a loss, in all the pictures I have seen of hell, whether the painter did not intend something ludicrous." [43]

Burke points out that it "is one thing to make an idea clear, and another to make it affecting to the imagination." The mystic in him maintains that clarity helps but little in affecting the passions, as it is a kind of "enemy to all enthusiasm." Like Kames and Jefferson himself, he appears to have subordinated the art of painting—without in the least meaning to—to the art of literature, an attitude inevitable to men who saw first and foremost the "literary" value in painting, and who were primarily litterateurs; an attitude incidentally, into which men like Hogarth and Reynolds, who were painters first and writers afterwards, never fell.

In Jefferson, then, is found a taste for painting consonant with the general world-view of the statesman, the revolutionary, the philosopher. It is a taste which stems out of a period when painting was a documentary art, whose social function was still thought of as exhortation—whether religious or political—and portraiture—whether royal or democratic. In this view, content was firmly wedded to form; problems of form, color and spatial organization could not be divorced from the "meaning" or the "message." It was therefore possible for Jefferson to profess ignorance in the subject—he described himself as "ignorant" to the painter Mme. de Brehan—and at the same time to evince the most lively awareness of the role that painting could play in the social life of a republic and in the education of the taste of free citizens for an ampler life. As Dr. Kallen points out "the painting he did prefer was . . . statuesque and commemorative." In this he was at one with the neoclassic age. In David's spacious and reasoned art he found the same qualities, so congenial to the republican, which he admired in Palladio, qualities of strength and simplicity, of chastity and logic, of humanism, grace and social virtue. In fine, his taste in painting was an extension of his taste

in sculpture and architecture—grounded in the Hellenic as
against the Gothic, in the Renaissance as against the
Baroque, in the democratic antique as against the aristocratic
rococo.

CHAPTER FIVE

1. Fiske Kimball: "Jefferson and the Arts," pp. 238-239, Vol. 87, No. 3, *Proceedings* of the American Philosophical Society, July (1943).

2. Jefferson's *Library Catalogue of 1815:* Jonathan Elliott, Washington (1815).

3. Fiske Kimball: "Jefferson and the Arts," p. 241.

4. *Ibid.*, p. 242.

5. *Ibid.*, p. 242.

6. Paul Wilstach: *Jefferson and Monticello,* pp. 108-109, New York (1928).

7. To Thomas Sully: Monticello, Jan. 8, 1812, ME, XIII, p. 120.

8. H. M. Kallen: "The Arts and Thomas Jefferson," p. 275.

9. William Wirt: *Eulogy on Jefferson,* ME, XIII, xlvii.

10. Memo of Jefferson's taxable property in Albemarle: March 1815, ME, XVIII, p. 285.

Note: For a detailed description see Marie Kimball: *The Furnishings of Monticello* (1940).

11. John Trumbull: *Autobiography, Reminiscences and Letters,* pp. 95-96, New York (1841).

12. *Ibid.*, p. 416.

13. *Ibid.*

14. To Samuel Adams Wells: Monticello, June 23, 1819, Ford, Fed. Ed., XII, p. 127.

15. To Ellen W. Coolidge: Monticello, Nov. 14, 1825, ME, XVIII, pp. 349-350.

16. Lord Kames: *Elements of Critiicsm,* pp. 52-53 (Edition 1883).

17. To Jared Mansfield: Monticello, Feb. 15, 1821, ME, XV, pp. 313-314.

18. To William Thornton: Monticello, July 17, 1816, ME, XVIII, pp. 296-297.

19. To Dr. Joseph Priestley: Philadelphia, Jan. 27, 1800, ME, XV, p. 148.

20. H. M. Kallen: "The Arts and Thomas Jefferson," p. 275.

21. Andrew D. White: *A History of Warfare of Science with Theology in Christendom,* II, pp. 334-335, New York (1936).

22. H. M. Kallen: "The Arts and Thomas Jefferson," p. 277.

23. To Mme. de Brehan: Paris, March 14, 1789, ME, VII, pp. 307-308.

24. H. M. Kallen: "The Arts and Thomas Jefferson," p. 277.
25. To General Washington: Paris, Aug. 14, 1787, ME, VI, p. 275.
26. To Nathaniel Macon: Monticello, Jan. 22, 1816, ME, XIV, p. 408.
27. Travelling Notes for Messrs. Rutledge and Shippen: June 3, 1788, ME, XVII, pp. 291–292.
28. Letter from Jefferson to Trumbull: Paris, June 1, 1789, in Trumbull's *Autobiography*, p. 157, New York (1841).
29. Letter from Trumbull to Jefferson: London, June 11, 1789, *Ibid.*, p. 158.
30. John Trumbull: *Autobiography*, pp. 169–172.
31. H. M. Kallen: "The Arts and Thomas Jefferson," p. 276.
32. Fiske Kimball: "Jefferson and the Arts," p. 243.
33. To Nathaniel Burwell: Monticello, March 14, 1818, Ford, Fed. Ed., XII, p. 92.
34. To John Page: Philadelphia, July 20, 1776, ME, IV, pp. 266–267.
35. To Benjamin Franklin: Paris, Jan. 27, 1786, ME, V, pp. 270–271.
36. To Joseph Delaplaine: Monticello, Aug. 28, 1814, ME, XIV, pp. 175–179.
37. To Joseph Delaplaine: Monticello, May 3, 1814, ME, XIV, pp. 131–134.
38. To John Trumbull: Monticello, Jan. 8, 1818 (MSS. Franklin Collection, Yale University) from Koch and Peden: *The Life and Selected Writings of Thomas Jefferson*, pp. 683–684, New York (1944).
39. Extempore Thoughts and Doubts on very Superficially Running over the *Bankrupt Bill*: ME, XVII, pp. 331–332.
40. *Notes on Virginia*: ME, II, p. 195.
41. H. M. Kallen: *Art and Freedom*, I, p. 171.
42. William Hogarth: *Analysis of Beauty*, Plate 31, Figure 3.
43. Edmund Burke: *Essay on the Sublime and Beautiful*, p. 132.

JEFFERSON ON THE USES OF SCULPTURE

JEFFERSON'S attitude towards sculpture paralleled, in the main, his attitude towards painting. Here, too, there was to begin with, a purely esthetic appreciation, coupled with a pervading awareness of the role that the art could play in the life of a free and enlightened people. His emotional response to sculpture was apparently greater than his response to painting; Dr. Kallen intimates that he "seems to have preferred the sculptor's monuments to the painter's." Certainly the plasticity of sculpture could not but appeal strongly to one who was as sensitive to architecture as Jefferson; the "workman" in him responded to the feel of stone and bronze much more naturally than to the more subtilized effects of canvas and color. Finding himself "on the vaunted scene of Europe" he writes Bellini from Paris: "Were I to tell you how much I enjoy their [the French] architecture, sculpture, painting, music, I should want words." [1] One should not perhaps place too much emphasis upon the order of words in a spontaneously written letter; but it is not without some significance that architecture and sculpture in this enumeration come before painting and music. His taste in sculpture seems to have been as eclectic as his taste in painting. He revered the masters; gave Houdon the same kind of admiration he lavished upon

94

David—he called him "among the foremost, or perhaps the foremost artist in the world" [2]—yet confided to Mme. de Tesse that he had fallen in love with a *Diana*—"a delicious morsel of sculpture" by M. A. Slodtz.[3] In this connection, it should be pointed out that Jefferson was far less the esthete, in the narrow sense of the term, than either Diderot or Grimm. Nor, in view of his time and place, is this hard to understand. Functioning in an effete and overly sophisticated culture, the latter applied themselves to the niceties of discrimination and evaluation. But in the then state of culture in the United States, the issue was not whether a Giorgione was to be preferred to a Titian, or a Canova to a Houdon. In that pioneer civilization, merely to display an interest in any painting or any piece of sculpture was already an affirmative act. Jefferson's function, therefore, must on no account be confused with the function of a Grimm or Diderot. His historical mission was to lead his countrymen, by every means in his power, to the threshold of the realm of art. Once they got there, other prophets would arise to lead them within, and guide them down this path rather than that. In this context, therefore, his general interest in art is the decisive point, rather than the correctness or error of his judgment in regard to this or that artist.

The considerations which led Jefferson to appreciate the symbolical, commemorative role that painting might play in the life of the young republic, applied with equal—if not greater—force in the role of sculpture. The founding fathers had to be immortalized for posterity; and statues, which reached the passer-by in the open, were even more viable as a means to this end than painting, which, after all, was an indoors art, for the walls of houses, museums and public buildings. Through sculpture, as through architecture, Jefferson hoped to achieve the monumental style which he considered worthy of the republic. Here, then, the attitude is social as much as esthetic; the preoccupation is with a content which shall determine the form; the approach, like that of Kames, Burke, and all the other litterateurs who have written on the other arts is unmistakably "literary"; the immanent qualities and problems of the art-style are seen in relation to values and symbolisms which in today's opinion are beyond the domain of the art. In short, Jefferson integrates sculpture—as he does painting, literature and science —with life in its wholeness, with liberty, with the happiness of man.

Jefferson's library catalogue of 1815 includes, in addition to the books on painting and sculpture listed in the section on painting, Richardson's *Account of paintings, statues, etc., in Italy*; François Perrier's folio *Signa et Statua Antiqua*, Winckelmann's *History of Art* and Addison's *Remarks on Several Parts of Italy*.[4] Fiske Kimball records the statues which Jefferson listed in his building notebook before he went abroad as objects he desired for the adornment of Monticello. These are: "Venus of Medicis, Florence; Hercules of Farnese, Rome; Apollo of Belvedere, Rome; Antinous, Florence; Dancing Faunus; Messenger pulling out a thorn; Roman slave whetting his knife; The Gladiator at Montalto; Myrmillo expiring; The Gladiator reposing himself after the engagement (companion to the former); Hercules and Antaeus; The two wrestlers; The Rape of the Sabines (3 figures)."[5]

This list, now, would undoubtedly be "cliché"; a century and a quarter ago it represented, without question, the highest level of taste in this country. It is interesting to note, in connection with the list, that Hogarth, writing in the *Analysis*, in his chaper "Of Proportion" described the *Antinous* as the most perfect figure of antiquity in "utmost beauty of proportion"; asserting that "The *Antinous* fills the spectator with admiration only while the *Apollo* strikes him with surprise . . . of something more than human." [6]

Kames' approach to sculpture was, as has been noted, as literary as his approach to painting. Poetry, according to him, occupied the first place among the fine arts for its power of arousing emotions. Painting and sculpture were more circumscribed, having the command of "no emotions but of what are raised by sight." They were peculiarly successful in expressing "painful passions, which are displayed by external signs extremely legible." [7] As we see it today, this habit of comparing the various arts, when each possesses properties which of necessity cannot be translated into terms of the other, was a shortcoming not only of eighteenth-century esthetics, but one that persists right up to our own time. From it comes the result that modern criticism has a long and painful struggle to establish the primacy of each art in its own field, completely independent of the rest. Noteworthy, too, is Kames' remark about the aptness of painting and sculpture to express "painful passions"—an attitude suggestive of that which led Jefferson to include in the list of sculptures he desired for Monticello such pieces as *Myrmillo Expiring, Messenger Pulling out a Thorn,* and *The Rape of the Sabines.* This attitude, of course, is not confined to the late eighteenth century. In all ages there have been ten tragedies to one comedy, and ten tearful operas to one *Falstaff.*

Burke's emphasis, too, was upon content rather than upon the "pure" problems of space and form. He treated of the fine arts under the category of imitation and "sympathy." A rectitude of judgment in the arts, he declared, depended in a large measure "upon sensibility; because if the mind has no bent to the pleasures of the imagination, it will never apply itself sufficiently to works of that species to acquire a competent knowledge in them." [8] In one of Burke's truly rare progressive passages, he abandoned the aristocratic line about the immutable qualities of human nature, and made taste dependent upon experience and observation "and not on the strength or weakness of any natural faculty; and it is from this difference in knowledge, that what we commonly, though with no great exactness, call a difference in taste proceeds." [9] It was in sympathy with a view such as this that Jefferson demanded a public gallery and school of fine arts. He knew the truth of the value of experience and observation from his own experience: how much greater joy he found in art amidst the opulence of Paris than in the comparative aridity of Williamsburg and Charlottesville and Richmond!

One of the first tasks of sculpture for America was, to Jefferson, to perpetuate the semblance of the Father of his Country. He addressed himself to the project with his usual thoughtfulness and thoroughness. From Paris, in 1785, he got the project under way. "There could be no question raised," he wrote to Governor Harrison, "as to the Sculptor who should be employed; the reputation of Mons. Houdon of this city, being unrivalled in Europe." [10]

We noticed, in connection with Trumbull's *Declaration of Independence* to how great a degree the concern for verisimilitude of the historically minded statesman shaped the esthetic attitudes of the art lover. The same concern manifests itself here: "Dr. Franklin and myself became satisfied that no statue could be executed so as to obtain the approbation of those to whom the figure of the original is known, but on actual view by the artist." [11] Statues made from portraits were always condemned by those who knew the original for their "want of resemblance." Therefore, M. Houdon must go to America "to take the true figure by actual inspection and mensuration."

The question of expense could never for long be lost sight of in the straitened circumstances of the new republic. Jefferson believed, from Houdon's character, that he would not "propose any very considerable sum for this journey, probably two or three hundred guineas." He reminded Governor Harrison of Virginia that "things that are handsome or just should never be done by halves. We shall regulate the article of expense as economically as we can with justice to the wishes of the world." [12]

In both the Kamesian and Burkian esthetic, grandeur was associated with bigness. The reasons for Jefferson's decision to resist the temptation to make the statue larger than life are of particular interest because "as they are generally a little elevated, they appear smaller, but we think it important that some one monument should be preserved of the true size as well as figure, from which all other countries, and our own, at any future day when they shall desire it, may take copies, varying them in their dimensions as may suit the particular situation in which they wish to place them." [13]

With characteristic attention to detail, Jefferson writes John Adams in London to insure the artist's life while he is engaged on the project. Nor does he neglect to prepare General Washington: "he [Houdon] comes now for the purpose of lending the aid of his art to transmit you to posterity . . . he has had a difficulty to withdraw himself from an order of the Empress of Russia, a difficulty however, which arose from a desire to shew her respect, but which never gave him a moment's hesitation about his present voyage which he considers as promising the brightest chapter of his history." [14] Jefferson points out that Houdon will have to see his distinguished sitter much while he is working on the statue; but "his eminence and merit gives him admission into genteel societies here." It is interesting that Jefferson, whose voluminous writings can be examined from beginning to end with hardly a trace of snobbism, becomes conscious of class, perhaps out of deference, when he writes to George Washington: "he [Houdon] brings with him a subordinate workman or two, who of course will associate with their own class only. . . ." [15]

Thirty years after his efforts to obtain Houdon's skill, Jefferson is still devoting thought to a new Washington statue; now the project has an even greater importance, for his old companion-in-arms is long since dead. He is for using Carrara marble, and for engaging a foreign sculptor. "I do not know that there is a single marble statuary in the United States, but I am sure there cannot be one who would offer himself as qualified to undertake this monument of gratitude and taste." [16] He suggests to Macon "old Canova, of Rome . . . for thirty years, within my own knowledge, he has been considered by all Europe as without a rival." The septuagenarian was being somewhat fickle here; he was forgetting that he had called Houdon "among the foremost, or

perhaps the foremost artist in the world." In this letter to
Macon, incidentally, we learn that Houdon, despite Jefferson's assurance to Governor Harrison that they would get
away with a bargain, "solemnly and feelingly protested
against the inadequacy of the price." Perhaps this circumstance had something to do with the fact that Jefferson now
refers to Houdon merely as "the first artist in France," and
explains that he had been taken because Canova would not
come to America and measure Washington from life. It is
in this same letter that there occurs the passage already
quoted in the chapter on painting in which Jefferson reverses
his previous opposition to the use of Roman costume for
contemporary characters on the ground that "our boots and
regimentals have a very puny effect."

It is not without interest to recollect the unfortunate
Ceracchi. Randall tells how Guiseppe Ceracchi, "the disciple, if not rival, of Canova" was among the sculptors who
came to America in the hope of executing an heroic com-
memoration of the Revolution soon after Congress voted
such monument in 1783. He was not merely "panting after
glory" like Houdon, but was an ardent libertarian who
wished "to link his fame with an undertaking so peculiarly
congenial to his tastes and feelings." He showed a model for
a structure 100 feet high, "sculptured with the deeds of
General Washington, with busts and basso-relievos of eminent American generals and statesmen and surmounted by
a colossal figure of the Pater Patriae." Its execution would
require ten years and its cost would be $100,000.00. The
plan was so much admired that Ceracchi spent $25,000.00
in preparations, and took twenty-seven models of the heads
of eminent revolutionary characters. An unfortunate inci-

dent wherein Wolcott persuaded Ceracchi he had been duped by General Washington, Madison, Hamilton, Jefferson and others, caused Ceracchi to leave the United States in disgust. Wolcott's persuasions were, of course, false. General Washington was displeased by the colossal marble bust Ceracchi made of him, and Jefferson refused the gift of his own marble bust which Ceracchi offered and had the price placed at its full value and paid it. "This was the magnificent bust afterwards obtained by Congress and placed in its library and destroyed there by fire in 1851." [17]

Randall further relates that Ceracchi, because of his patriotic zeal for an Italian Republic, was forced to leave his own country in 1799 and went to Paris. There he was commissioned to execute a bust of Bonaparte, then First Consul. The young artists of Paris with whom Ceracchi formed political affiliations induced him to enter a conspiracy to kill Bonaparte, in Ceracchi's mind the oppressor of Italy. Ceracchi was arrested, and entering no defense for himself except monosyllabic answers to the court, marched to the guillotine in February, 1801. His artistic credo takes one form in an excerpt from a letter to Governor Clinton of New York in 1792 when he stated: "The greatest ancient nations erected monuments to their Heroes while living in order to produce emulation." [18]

Always keenly aware of the symbolic function of art—particularly of an art such as sculpture—Jefferson expresses this awareness in a letter to Abigail Adams, who had requested him to purchase a group of statues for her use as table decorations at the American Embassy in London. He could find only three of those she had named, Minerva, Diana and Apollo; and was obliged to add a

fourth, unguided by her choice. "They offered me a fine
Venus; but I thought it out of taste to have two at table at
the same time." The reference is to Abigail's daughter who
was much admired for her beauty. "Paris and Helen were
represented. I conceived it would be cruel to remove them
from their peculiar shrine." It came about that "At length
a fine Mars was offered, calm, bold, his faulchion not drawn
but ready to be drawn. This will do, thinks I, for the table
of the American Minister in London, where those whom it
may concern may look and learn that though Wisdom is
our guide, and the Song and Chase our supreme delight, yet
we offer adoration to that tutelar God also who rocked the
cradle of our birth . . . and has shown himself the patron
of our rights and avenger of our wrongs." The group was
happily dispatched, but "envy and malice will never be
quiet." Already he hears it whispered that in admitting
Minerva to Abigail's table he had departed from the principle which made him reject Venus: "in plain English that I
have paid a just respect to the daughter but failed to the
mother. No Madam, my respect to both is sincere. Wisdom,
I know, is social. She seeks her fellows, but Beauty is jealous,
and illy bears the presence of a rival." [19]

Jefferson was concerned not only with the proper style of
statuary (and of architecture) "dedicated to the sovereignty
of the people" [20] but he also gave his attention to the closely
related problem of the "lapidary style." It appears that
Houdon remonstrated against the length of the inscriptions
on the statues he had made of Washington and Lafayette.
The teacher in Jefferson was too strong to yield to such a
"purely" esthetic argument. Despite his enormous respect
for Houdon's talent, he could not agree that the story of

these soldiers' valor, told on their statues, should be curtailed.[21] The Frenchman's remonstrances, however, seem not to have been forgotten. Almost thirty years later he wrote to James Monroe: "If it be proposed to place an inscription on the capitol, the lapidary style requires that essential facts only should be stated, and these with a brevity admitting no superfluous word. The essential facts in the two inscriptions proposed are these: 'FOUNDED 1791 —BURNT BY A BRITISH ARMY 1814—RESTORED BY CONGRESS 1817.' " [22] The reasons he adduces for this brevity are, first, that the letters must be large to be read from below; second, that there is not much space for them in a pediment or frieze; and third "that no passion can be imputed to this inscription, every word being justifiable from the most classical examples." By this time, clearly, his attitude in this matter was poles apart from that of Dr. Samuel Johnson, who held the opinion that "in lapidary inscriptions a man is not upon oath." [23]

Jefferson's love of antique sculpture seems never to have left him. In the last year of his life he joyfully communicated to his grandson-in-law Joseph Coolidge, Jr., the news received from his friend Appleton in Europe that "several statues of the highest order of sculpture" had been reported found in a subterranean vault in Athens along with two thousand papyri of classic Greek authors in a "great state of perfection." [24]

Nor did he lose the feeling, so consonant with the predominantly agrarian outlook of the leader of a country which was only beginning to be industrialized—that statuary as such was still too expensive an undertaking for pioneer America. He included "statuary" along with painting when he advised Rutledge and Shippen that since they "are too expensive for the state of wealth among us . . . they are worth seeing but not studying." In similar vein he wrote Thomas Appleton twenty-eight years later, that even though he wished the sculptor Bartholin could be gainfully employed in the United States in a manner worthy of his talent, there simply were too few individuals of great wealth—and among these, too few with a taste for the fine arts—to sustain the activity of a sculptor.[25] It would appear he did not consider Bartholin competent for any of the sculpture work on the Capitol then rebuilding.

Just as Jefferson's interest in painting extended to the cognate art of engraving, so his predilection for sculpture, for obviously utilitarian reasons, took in also the subsidiary techniques of casting coins and medals.

He closely observed the minting of coins while abroad; any ideas of value that he picked up there might be applied with profit after he came home. To Francis Hopkinson, the first known American composer, who later became Director of the United States Mint, he wrote from Paris that a method had been invented there for making a "coin as beautiful as a medal" and more cheaply; and that he would endeavor to procure a sample for Congress to use as a model.[26]

Equally important was the problem of medals, which had a symbolic use as gifts to visiting diplomats. Since these were to be instrumental in establishing the dignity of the young republic among the ambassadors of the sovereigns who would like nothing better than to deny that dignity, the matter merited careful attention. He discussed the project with William Short, describing in detail an appropriate design: "One suggestion has been a Columbia (a fine female figure) delivering the emblems of peace and commerce to a Mercury, with a legend 'Peace and Commerce' circumscribed, and the date of our republic, to wit, 4th July, MDCCLXXVI, subscribed as an exergum; but having little confidence in our own ideas in an art not familiar here, they are only suggested to you, to be altered, or altogether postponed to such better device as you may approve, on consulting with those who are in the habit and study of medals." [27] He recommended Duvivier and Dupré as the best available workmen; the latter, whom he designated as "perhaps the better of the two," he knew as the artist who had executed medals for John Paul Jones.[28]

Interestingly, it was in his *Notes for the Establishment of a Money Unit and a Coinage for the United States*, written as a result of his researches into techniques of coining, that Jefferson delivered himself of the famous dictum that "taste cannot be controlled by law."

Jefferson's recognition of the talent for painting among Indians has been noted. In his *Notes on Virginia* occurs a parallel passage about their capacity for sculpture, in which he makes the observation that "the Indians . . . will often carve figures on their pipes not destitute of design or merit." [29] His life-long interest in and appreciation of the qualities of the Indian tribes is nowhere better expressed than in his letter of thanks to Harry Innes: "The statue you have been so kind as to send me, and for which I beg you to accept my thanks, would, because of the hardness of the stone, be a better proof of the use of iron, than I ever yet saw; but as it is a solitary fact, and possible to have been made with implements of stone, and great patience, for which the Indians are remarkable I consider it to have been so made. It is certainly the best piece of workmanship I ever saw from their hands." [30]

In the description of the interior furnishings of Monticello by visitors during Jefferson's lifetime, it was recorded that in the summer of 1816 he had a large collection of Indian curiosities, including "busts of a male and female, sitting in Indian position. They are supposed to be of great antiquity, and to have been formed by the Indians; they were ploughed up in the state of Tennessee; are of very hard stone and are considerably defaced. There is also in the hall a representation of battle between the Panis and Osages, also a map of the Missouri and its tributary streams, both executed by Indians on dressed buffalo hides; bows, arrows, poisoned lances, pipes of peace, wampum belts, mockasins, etc., several dresses and cooking utensils, of the Mandan and other nations of the Missouri." [31]

Monticello contained at the same time a colossal bust of Jefferson in the hall on a "truncated column, on a pedestal of which are represented the 12 tribes of Israel and the 12 signs of the Zodiac." In addition, there was a full-length figure of Cleopatra reclining after she had applied the asp, a model of one of Egypt's pyramids, and plaster busts of Voltaire and Turgot. Placed in the parlor were busts of the "Emperors Alexander of Russia and Napoleon of France sitting on columns, and a sleeping Venus" while the bow of the dining room held busts of General Washington, Dr. Franklin, Marquis de Lafayette and Paul Jones in plaster. [32]

Among the arts and crafts allied to sculpture, modelling in wax enjoyed widespread popularity. Preeminent in this field was an American, Patience Lovell Wright, a niece of

John Wesley, born among Quakers in Bordentown, New
Jersey. She was enormously successful in London, where her
likenesses achieved a wide reputation; she moved in Benjamin West's circle, and for a time had access to George the
Third, although she lost that monarch's favor by scolding
him for having sanctioned the American war. Despite her
English connection, she remained demonstratively American,
as is evidenced by the letter she wrote to Jefferson in Paris in
1785: "Honoured sir: . . . I most sincerely wish not only
to make the likeness of Washington, but of those *five* gentlemen, who assisted at the signing the treaty of peace, that
put an end to so bloody and dreadful a war. The more public
the honours bestowed on such men by their country, the
better. To shame the English king, I would go to any trouble
and expense to add my mite in the stock of honour due to
Adams, Jefferson and others, to send to America; and I
will, if it is thought proper to pay my expense of travelling
to Paris, come myself and model the likeness of Mr. Jefferson." [33] The project she suggested did not materialize;
Patience Wright died in London that same year.

She was a forerunner of a new generation of Americans,
who, in the plastic arts and crafts, within the space of a
few decades, laid the foundation for an indigenous art. As
the republic grew in wealth and power, arts such as painting
and sculpture which Jefferson had regarded as too expensive
for a youthful nation became increasingly accessible; this
development was enormously accelerated by the rapid in-
dustrialization of the North and the development of the
West. As late as 1820 John Trumbull believed that "nothing
in sculpture would be wanted in this country for yet a hundred years"; but his was a rabidly conservative view. He

and those who thought like him "overlooked two facts: first, the growing demand for statues and memorials to commemorate the struggle for independence; and, second, the pioneer work already done by Americans who had learned to model in wax, wood or clay. From this group of early modelers, few in number, came the inspiration for our first native sculptors. . . . Craftsmen working in wood or stone were the immediate forerunners of the professional sculptor." [34] Particularly worthy of mention among this advance guard were William Rush, who became famous for his ships' figureheads; Hezekiah Augur, who did a copy of the bust of Apollo in Carrara marble; and John Browere, whose aim was to create a national gallery of famous Americans through his life-casts of the human face.

Despite these and other craftsmen in stone and wood who did excellent work on the trim of the finer houses and a few of the public buildings, there were no American sculptors competent, in Jefferson's opinion, for the interpretation of the classical style on public buildings as he conceived it. During Jefferson's second term as President he suggested that Benjamin Latrobe write Philip Mazzei, his old neighbor and friend then long resident in Italy, for his aid in securing qualified sculptors for the Capitol. This correspondence between Latrobe and Mazzei resulted in contracts with Giuseppe Franzoni, son of the President of the Academy of Fine Arts at Carrara and nephew of Cardinal Franzoni, as well as Giovanni Andrei, said to be his brother-in-law and instructor. They reached Washington in 1806. The Italians were responsible for most of the sculptured work on the Capitol which was destroyed when the British burned it in August, 1814, but their small preliminary models were saved. After Giuseppe Franzoni's death in Washington in 1815, Andrei went to Italy and brought back two more sculptors, Francisco Iardella and Carlo Franzoni, brother of Giuseppe. They were followed by Luigi Persico, Enrico Causici, Antonio Capellano, Giuseppe Valaperti and the Frenchman Nicholas Gevelot, all of whom worked on the sculptures of the rebuilt Capitol. Not until 1832 did Horatio Greenough become the first American sculptor to receive a public commission from Congress.[35]

Browere's attempt to take Jefferson's life mask almost turned into disaster. The Sage of Monticello was then eighty-two. This marked his farewell to posing: "I was taken in by Mr. Browere. He said his operation would be of about twenty minutes and less unpleasant than Houdon's method. I submitted without enquiry. But it was a bold experiment on his part on the health of an octogenary worn down by sickness as well as age. Successive coats of grout plastered on the naked head and kept there an hour would have been a severe trial of a young and hail man. He suffered the plaster also to get so dry that separation became difficult and even dangerous. He was obliged to use freely the mallet and chisel to break it into pieces and get off a piece at a time. These strokes of the mallet would have been sensible almost to a loggerhead. The family became alarmed and he confused till I was quite exhausted, and there became real danger that the ears would tear from the head sooner than from the plaster. I now bid adieu forever to busts and even portraits." [36]

We see then, throughout Jefferson's attitudes towards the fine arts, the impulse of the humanist, the statesman, the lover of culture, and the teacher. Where the esthete sep-

Fig. No. 9.

DRAWING BY THOMAS JEFFERSON OF HIS INVENTION—THE MOLD-BOARD PLOW

Courtesy of the Massachusetts Historical Society, Boston, Massachusetts

Fig. No. 10.

WILLIAM NOGARTH'S SERPENTINE OR "S" LINE

Courtesy of Mr. A. A. Ostrander and the Silver Lotus Press, Pittsfield, Massachusetts

arates art from life, and uses his artistic sensitivities to affirm his superiority to the common run, Jefferson would bring art close to life, to the daily experience, the aspirations and dreams of mankind at large. Where the esthete seeks to exclude, Jefferson seeks to include. True, Jefferson is far from impeccable in his judgments; but his instinct is thoroughly healthy, and his own unspoilt delight in art is allied to a social-mindedness which impels him to share it with his countrymen. It is for this reason that, even though he did not formulate a system or a body of doctrine on esthetic experience, we may well consider him in the fore-front of America's practical estheticians—and probably the first.

CHAPTER SIX

1. To Charles Bellini: Paris, Sept. 30, 1785, ME, V, pp. 152–154.
2. *Ibid.*
3. To Comtesse de Tesse: Nismes, March 20, 1787, ME, VI, p. 102.
4. Jefferson's *Library Catalogue of 1815:* Jonathan Elliott, Washington (1815).
5. Fiske Kimball: *Thomas Jefferson, Architect,* fig. 79, privately printed, Boston (1916).
6. William Hogarth: *Analysis of Beauty,* p. 146.
7. Lord Kames: *Elements of Criticism,* II, p. 464, Edinburgh (1774).
8. Edmund Burke: *Essay on the Sublime and Beautiful,* p. 79.
9. *Ibid.,* p. 73.
10. To Governor Harrison of Virginia: Paris, Jan. 12, 1785, from Gilbert Chinard: *Houdon in America,* pp. 5–6, Baltimore (1930).
11. *Ibid.*
12. *Ibid.*
13. *Ibid.*
14. To George Washington: Paris, July 10, 1785, ME, XIX, pp. 8–10.
15. *Ibid.*
16. To Nathaniel Macon: Monticello, Jan. 22, 1816, ME, XIV, pp. 408–410.
17. Henry G. Randall: *Life of Thomas Jefferson,* II, pp. 199–200, New York (1858).
18. *Ibid.,* III, pp. 596–597.

19. To Abigail Adams: Paris, Sept. 25, 1785, Ford, Fed. Ed., IV, pp. 463-464.

20. To B. H. Latrobe: Monticello, July 12, 1812, ME, XIII, pp. 178-179.

21. To James Madison: Paris, Feb. 8, 1786, ME, V, pp. 280-281.

22. To James Monroe: Monticello, Oct. 16, 1816, ME, XV, pp. 78-79.

23. J. W. Krutch: *Samuel Johnson,* p. 30, New York (1944).

24. To Joseph Coolidge, Jr.: Monticello, Jan. 15, 1825, ME, XVIII, pp. 334-335.

25. To Thomas Appleton: Monticello, Jan. 14, 1816, ME, XIX, p. 229.

26. To Francis Hopkinson: Paris, Dec. 23, 1786, ME, XVI, pp. 21-22.

27. To William Short: New York, April 30, 1790, ME, VIII, p. 28.

28. To John Paul Jones: Paris, March 23, 1789, ME, XIX, pp. 54-60.

29. *Notes on Virginia:* ME, II, p. 195.

30. To Harry Innes: Philadelphia, March 7, 1791, ME, VII, pp. 135-136.

31. P. Wilstach: *Jefferson and Monticello,* pp. 108-109.

32. *Ibid.*

33. William Dunlap: *History of the Rise and Progress of the Arts of Design,* I, p. 136.

34. John Krout & Dixon Ryan Fox: *The Completion of Independence,* pp. 345-346, New York (1944).

35. I. T. Frary: *They Built the Capitol,* p. 86; pp. 107-130, Richmond (1940).

36. To James Madison: Monticello, Oct. 18, 1825, ME, XIX, pp. 286-287.

ARCHITECT JEFFERSON

IF, IN REGARD to painting and sculpture, Jefferson considered himself the amateur-onlooker, when it came to architecture and gardening he was definitely the participant and doer. "To his neighbors of Virginia his fame rests almost as solidly on the genius he displayed as an architect, and proud is the owner of an old estate who can claim Jefferson as designer of his buildings and perhaps of the grounds by which they are surrounded."[1] Among the great houses ascribed to architect Jefferson are Bremo, Barboursville, reputed to have been the most imposing estate in all Virginia, Edgehill, Edgemont, Farmington and Ampthill. For two other Presidents of the United States Jefferson designed houses, Ash Lawn for James Monroe near Monticello at a cost of $1,000.00 when he had little money, and Oak Hill after he became President, as well as Montpelier for James Madison. In building the philosopher-statesman joined hands with the practical man of affairs, the social reformer with the methodical promoter of his country's welfare. Building gave his predilection for the classical in art its widest scope and profoundly affected the course of American architecture. Indeed, he has been considered to have started, singlehanded, "the classical revival not only in America but in the world."

Architecture in the American colonies, up to the close of the Revolution, was a gentleman's avocation rather than a profession, and a desirable, though not essential feature of a well-rounded education. Because of the prevalence of this attitude, many of the important houses were designed by the owners themselves. For Jefferson, architecture was a lifelong study as well as an absorbing interest. As he himself said: "Architecture is my delight, and putting up and pulling down one of my favorite amusements."

The art appealed to everything in him that loved order, harmony and logical arrangement. In the realm of spatial relationships it represented the same internal organization and coordination of parts in a whole which, on a more abstract plane, was afforded him by his "favorite study" of mathematics. As Fiske Kimball and Frary have pointed out, architecture for Jefferson was largely a matter of formulas and mathematics; his proportions were calculated mathematically, and on the backs of his drawings are to be seen "set down in his precise handwriting the results of those calculations." The length and breadth of the building, the height of the entablature, the diameter of the column—these were visible manifestations, in the realm of matter, of the harmony of numbers.

But allied to the intellectual appreciations of the master planner was the direct emotional response of the artist, a response which he describes to the Comtesse de Tesse in one of his most playful letters: "Here I am, Madam, gazing whole hours at the Maison Quarrée, like a lover at his mistress. The stocking weavers and silk spinners around it consider me a hypochondriac Englishman, about to write with a pistol the last chapter of his history. . . . While in

Paris, I was violently smitten with the Hotel de Salm, and used to go to the Tuileries almost daily, to look at it. The loueuse des chaises, inattentive to my passion, never had the complaisance to place a chair there, so that, sitting on the parapet, and twisting my neck round to see the object of my admiration, I generally left it with a torti-colli." He continues: "From Lyons to Nismes I have been nourished with the remains of Roman grandeur. They have always brought you to my mind, because I know your affection for whatever is Roman and noble. At Vienne [2] I thought of you. But I am glad you were not there; for you would have seen me more angry than, I hope, you will ever see me. The Praetorian Palace, as it is called, comparable, for its fine proportions, to the Maison Quarrée, defaced by the barbarians who have converted it to its present purpose, its beautiful fluted Corinthian columns cut out, in part, to make space for Gothic windows, and hewed down, in the residue, to the plans of the building, was enough, you must admit, to disturb my composure . . . I am immersed in antiquities from morning to night. For me, the city of Rome is actually existing in all the splendor of its empire. I am filled with alarms for the event of the irruptions daily making on us, by the Goths, the Visigoths, Ostrogoths, and Vandals, lest they should re-conquer us to our original barbarism. If I am sometimes induced to look forward to the eighteenth century, it is only when recalled to it by the recollection of your goodness and friendship." [3]

Jefferson's sensitivity to architecture seems at an early period to have made him aware of the deplorable state of the art in colonial Virginia. This awareness culminated in the trenchant criticisms contained in his Notes on Virginia.

But an awareness of deficiencies was bound up, for him, with the strong wish to remedy them. An opportunity for a new style came to him with plans for the building of Monticello. The mountain-top home which became the concrete embodiment of his vision and his taste, introduced a new tone into eighteenth-century building in America, and has remained a monument to the creative impulse of its builder.

Jefferson's early comments on the architecture of his native state evince a clear grasp of the shortcomings, and a rankling recognition of the opportunities neglected: "The private buildings [in Virginia] are very rarely constructed of stone or brick, much the greater portion being of scantling and boards, plastered with lime. It is impossible to devise things more ugly, uncomfortable, and happily more perishable. . . . The first principles of the art are unknown, and there exists scarcely a model among us sufficiently chaste to give an idea of them." [4]

The root of the evil, he holds, is the "unhappy prejudice" that houses of brick or stone are less wholesome than those of wood. "A dew is often observed on the walls of the former in rainy weather, and the most obvious solution is, that the rain has penetrated through these walls." With his usual exactitude of observation, he brings arguments to show that this impression is erroneous and that "the inhabitants of Europe, who dwell chiefly in houses of stone or brick, are surely as healthy as those of Virginia." Even here his permeating social-mindedness comes through: he points out that "A country whose buildings are of wood, can never increase in its improvements to any considerable degree. . . . Whereas when buildings are of durable materials, every new edifice is an actual and permanent acquisition to the State, adding to its value as well as to its ornament." [5]

Going from private to public buildings, he finds the picture as dreary: "The only public buildings worthy of mention are the capitol, the palace, the college, and the hospital for lunatics, all of them in Williamsburg, heretofore the seat of our government." His comments on the colonial Capitol show an exquisite sensibility to proportion and style: "The capitol is a light and airy structure, with a portico in front of two orders, the lower of which, being Doric, is tolerably just in its proportions and ornaments, save only that the intercolonations are too large. The upper is Ionic, much too small for that on which it is mounted, its ornaments not proper to the order, nor proportioned within themselves. It is crowned with a pediment, which is too high for its span. Yet, on the whole, it is the most pleasing piece of architecture we have. The palace is not handsome without, but it is spacious and commodious within, is prettily situated, and with the grounds annexed to it, is capable of being made an elegant seat." [6]

As for the college and hospital, they are "rude, misshapen piles which, but that they have roofs, would be taken for brick-kilns." He concludes in dismay "The genius of architecture seems to have shed its maledictions over this land" yet refuses to abandon hope: "Perhaps a spark may fall on some young subjects of natural taste, kindle up their genius, and produce a reformation in this elegant and useful art." [7]

The vision which Jefferson opposed to this lamentable tastelessness was founded on his "lifelong devotion to classic architecture and to that exponent of its principles, Andrea Palladio, sixteenth century Italian architect to whose published works devotees of classicism have ever since more or less pinned their faith." I. T. Frary goes on to remark: "To Jefferson, Palladio was a prophet, his books the Bible of Architecture. Five editions of this work were in the Monticello library, three in English, two in French. Upon the formulae laid down by the architect of Vicenza in the sixteenth century were based the designs by the architect of Monticello in the eighteenth century." [8]

As Dr. Kallen has pointed out, the Palladian outlook fitted in perfectly with the deepest strivings of the Age of Reason: "To an intellectual class all whose thinking was suffused with the idea of a Nature whose architecture had the clear and distinct construction revealed by Newton's *Principia*, Palladio's designs for building were readily enough expressions of the same simple, harmonious mechanism, which alone made good sense. For these liberated minds 'classic' had come to symbolize scientific knowledge, social order, power and loving kindness. . . . 'Classic' stood for the vitality of commonsense, the inner light which must burn of itself and cannot take fire from without. In that light, to that generation, form is the consequence of function, and function follows the laws of a Newtonian Nature. Now concerning these matters Jefferson was a child of that generation of English intellectuals. He took his Newton literally, and he read his Pope as well as he studied his Palladio." [9]

Rejecting the Georgian Baroque which he found as odious as the "Gothic," Jefferson early set about adapting the Palladian patterns to the needs of his own country. "He rarely permitted originality on his own part to take prece-

dence over tradition," says I. T. Frary, "yet he displayed
great originality and ingenuity in carrying out and adapting
the ideas which he borrowed from antiquity. . . . Jefferson's
architecture is therefore a direct adaptation of classic models
to present and local needs. The white columns with which
he relieved the red brickwork of his walls, the mouldings
with which he accented them, the detail with which he
sparingly enriched plain surfaces, were all painstakingly
abstracted from the plates of Palladio and other authorities,
but principally from those of Palladio." [10]

The construction of Monticello proceeded as rapidly as
possible following Jefferson's marriage to Martha Skelton
on New Year's Day of 1772. "The plan of the house at
Monticello can be traced definitely to plans in Palladio's
books." [11] This was a two-story brick pavilion with wings,
entered front and back by columned porticoes. Command-
ing a superb view of the Blue Ridge mountains to the west
and of Charlottesville in the valley below, Monticello, as
has been pointed out, adequately fulfilled Kames' dictum
about the beauty of a view that can be taken in at one
glance. Its classical simplicity amply illustrates the Scottish
esthetician's interdiction against profuseness of ornament:
"In all the works of nature, simplicity makes an illustrious
figure. It also makes a figure in works of art: profuse ornament in painting, gardening, or architecture, as well as in
dress or in language, shows a mean or corrupted taste:

> Poets, like painters, thus unskill'd to trace
> The naked nature and the living grace,
> With gold and jewels cover every part,
> And hide with ornaments their want of art.
> *Pope's Essay on Criticism.*" [12]

Kames called attention to the fact that architecture, which for many ages was a "useful art merely" was now improved into a fine art: it could now be considered as either. "There is a beauty in utility; and in discoursing of beauty, that of utility must not be neglected." Buildings could be "destined for use solely, for beauty solely, or for both." Such variety of destination "bestows upon these arts a great command of beauties, complex no less than various." In a curious comparison of architecture with gardening—a comparison which would be almost unthinkable to a twentieth-century mind, Kames states that in architecture "the beauties of regularity, order and proportion are still more conspicuous than in gardening: but as to the beauty of colour, architecture is far inferior." Grandeur, he concedes, could be expressed in a building "perhaps more successfully than in a garden, but as to the other emotions above mention"—sweetness, gaiety, melancholy, wildness, surprise or wonder all of which could be expressed in landscape— "architecture hitherto has not been brought to the perfection of expressing them distinctly." To balance this deficiency, architecture displayed "the beauty of utility in the highest perfection." He ends the comparison with the assertion that a building "even the most magnificent, is necessarily confined to one expression." [13]

Jefferson shared with Lord Kames not only a love of simplicity but also the predilection for a functional style. Kames taught that "every building [should] have an expression corresponding to its destination: A palace ought to be sumptuous and grand; a private dwelling, neat and modest; a play-house, gay and splendid; and a monument, gloomy and melancholy." [14]

It is significant that Hogarth, whom Dr. Kallen has called "the first of the true moderns among painters," failed to share the enthusiasm of his time for the Palladian style precisely on the grounds of functionalism. He protested against the indiscriminate use of the antique whether it was relevant to the particular function of the building or not: ". . . churches, palaces, hospitals, prisons, common houses and summer houses, might be built more in distinct characters than they are, by contriving orders suitable to each; whereas, were a modern architect to build a palace in Lapland or the West Indies, Palladio must be his guide, nor would he dare to stir a step without his book." [15]

Hogarth actually was far closer to the Baroque and the Romantic than to the classical; his rococo, as has frequently been pointed out, was essentially pre-romantic. He preferred St. Paul's in London to St. Peter's in Rome; and was certainly modern in his opinion that many Gothic buildings have consistent beauty, due perhaps to "a series of improvements made from time to time by the natural persuasion of the eye, which very nearly often answers the end of working by principles, and sometimes begets them." [16] Such views were diametrically opposed to those of Jefferson and the Enlightenment. Kames seems to have occupied an intermediate position. The old Gothic form of building seemed to him well suited "to the rough uncultivated regions where it was invented." The only lapse in taste of the Gothic style was "the transferring this form to the fine plains of France and Italy, better fitted for buildings in the Grecian taste." [17] In Inverary, on the contrary, "the profuse variety of wild and grand objects . . . demanded a house in the Gothic form." Kames, therefore, already sensed what Jefferson's deeply ingrained utilitarianism enabled him to avoid—"the structural irrelevancy of building to scene of which Hogarth complained."

The building of Monticello challenged the "workman" in Jefferson as well as the gentleman-esthete: "Jefferson trained the laborers on his estate as brick-layers, stonecutters, carpenters, cabinet-makers and ironworkers. Nails from the Monticello shop were used throughout the neighborhood. He sent away for master workmen, but depended upon his own men for most of the work. He studied the problems of brick-making, mortar mixing and building construction. The extraordinary character of his achievement in all these lines is evident to anyone who will examine the work at Monticello." [18]

Here, too, the utilitarian whose aim was to use science for the advancement of human happiness found a fertile field, through "numberless ingenious devices by means of which it [Monticello] was made livable and enjoyable," according to the standards of the time—"clever inventions that reveal the man's human side and his fondness for playing with the problems that he encountered." [19]

Among these devices were the large compass on the east porch which, connected with a weather vane on the roof above, gave the direction of the wind; the clock over the east entrance which, one dial on the hall and another on the porch side, indicated the days of the week as well as the hours of the day; the double doors between hall and drawing-room which open and close as either one is moved; the two miniature dumb-waiters, built into the dining-room mantel, which descend into the wine cellar bearing down an empty bottle as a full one is brought up; Jefferson's bed, placed in an open alcove between study and dressing room, to afford good circulation of air. There were also the recesses in the other sleeping-rooms for the beds which, resting on ropes strung from iron hooks, could be moved out of sight during the day; the placement of kitchen and service quarters in the low wings flanking the lawn, connected with the mansion by a tunnel; triple sashes set into the first-story windows to secure flexible adjustment in controlling ventilation; and the stairways tucked away into inconspicuous nooks. The extraordinary diversity of interests of Jefferson's mind ranged from the testing of various methods of seasoning lumber to the designing of an astronomical observatory. "Whatever he undertook was grasped with amazing thoroughness," says Frary. From the hencoops on his Pantops farm to the barometer which he constructed himself, to the double thermometer for comparing external and internal temperatures, which was built from his own specifications "nothing was too great or too small, too complex or too simple to command his attention." [20]

If, through Monticello, Jefferson inaugurated a new style for the great houses of Virginia which soon spread over the Union, through his preoccupation with public buildings he established the monumental style of antiquity as the appropriate one for the official structures of the Republic. Already as Governor of Virginia he projected "a transformation of the Palace at Williamsburg," suggesting a plan for a temple with pedimented porticoes of eight columns. But the decisive opportunity came to him with the building of the Virginia State Capitol. Writes M. Louis Réau: "The Capitol of Virginia is in effect the first monument of the classical renaissance in the United States, and one might add, in the world." [21]

In explaining his choice of a model for the Capitol, Jefferson advanced an argument used by Edmund Burke—that the style has the approbation of the centuries, and must therefore be commended over designs which have not withstood the test of time. It is interesting that only in matters of art does Jefferson have recourse to the judgment of ancestors; in matters of science and politics he expostulates again and again that we must not be bound by the fetters of tradition, and that the new is infinitely preferable to the old. James Madison is told, "We took for our model what is called the Maison Quarrée of Nismes, one of the most beautiful, if not the most beautiful and precious morsel of architecture left us by antiquity. It was built by Caius and Lucius Caesar, and repaired by Louis XIV, and has the suffrage of all the judges of architecture who have seen it, as yielding to no one of the beautiful monuments of Greece, Rome, Palmyra, and Balbec, which late travellers have communicated to us. It is very simple, but it is noble beyond expression, and would have done honor to our country, as presenting to travellers a specimen of taste in our infancy, promising much for our maturer age." [22]

This was the plan which Jefferson had in mind when he received an application for a design for a State Capitol from the directors of the public buildings in Virginia: "I shall send them one taken from the best morsel of ancient architecture now remaining. It has obtained the approbation of fifteen or sixteen centuries, and is therefore preferable to any design which might be newly contrived. . . . It will be superior in beauty to anything in America, and not inferior to anything in the world. It is very simple." [23]

As he was busily drawing up the plans in Paris, Jefferson was much upset by the news that the legislators in Rich-

mond had decided not to wait for him, and that work on
the Capitol had indeed been begun: "I have been much
mortified with information, which I received two days ago
from Virginia, that the first brick of the capitol would be
laid within a few days. But surely, the delay of this piece of a
summer would have been repaired by the savings in the
plan preparing here, were we to value its other superiorities
as nothing." In exhorting Madison to have the work stopped
till his plans could reach Richmond, Jefferson returns to
the argument previously indicated: "Do . . . exert yourself to get the plan [of the Capitol] begun on, set aside
and that adopted which was drawn here. It was taken from
a model which has been the object of as many pilgrimages
as the tomb of Mahomet; which will give unrivalled honor
to our State, and furnish a model whereon to form the
taste of our young men." For Jefferson the Capitol at Richmond presented a golden opportunity to instruct his com-
patriots. "How," he demands of Madison, "is a taste in
this beautiful art to be formed in our countrymen unless
we avail ourselves of every occasion when public buildings
are to be erected, or presenting to them models for their
study and imitation?" How could the legislators at Richmond be so blind as to wish to go ahead when he was preparing for them a new vision of beauty? He was prepared
to move heaven and earth to halt their ill-timed activity,
and implored Madison to effect the stopping of the project.
The loss would be only of the bricks already laid; and even
these could be used in the interior walls: "This loss is not
to be weighed against the saving of money which will arise,
against the comfort of laying out the public money for something honorable, the satisfaction of seeing an object and

proof of national good taste, and the regret and mortification of erecting a monument of our barbarism, which will be loaded with execrations as long as it shall endure." [24]

The legislators finally heeded his exhortations; Jefferson breathed more easily. He always wrote of this achievement with pride: "The capitol in the city of Richmond, in Virginia, is the model of the Temples of Erectheus at Athens, of Balbec, and of the Maison Quarrée of Nismes. All of which are nearly of the same form and proportions, and are considered as the most perfect examples of cubic architecture, as the Pantheon of Rome is of the spherical. Their dimensions not being sufficient for the purpose of the Capitol, they were enlarged, but their proportions rigorously observed." [25]

When Jefferson went to London to join Adams in a vain attempt to negotiate a treaty with the "mulish" George III, his sensitive eye at once passed judgment on the state there of the "beautiful art": "[English] architecture is in the most wretched style I ever saw, not meaning to except America, where it is bad, nor even Virginia, where it is worse than in any other part of America which I have seen." [26]

In the "Dialogue between my Heart and my Head"—addressed by Jefferson to Maria Cosway when she left France—architecture is described as a competitor to love in the passage where Heart blames Head for having brought about the beginning of the pleasant relationship which had now left it so bereft: "*Heart.* Accordingly, Sir, this acquaintance was not the consequence of my doings. It was one of your projects which threw us in the way of it. It was you, remember, and not I, who desired the meeting at

Legrand and Motinos. I never trouble myself with domes
nor arches. The Halle aux Bleds might have rotted down
before I should have gone to see it. But you, forsooth, who
are eternally getting us to sleep with your diagrams and
crotchets, must go and examine this wonderful piece of
architecture; and when you had seen it, oh! it was the most
superb thing on earth! . . . *Head*. It would have been
happy for you if my diagrams and crotchets had gotten you
to sleep on that day, as you are pleased to say they eternally
do. My visit to Legrand and Motinos had public utility
for its object. A market is to be built in Richmond. What a
commodious plan is that of Legrand and Motinos; especially if we put on it the noble dome of the Halle aux Bleds.
If such a bridge as they showed us can be thrown across
the Schuylkill at Philadelphia, the floating bridges taken
up, and the navigation of that river opened, what a copious
resource will be added, of wood and provisions, to warm
and feed the poor of that city!" [27]

This colloquy is placed, be it remembered, in a personal
letter to a very dear friend who had never been in America.
Heart recalls the pleasures of the friends' first excursion together to St. Germains and their occasions are mostly architectural. "*Heart*. Oh! my dear friend, how you have re-
vived me by recalling to my mind the transactions of that
day! How well I remember them all, and that, when I came
home at night and looked back to the morning, it seemed
to have been a month agone. Go on, then, like a kind com-
forter, and paint to me the day we went to St. Germains.
How beautiful was every object! the Port de Reuilly, the
hills along the Seine, the rainbows of the machine at Marly,
the terrace of St. Germains, the chateaux, the gardens, the

statues of Marly, the pavillon of Lucienne. Recollect, too, Madrid, Bagatelle, the King's garden, the Dessert. How grand the idea excited by the remains of such a column! The spiral staircase, too, was beautiful." [28]

In 1787 and 1788 Jefferson travelled through France to Italy, and through Germany to Holland, in addition to his trip to England. His "memoranda" are an amazing sequence of observations on the life of the people, the condition of the soil, farming, wine pressing, husbandry and manufacture. Nothing of moment escapes his eye—an ingenious gate at Düsseldorf, scaffold poles for the upper parts of a wall at Genoa, an economical curtain bedstead at Mannheim. His notes on the architecture of the various places he passed through show the interests of the antiquarian, the artistic amateur, and the professional technician: *"Champagne. Few chateaux; no farm houses, all the people being gathered in villages. . . . Dauphine.* The Praetorian palace at Vienne is forty-four feet wide, of the Corinthian order, four columns in front, and four in flank. It was begun in the year 400, and finished by Charlemagne." There follows the most minute description of the Sepulchral pryamid a little way out of the town, with measurements of the pedestals, columns, capitals, arches and pilasters. There is a professional touch in Jefferson's every remark on architecture. He might have considered himself an "ignorant" when it came to painting and sculpture. Here, certainly, he is on home ground. At Arles he notes, in an ancient church in the suburbs, the hundreds of ancient stone coffins along the roadside. Also: "Within the town, are a part of two Corinthian columns, and of the pediment with which they were crowned, very rich, having belonged to the ancient capitol of the place. But the principal monument here, is an amphitheatre, the external portico of which is tolerably complete." [29]

At Milan Jefferson remarks on the many houses painted *al fresco*, among which the Casa Roma and Casa Candiani by Appiani and Casa Belgioiosa by Martin "are superior." At Genoa he notes the strawberries, the use of slate for stairs and for fixed Venetian blinds, and the benches with straight legs. A superb road, he writes, might be made along the margin of the sea from Laspeze to Nice, whereby "travellers would enter Italy without crossing the Alps"—an idea, it may be added, which was subsequently put into effect. At Tours he called upon the secretary of the "Intendance" to discuss with M. Gentil the theory of Voltaire "in his Questions Encyclopediques, article Coquilles, relative to the growth of shells unconnected with animal bodies, at the Chateau of M. de la Sauvagiere, near Tours." He notes at Amsterdam joists of houses placed "not with their sides horizontally and perpendicularly, but diamond wise," and makes a sketch of the arch. There is a sketch of a hanging bridge, as well as of a Dutch wheelbarrow, and of Hope's house near Haarlem, and he observes how the separation between middle building and wings in the upper story gives "a capricious appearance yet a pleasing one." At Hanau "The streets are cleaner than a German floor, because nobody passes them"; at Rudesheim is a tower of which he also carries away a sketch. The chateau at Heidelberg "is the most noble ruin I have ever seen, having been reduced to that state by the French in the time of Louis XIV, 1693. Nothing remains under cover but the chapel. The situation is romantic and pleasing beyond expression. It is on a great scale much like the situation of Petrarch's chateau, at Vaucluse, on a small one." [30]

These are a few among the wealth of details. That year, in his memoranda to Mr. Rutledge and Mr. Shippen, he advises them on their travels: "5. Architecture worth great attention. As we double our numbers every twenty years, we must double our houses. Besides, we build of such perishable materials, that one half of our houses must be rebuilt in every space of twenty years, so that in that time, houses are to be built for three-fourths of our inhabitants. It is, then, among the most important arts; and it is desirable to introduce taste into an art which shows so much." [31]

Upon his return to America, Jefferson became Washington's Secretary of State. With the selection of the site of the new capital—a choice which Nock in his biography inaccurately attributes to Jefferson—there opened up for the statesman a project of building and city planning worthy of his best efforts. The problems of laying out the city of Washington immediately summoned from him a series of carefully thought out, progressive and "common sense" opinions which he communicated in a letter of advice to the Frenchman, Major L'Enfant, who had been charged with the task of drawing up the plans for the capital: "I have examined my papers, and found the plans of Frankfort-on-the-Mayne, Carlsruhe, Amsterdam, Strasburg, Paris, Orleans, Bordeaux, Lyons, Montpelier, Marseilles, Turin, and Milan, which I send in a roll by the post. They are on large and accurate scales, having been procured by me while in those respective cities myself." [32] Considerations of utility and beauty go hand in hand with his judgment about the seat of government: "I should propose these [streets of the Federal Capital] to be at right angles, as in Philadelphia, and that no street should be narrower than one hundred feet, with foot ways of fifteen feet. Where a street is long and level, it might be one hundred and twenty feet wide. I should prefer squares of at least two hundred yards every way, which will be about eight acres each." He doubts whether the obligation to build the houses at a given distance from the street contributes to its beauty. "It produces a disgusting monotony; all persons make this complaint against Philadelphia." Here we are in the atmosphere of the rococo, with its hatred of straight lines, which came out so clearly in Jefferson's remarks on English gardens. "The contrary practice varies the appearance, and is much more convenient to the inhabitants." [33]

With customary foresight, he provides against the hazard of fire: "I cannot help again suggesting one regulation formerly suggested, to wit: To provide for the extinguishment of fires, and the openness and convenience of the town, by prohibiting houses of excessive height; and making it unlawful to build on any one's purchase any house with more than two floors between the common level of the earth and the eaves." [34]

The city plan must be related to the health no less than the happiness of mankind. In 1803 he is writing to Governor Harrison in relation to a projected city: "You mentioned the plan of the town which you had done me the honor to name after me, and to lay out according to an idea I had formerly expressed to you. I am thoroughly persuaded that it will be found handsome and pleasant, and I do believe it to be the best means of preserving the cities of America from the scourge of the yellow fever, which being peculiar to our country, must be derived from some peculiarity in it. That peculiarity I take to be our cloudless skies. In Europe, where the sun does not shine more than half the number of days in the year which it does in America, they can build their town in a solid block with impunity; but here a constant sun produces too great an accumulation of heat to admit that. Ventilation is indispensably necessary. Experience has taught us that in the open air of the country the yellow fever is not only not generated, but ceases to be infectious. I cannot decide from the drawing you sent me, whether you have laid off streets round the squares thus: [in checkerboard design] or only the diagonal streets therein marked. The former was my idea, and is, I imagine, most convenient." [35]

Two years later he makes the same point to Count Volney: "Yellow fever . . . is generated only in low, close and ill cleansed parts of a town, I have supposed it practicable to prevent its generation by building our cities on a more open plan. Take . . . the chequer board for a plan. Let the black squares only be building squares and the white ones . . . left open in turf and trees." [36]

Jefferson is proud of the plans for Washington, and eager to exhibit to the experts of the Old World how the free citizens of the New go about planning their federal capital. He makes arrangements with Thomas Pinckney for showing the plans of the new city in London, Edinburgh, Glasgow, Bristol and Dublin; while Gouverneur Morris is to see to it that Paris, Lyons, Rouen and the large seaport towns of France have an opportunity to view them.

In the competition for the design of the Capitol building at Washington, Jefferson gave careful consideration to the contestants. The "grandeur, simplicity and beauty" of Dr.

Thornton's plan led him to prefer it to James Hoban's and Stephen Hallet's. Even though he preferred Thornton's plan, he desired that Hallet should be "liberally rewarded for the time and labor he has expended" and that his feelings be "saved and soothed as much as possible." Jefferson manifested the same consideration for Hallet, despite his uncooperative attitude, as he did for Trumbull. Indeed, consideration marked all his dealings with artists.

Thornton's design was chosen, although Thornton was an amateur at architecture. He was to have as his assistants the Frenchman Stephan Hallet; the Englishman George Hadfield, brother of Jefferson's friend Maria Cosway; Robert Mills, the American; and Benjamin Latrobe, English-born son of French Protestant emigrés, an architect of considerable imagination, refinement of taste and engineering ability. Talbot Hamlin tells us that "the competition for the national Capitol may well be considered the birth of the profession of architecture in this country." Hamlin attributed to Jefferson an enormously important role in the formation of a distinctive American style. His reason: that Jefferson intended "a conscious separation from Europe," that he had "a fierce will to be American. . . . The contribution to American architecture made by Thomas Jefferson, seconded by Washington, in the plans for the new Federal capital was epoch-making. L'Enfant . . . would have been much less purely classic if Jefferson had not been so constantly interested and eager in giving advice, counsel and inspiration. . . . To the problem of the Washington architecture he brought all the knowledge he had gained through nearly twenty years of experimentation in his own house, Monticello, and all the inspiration of his years of residence in France, his admiration for the brilliance of French planning, and his almost worshipful veneration of the one important Roman ruin he had seen. . . . In Domestic architecture . . . his influence produced a type of large mansion in Maryland and Virginia that undoubtedly made simpler the transition to the later Greek Revival. . . . Exactly how great was Jefferson's influence on the work of Dr. Thornton and Latrobe we may never know, but his association with them was close. . . . Robert Mills, who claimed to be the first native-born American to be trained specifically for a career as a professional architect, came under Jefferson's influence even more closely while working as a draftsman for him for two years, and during the lifetime of both there remained between them a relationship warm and vivid." [37]

Fiske Kimball tells us "Jefferson submitted a plan anonymously for the President's house based on Palladio's Villa Rotonda, and he was responsible while he occupied the White House for its circular portico toward the Potomac and its long flanking colonnades." [38]

Hamlin considers Jefferson largely responsible for the birth of American architecture because of his hatred of "what seemed to him the frivolities of English Baroque architecture" and because "to him the dignity of the simple orders which he found in his Palladio and the bigness of conception of the Roman buildings seemed the only fitting inspiration . . . to satisfy the wants of a new republic."

That the Jeffersonian influence spread widely is evidenced by a quotation brought by Hamlin from the Russian author, diplomat and artist Pavel Svinin, who was in America from 1811 to 1813: "English architecture prevails here throughout. . . . As regards country homes, the Americans have for some time adopted the Italian style, and I have found here many such homes of the most modern and very pleasant style of architecture." [39] As Hamlin observes "classicism was the 'modern' in that period" and Jefferson's influence was so widely felt that it superseded the "English" style with surprising rapidity. Latrobe's ideas were completely congenial to Jefferson. For Latrobe "the inspiration of ancient classic forms offered a spacious pathway out of the dulness of an outworn Baroque tradition, and this idea— that the Classic Revival forms were not new set categories imposing a new slavery of design, but rather a powerful means of breaking off the shackles of the past—became a controlling factor in the American Classic Revival." [40] Thus, "at the very beginning of the building of Washington, classicism and monumentality were determined upon and fixed the ideals of American governmental architecture." [41] With Latrobe Jefferson was able to discuss all the special problems of the edifice. In 1804 he writes him: "Though the spheroidical dome presents difficulties to the executor, yet they are not beyond his art; and it is to overcome difficulties that we employ men of genius. . . . Would it not be best to make the internal columns of well-burnt brick, moulded in portions of circles adapted to the diminution of the columns? Burlington, in his *Notes on Palladio,* tells us that he found most of the buildings erected under Palladio's direction, and described in his architecture, to have their columns made of brick in this way and covered with stucco." [42]

In line with Jefferson's consistent encouragement of the arts and inventive genius were his appointments of Latrobe to the post of Surveyor of Public Buildings and Thornton to develop a system of handling patents. These were no mere political gestures, but based on appreciation of talent.

It is generally assumed that it was at Jefferson's suggestion that Latrobe created the new and specifically American architectural orders based upon the tobacco and the maize, but Frary thinks this attribution disproved by a letter written by Latrobe to Jefferson. This is dated August 28, 1809, in which he tells Jefferson the design for the "capital of the columns of the lower vestibule of the Senatorial department of the North wing of the Capitol" is composed of maize, but christened "Corn-cob capitals" by members of Congress "whether for the sake of alliteration I cannot tell, but certainly not very appropriately." [43] The tobacco leaf is used on the capitals of the small rotunda on the floor above. The period of the building of the maize and tobacco leaf capitals is fixed in a letter from Latrobe to Jefferson dated November 5, 1816, in which he states: "I have therefore composed a capital of leaves and flowers of the tobacco plant which has an intermediate effect approaching the Corinthian order and retaining the simplicity of the Clepsydra or Temple of the Winds. Iardella, a sculptor . . . has made an admirable model for execution in which he has well preserved the botanical character of the plant, although it has been necessary to enlarge the proportion of the flowers to the leaves, and to arrange them in clusters of three." [44]

The tobacco-leaf and "corn-cob" capitals impressed even Englishwoman Mrs. Trollope, who writes in her sneering *Domestic Manners of the Americans:* "In a hall leading to some of these rooms [of the Capitol] the ceiling is supported by pillars, the capitals of which struck me as peculiarly beautiful. They are composed of the ears and leaves of Indian corn, beautifully arranged, and forming as graceful an outline as the acanthus itself." [45]

When a good part of the noble work was achieved, Jefferson wrote warmly to Latrobe: "I shall live in the hope that the day will come when an opportunity will be given you of finishing the middle building in a style worthy of the two wings, and worthy of the first temple dedicated to the sovereignty of the people, embellishing with Athenian taste the course of a nation looking far beyond the range of Athenian destinies." [46] Exactly two years, one month and twelve days after Jefferson expressed this hopeful vision came the wanton destruction by the British of the "first temple dedicated to the sovereignty of the people."

The Britishers' burning of Washington's public buildings is one of warfare's most utterly senseless and vulgar deeds. The Capitol and the President's House were fired on August 24, 1814, upon orders of the ineffable Admiral Cockburn, who stalked with his muddy boots into the House of Representatives and declaimed from the Speaker's chair to the soldiers who followed him: "Shall this harbor of Yankee democracy be burned? All for it will say 'aye.'" By unanimous vote of these captors of the city the Capitol was set ablaze. The artist C. Turner commemorated this act by an engraved portrait of Cockburn of which he made a servile presentation to the Earl St. Vincent by permission. This portrait shows His Majesty's Lord of the Admiralty, Sir George Cockburn, G.C.B., warming his coattails before a remarkably accurate drawing of the burning buildings of Washington, which was probably sketched by an eyewitness. [47]

Latrobe gives his account of the appearance of the Capitol after its destruction: "In the Hall of Representatives the devastation has been dreadful. There was no want of materials for the conflagration, for when the number of members of Congress was increased the old platform was left in its place and another raised over it, giving an additional quantity of dry and loose timber. All the stages and seats of the galleries were of timber and yellow pine. The mahogany desks, tables, and chairs were in their places. At first rockets were fired through the roof, but they did not set fire to it. They sent men on it, but it was covered with sheet iron. At last they made a great pile in the center of the room of the furniture and, retiring, set fire to a quantity of rocket stuff in the middle. The whole was soon in a blaze, and so intense was the flame that the glass of the lights was melted, and I have now lumps weighing many pounds run into a mass. The stone is, like most freestone, unable to resist the force of flame, and I believe no known material would have been able to resist so sudden and intense a heat. The exterior of the columns and entablatures scaled off, and not a vestige of sculpture or fluting remained." [48]

During this holocaust Thornton is credited with having saved the Patent Office in a deed of singular heroism. "According to the story, he saw a British officer wheel a cannon into position to fire on the building, whereupon he dashed up, threw himself from his horse directly before the mouth of the cannon, and demanded, 'Are you Englishmen, or Goths and Vandals? This is the Patent Office, the repository of the inventive genius of America, in which the whole civilized world is concerned. Would you destroy it? If so, fire away and let the charge pass through my body.' " The pleader was the scholarly writer on medicine, philosophy, language, astronomy, government, finance and art, whose book *Cadmus* had won him the Magellanic gold medal from the American Philosophical Society; whose contemporaries had called him "a wit, a painter and a poet" and "whose company was a complete antidote to dullness." [49]

The rebuilding of the Capitol started when Congress, on February 15, 1815, authorized President Madison to borrow half a million dollars to restore the public buildings of Washington, and work has continued down to the present day. Frary says, "The Capitol has passed through the control of men variously endowed and with conflicting ideals, yet, curiously enough, it has retained as a whole a consistent character. It has its faults, and critics at various times have suggested changes that might bring it nearer to perfection. However, in spite of possible slips from absolute flawlessness, it is generally regarded as one of the beautiful buildings of the world. We have a sentimental attachment for the Capitol that is amply justified. The north and south wings of the old building stand today as they appeared, and as they were in 1814, when British vandals sought their destruction. The east portico and steps have provided a setting through many generations for presidential inaugurations. The great Dome has been the dominating feature of the city since midway in that regrettable struggle between North and South. The Capitol has been a symbol of our Nation's greatness and growth through all the years that have elapsed since the days when President Washington laid its corner stone. As such we cherish it." [50]

With the founding of the University of Virginia—"The

last act of usefulness I can render"—came a new architectural task to be met, as the others had been, by combining beauty and function. To Dr. Thornton Jefferson wrote: "We propose to lay off a square of about 700 or 800 feet, on the outside of which we shall arrange separate pavilions. . . . Between pavilion and pavilion a range of dormitories for the boys, one story high, giving to each a room. . . . The whole . . . to be united by a colonnade in front, of the height of the lower story of the pavilions, under which they may go dry from school to school. The colonnade will be of square brick pilasters (at first) with a Tuscan entablature. . . . These pavilions . . . shall be models of taste and good architecture, and of a variety of appearance, no two alike, so as to serve as specimens for the architectural lectures." [51]

This final project, to which Jefferson gave all the energies of his declining years, was not only, as he himself considered it, the fitting culmination of his long public activity; it was the concretization of the major tenets of his humanism and naturalistic rationalism. The establishment of a free system of public education had been one of a group of social reforms—separation of church and state, establishment of religious liberty, and the division of the great landed estates through the abolition of entail and primogeniture had been among the others—which had exercised young Jefferson's talents in the Virginia Legislature during the late 1770's. There was something eminently appropriate in his return to what was the most cherished of these projects, four decades later: "A system of general instruction, which shall reach every description of our citizens from the richest to the poorest, as it was the earliest, so will it be the latest of all the public concerns in which I shall permit myself to take an interest." [52]

The Legislature, which was a bit slow in perceiving "the important truths that knowledge is power, that knowledge is safety, and that knowledge is happiness," held up the necessary appropriations. In the meantime, Jefferson pushed on the building of the Central College, of which he was rector, to operate as a privately supported institution till the lawgivers were ready to take it over as a state-supported university. As always, he shifted easily and flexibly from the theoretical aspects of the over-all plan to the carrying out of the practical details: "Our Central College gives me more employment than I am equal to. The dilatoriness of the workmen gives me constant trouble. It has already brought into doubt the completion this year of the building begun, which obliges me to be with them every other day. . . . I drew a plan of a college in its dormitories, such as the bill calls for, to demonstrate that it will not cost more than the sum allotted." [53]

The bitter opposition aroused by the plan only because Jefferson was associated with it has its parallels in the history of our struggle to realize the American dream: "Would it promote the success of the institution most for me to be in or out of it? Out of it, I believe. . . . There are fanatics both in religion and politics, who, without knowing me personally, have long been taught to consider me as a rawhead and bloodybones, and . . . we can afford to lose no votes." [54]

Finally, on January 25, 1819, the Legislature confirmed the project; and on March 29, at the age of seventy-six, Jefferson was elected rector of the University of Virginia.

The great undertaking was under way: "The plan of building is not to erect one single magnificent building to contain
everybody and everything, but to make of it an academical
village in which every professor should have his separate
house (or 'pavilion'), containing his lecturing room with
two, three or four rooms for his own accommodation according-
ing as he may have a family or no family, with kitchen,
garden, etc.; distinct dormitories for the students, not more
than two in a room; and separate boarding houses for diet-
ing them by private housekeepers." [55]

He was soon at work drawing up the plans, adapting the
design of the Temple of Nerva Trajan by retaining its general proportions while simplifying its style. At seventy-six
he is consulting the same architectural authority who formed
the inclinations of his youth. He pronounced, in making
the reference to Palladio, a typically Kamesian view regarding ornament: "Our University, four miles distant,
gives me frequent exercise, and the oftener, as I direct its
architecture. Its plan is unique, and it is becoming an object
of curiosity for the traveler.[56a] Pavilion No. X [is to be
modeled on the] East Doric of the Theatre of Marcellus.
The columns to have no bases. . . . I have never seen an
attic pilaster with the measures of its parts minutely expressed except that of the Temple of Nerva Trajan (Palladio, Book III, Plate 18). That temple is overloaded with
ornaments, and its pilaster frittered away so minutely in its
mouldings as to lose all effect. I have simplified these mouldings to suit our plainer style, still, however, retaining nearly
their general outlines and proportions.[56b] Seven of the ten
pavilions destined for the professors, and about thirty (one-
room) dormitories, will be completed (in 1820), and three

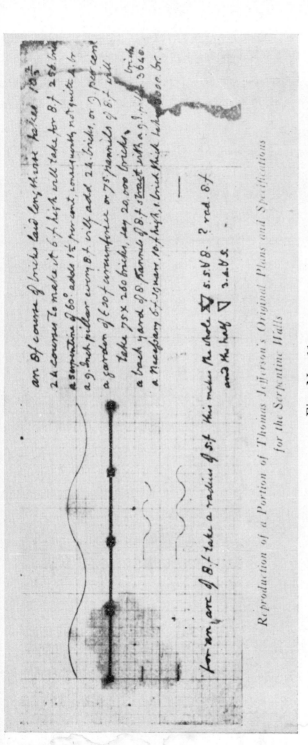

Fig. No. 11.

REPRODUCTION OF A PORTION OF THOMAS JEFFERSON'S ORIGINAL PLANS AND SPECIFICATIONS FOR THE SERPENTINE WALLS

Courtesy of Mr. Samuel Herbert McVitty of Ridgewood Farm, Salem, Virginia

Fig. No. 12.

Maison Quarrée in Nimes, from South West. Early first century A.D.

From the Bettman Archive

other, with six hotels for boarding, and seventy other dormitories, will be completed the next year . . ." [56c]

There is the eighteenth-century libertarian pride in his word to Destutt de Tracy that "this institution of my native state, the hobby of my old age, will be based on the illimitable freedom of the human mind to explore and to expose every subject susceptible of its contemplation." [57] Obstructions and difficulties were not lacking: "The serious enemies are the priests of the different religious sects. . . . Their pulpits are now resounding with denunciations against the appointment of Dr. [Thomas] Cooper, whom they charge as a monotheist in opposition to their tritheism. But in despite of their fulminations against endeavors to enlighten the general mind, to improve the reason of the people and encourage them in the use of it, the liberality of this state will support this institution . . . this beautiful and hopeful institution *in ovo*." [58]

Year in, year out, he held on to this high purpose with indomitable courage, determined to see it attained: "The time of opening our University is still as uncertain as ever. All the pavilions, boarding-houses, and dormitories are done. Nothing is now wanting but the central building (the Rotunda) for a library and other general purposes. For this we have no funds, and the last legislature refused all aid." [59] He does not falter: "But the gloomiest of all prospects is in the desertion of the best friends of the institution, for desertion I must call it. . . . What object of our lives can we propose so important? What interest of our own which ought not to be postponed to this? Health, time, labor, on what in the single life which nature has given us, can these be better bestowed than on this immortal boon to our country? The exertions and the mortifications are temporary; the benefits eternal. If any member of our college of visitors could justifiably withdraw from this sacred duty it would be myself, who . . . have neither vigor of body nor mind left to keep the field; but I will die in the last ditch." [60]

Jefferson explains that it was necessary to have impressive buildings in order to attract distinguished scholars from abroad as well as from all over America: "The great object of our aim from the beginning has been to make the establishment the most eminent in the United States, in order to draw to it the youth of every state, but especially of the South and West. We have proposed, therefore, to call to it characters of the first order of science from Europe, as well as our own country. . . . Had we built a barn for a college, and log huts for accommodations, should we ever have had the assurance to propose to a European professor of that character to come to it?" [61]

To William Short he expresses his hope of the effect of the completed work: "It will be a splendid establishment, would be thought so in Europe, and for the chastity of its architecture and classical taste leaves everything in America far behind it." [62]

Finally, in 1825, his "bantling of forty years' nursing" was brought to completion. Jefferson, at eighty-two, designed an ingenious clock for the rotunda with a bell which rang the hours automatically, yet could also, for school needs, be rung independently. The same year he reflected on the future: "Withdrawn by age from all other public services and attentions to public things, I am closing the last scenes of life by fashioning and fostering an establishment for the instruction of those who are to come after us. I hope its influence on their virtue, freedom, fame and happiness will be salutary and permanent." [63]

If, in painting and sculpture, Jefferson attempted to unite art and life, architecture gave him the widest possible scope for the achievement of this goal. Here utility and beauty could combine to provide men with a proper setting for the conduct of their lives both as private individuals and as citizens of a republic. The Georgian Baroque was as repugnant to him as the Gothic. In the restraint and simplicity of the antique, and in the chastity of the Palladian style, he found the architectural equivalents of all that had delighted him in the monumental republicanism of David and Houdon. Through architecture, the political philosopher and statesman in Jefferson joined hands with the city planner, the builder of a new state upon the original nature of man with the artist of a new form upon the old tradition of form. That uncanny ability of his to take over elements of the old and recombine them into a pattern of the new perfectly adapted to his particular needs—an ability we have noticed again and again in his handling of philosophical and esthetic concepts—comes out clearly in his labors as architect. Frary has hit upon it when he remarks that Jefferson's mind "was a curious mingling of supreme independence and absolute dependence; independence of vision that saw and planned far beyond his time, yet complete dependence, so far as style and detail (in architecture) went, upon precedent and tradition of the past." [64] Out of this combination Jefferson created a style admirably adapted to the demands of the young democracy. True, the present-day visitor to Washington, oppressed by the dreary sameness of thousands upon thousands of Corinthian columns, may not be as grateful to Jefferson's influence as he should. But that is only because one can have too much of a good thing. Within the historic context, the Jeffersonian style in architecture projected the impact of the revolutionary age. It created something new— something demanded by the spirit of the time and the place.

CHAPTER SEVEN

1. I. T. Frary: *Thomas Jefferson: Architect and Builder*, p. 1, Richmond (1939).

2. Note: Correction of the text is mine. In the Bergh Memorial Edition version of Jefferson's letter to Mme. de Tesse, it is given as "Vienna." This is misleading, as well as impossible, because Jefferson, so far as is known, never visited Vienna, Austria. He does refer to *Vienne* in his travel notes and, in another connection, makes observations on the Praetorian Palace there.

3. To Comtesse de Tesse: Nismes, March 20, 1787, ME, VI, pp. 103–106.

4. *Notes on Virginia:* ME, II, p. 211; p. 213.

5. *Ibid.,* pp. 213–215.

6. *Ibid.,* p. 212.

7. *Ibid.,* p. 213.

8. I. T. Frary: *Ibid.,* pp. 2–3.

9. H. M. Kallen: "Jefferson's Garden Wall," p. 79.

10. I. T. Frary: *Ibid.,* pp. 2–3

11. I. T. Frary: *Ibid.,* p. 4.

12. Lord Kames: *Elements of Criticism,* p. 114, New York (Edition 1883).

13. Lord Kames: *Ibid.,* II, pp. 431–432, Edinburgh (Edition 1774).

14. *Ibid.,* II, pp. 467–468, Edinburgh (Edition 1774).

15. William Hogarth: *Analysis of Beauty,* p. 89.

16. *Ibid.,* pp. 89–90.

17. Lord Kames: *Ibid.,* II, p. 469, Edinburgh (Edition 1774).

18. I. T. Frary: *Ibid.,* p. 5.

19. *Ibid.,* p. 7.

20. I. T. Frary: *Ibid.,* p. 55.

21. Louis Réau: *L'Art francais aux Etats-Unis,* pp. 79–80, Paris (1927).

22. To James Madison: Paris, Sept. 20, 1785, ME, V, pp. 135–136.

23. To James Madison: Paris, Sept. 1, 1785, ME, V, p. 110.

24. To James Madison: Paris, Sept. 20, 1785, ME, V, p. 136

25. *An Account of the Capitol in Virginia*, Miscellaneous Papers, ME, XVII, p. 353.

26. To John Page: Paris, May 4, 1786, ME, V, pp. 304-305.

27. To Maria Cosway: Paris, Oct. 12, 1786, ME, V, pp. 432-433.

28. *Ibid.*, p. 434.

29. Memoranda taken on a Journey from Paris into the Southern Parts of France, and Northern of Italy in the year 1787: ME, XVII, pp. 153; 167-168; 168-170; 171-172.

30. Memoranda taken on a Tour from Paris to Amsterdam, Strasburg, and back to Paris, 1788, ME, XVII, p. 272.

31. Travelling Notes for Mr. Rutledge and Mr. Shippen; June 3, 1788, ME, XVII, p. 292.

32. To Major L'Enfant: Philadelphia; April 10, 1791, ME, VIII, p. 162.

33. *Opinion on Capital:* Nov. 29, 1790, Ford, Fed. Ed., VI, pp. 156-157.

34. *Opinion on Capital:* March 1791 from H. A. Washington: *The Writings of Jefferson,* VII, p. 513.

35. To Gov. Wm. H. Harrison: Washington, Feb. 27, 1803, ME, X, pp. 368-369.

36. To C. F. C. de Volney: Washington, Feb. 8, 1805, ME, XI, pp. 62-69.

37. Talbot Hamlin: *Greek Revival Architecture in America*, pp. 4-21, New York (1944).

38. Fiske Kimball: "Jefferson and the Arts," p. 244.

39. Talbot Hamlin: *Ibid.*, p. 20.

40. Talbot Hamlin: *Ibid.*, p. 28.

41. Talbot Hamlin: *Ibid.*, p. 28.

42. To B. H. Latrobe: Washington, Feb. 28, 1804, ME, XI, pp. 13-15.

43. I. T. Frary: *They Built the Capitol,* p. 80, Richmond (1940).

44. Letter from Latrobe to Jefferson, Nov. 5, 1816, quoted by I. T. Frary: *They Built the Capitol,* pp. 81-86.

45. Talbot Hamlin: *Ibid.*, p. 37.

46. To Benjamin Latrobe: Monticello, July 12, 1812, ME, XIII, pp. 178-179.

47. I. T. Frary: *Ibid.*, pp. 88-90.

48. I. T. Frary: *Ibid.*, p. 92.

49. I. T. Frary: *Ibid.*, pp. 51-53.

50. I. T. Frary: *Ibid.*, p. 258.

51. To William Thornton: Monticello, May 9, 1817, ME, XVII, p. 396.

52. To Joseph C. Cabell: Monticello, Jan. 14, 1818, Ford, Fed. Ed., XII, p. 87.

53. *Ibid.*, Monticello, Oct. 24, 1817, ME, XIX, pp. 250, 251-252.

54. To Joseph C. Cabell: Monticello, Feb. 26, 1818, in N. F. Cabell: *Early History of University of Virginia*, p. 128.

55. To Nathaniel Bowditch: Monticello, Oct. 26, 1818, ME, XIX, pp. 264-265.

56. Bernard Mayo: *Jefferson Himself*, p. 327, Boston (1942).
a. To John Adams: Monticello, August 15, 1820, ME, XV, p. 269.
b. Specifications for Pavilion X, MS. University of Virginia.
c. To William Short: Monticello, April 13, 1820, ME, XV, p. 245.
57. To A.C.V.C. Destutt de Tracy: Monticello, Dec. 26, 1820, Ford, Fed. Ed., XII, p. 183.
58. To William Short: Monticello, April 13, 1820, ME, XV, pp. 245-247.
59. To Dr. Thomas Cooper: Monticello, Nov. 2, 1822, ME, XV, p. 406.
60. To Joseph C. Cabell: Monticello, Jan. 31, 1821, ME, XV, pp. 311-312.
61. *Ibid.*, Monticello, Dec. 28, 1822: N. Cabell: *Early History of University of Virginia*, p. 260.
62. To William Short: Monticello, Nov. 24, 1821, ME, XVIII, p. 315.
63. To Augustus B. Woodward: Monticello, April 3, 1825, ME, XVI, p. 117.
64. I. T. Frary: *Thomas Jefferson: Architect and Builder*, pp. 2-3.

ON GARDENING AS A FINE ART

THE CONSIDERATIONS of use and beauty which so endeared the art of architecture to Jefferson operated no less effectively in the field of gardening. What other art so charmingly suffused beauty with use and use with beauty? If the backwoodsman in Jefferson occasionally rebelled against the sophistication and opulence of cities—historically the necessary concomitant and setting for all the other arts—to gardening he could give an undivided loyalty. Was not this the art closest to nature, was not its material the living things of the earth? "No occupation is so delightful to me as the culture of the earth," he wrote Charles Peale, "and no culture comparable to that of the garden. . . . Under a total want of demand except for our family table, I am still devoted to the garden. But though an old man, I am but a young gardener." [1] The old man and young gardener was in fact much more deeply concerned about the gardens that could be useful, than about gardens that would look well. In his various available remarks about gardening and gardens there are many hundreds of references. Of these most deal with vegetable gardening, the growth of fruits, roots, and only a comparative few refer to the fine art of landscape gardening. For Jefferson there were two kinds of gardening, one for food, one for beauty, and perhaps a combination of the two.

Jefferson's esthetic pleasure in gardening was organically related to his interest in agriculture and horticulture, and to his pride in the fertility of the as yet unexploited American continent. This feeling has one of its happiest statements in his letter to Mrs. Angelica Church from Paris in 1788: "I remember you told me when we parted, you would come to see me at Monticello. and tho' I believe this to be impossible, I have been planning what I would shew you: a flower here, a tree there; yonder a grove, near it a fountain; on this side a hill, on that a river. indeed madam, I know nothing so charming as our own country. the learned say it is a new creation; and I believe them; not for their reasons, but because it is made on an improved plan. Europe is a first idea, a crude production, before the maker knew his trade, or had made up his mind as to what he wanted." [2] The considerations of expense which made him feel that for Americans painting and sculpture "were worth seeing but not studying" he advances also, musician though he was, in regard to the idea of forming and maintaining orchestras in the New World. But they did not in the least affect his views of gardening. Gardening was an art most appropriate for a young land, and well worth the attention of an American because America was the one country where "the noblest gardens may be made without expense. We have only to cut out the superabundant plants." [3] As he wrote to Peale: "I have often thought that if heaven had given me choice of my position and calling, it should have been on a rich spot of earth, well watered, and near a good market for the production of the garden." [4]

Jefferson seems to have been actively interested in gardening since his earliest days. Indeed, of all Jefferson's memorandum books, his *Garden Book*, begun in 1766 and continued, despite the lapses and irregularities caused by his many and long absences from Monticello, over a space of fifty-eight years till the autumn of 1824, "contains the most varied entries." "Here is revealed what was probably the most absorbing of all the interests of one who . . . was possessed of a love of nature so intense that his observant eye caught almost every passing change in it. And whatever he saw rarely escaped being recorded. . . . The gardens and groves at Monticello became experimental plots where new plants were introduced and nurtured, and if they were found suitable for use or ornament, they were passed on to interested neighbors and friends in various parts of the country." [5] The Marquis de Chastellux who visited Jefferson at Monticello in 1782 describes the house on the summit of the mountain and says that although Jefferson owned a good deal of property in the neighborhood "there was nothing to prevent him from fixing his residence wherever he thought proper. But it was a debt Nature owed to a philosopher, and a man of taste, that in his own possessions he should find a spot where he might best study and enjoy her. He calls his house *Monticello* (in Italian, Little Mountain), a very modest title, for it is situated upon a very lofty one, but which announces the owner's attachments to the language of Italy; and, above all, to the fine arts of which that country was the cradle, and is still the asylum . . . we may safely aver that Mr. Jefferson is the first American who has consulted the fine arts to know how he should shelter himself from the weather. . . . Let me describe to you a man, not yet forty, tall and with a mild and pleasing countenance, but whose mind and understanding are ample substitutes for every ex-

terior grace. An American, who, without ever having quitted
his own country, is at once a musician, skilled in drawing, a
geometrician, an astronomer, a natural philosopher, legisla-
tor and statesman . . . a philosopher, in voluntary retire-
ment from the world and public business because he loves
the world, in as much only as he can flatter himself with
being useful to mankind, and the minds of his countrymen
are not yet in a condition either to bear the light or suffer
contradiction . . . before I had been two hours with him,
we were as intimate as if we had passed our whole lives together; walking, books, but above all, a conversation always
varied and interesting, always supported by the sweet satisfaction experienced by two persons, who, in communicating
their sentiments and opinions, are invariably in unison, and
who understand each other at the first hint, made four days
pass away like so many minutes. This conformity of opinions
and sentiments . . . was so perfect, that not only our taste
was similar, but our predilections also; those partialities
which cold methodical minds ridicule as enthusiastic, while
sensible and animated ones cherish and adopt the glorious
appellation. . . . Sometimes natural philosophy, at others
politics or the arts, were the topics of our conversation, for
no object had escaped Mr. Jefferson; and it seemed as if
from his youth he had placed his mind, as he had done his
house, on an elevated situation, from which he might contemplate the universe." 6

The distinguished and patriotic French nobleman, the
Duc de la Rochefoucauld-Liancourt, who had been President
of the National Assembly as well as Lieutenant-general of
France, spent some days of his exile at Monticello in June,
1796, and according to Jefferson's great-granddaughter

Sarah Randolph, the description left by the Duc is accurate except for one or two trifling mistakes regarding geographical names. He writes: "The house stands on the summit of the mountain, and the taste and arts of Europe have been consulted in the formation of its plan. . . . Monticello, according to its first plan, was infinitely superior to all other houses in America, in point of taste and convenience; but at that time Mr. Jefferson had studied taste and the fine arts in books only. His travels in Europe have supplied him with models; he has appropriated them to his design; and his new plan, the execution of which is already much advanced, will be accomplished before the end of next year, and then his house will certainly deserve to be ranked with the most pleasant mansions in France and England. Mr. Jefferson's house commands one of the most extensive prospects you can meet with. . . . The bounds of the view on this point, at so small a distance, form a pleasant resting-place, as the immensity of prospect it enjoys is perhaps already too vast. A considerable number of cultivated fields, houses, and barns, enliven and variegate the extensive landscape, still more embellished by the beautiful and diversified forms of mountains, in the whole chain of which not one resembles another. The aid of fancy is, however, required to complete the enjoyment of this magnificent view; and she must picture to us those plains and mountains such as population and culture will render them in a greater or smaller number of years. The disproportion existing between the cultivated lands and those which are still covered with forests as ancient as the globe, is at present much too great; and even when that shall have been done away, the eye may perhaps further wish to discover a broad river, a great mass of

water. . . . On this mountain, and in the surrounding valleys on both banks of the Rivanna, are situated the five
thousand acres of land which Mr. Jefferson possesses in
this part of Virginia. Eleven hundred and twenty only are
cultivated. . . . Its situation on the declivities of hills and
mountains renders a careful cultivation more necessary than
is requisite in lands situated in a flat and even country. . . .
This forms at present the chief employment of Mr. Jefferson. But little accustomed to agricultural pursuits, he has
drawn the principles of culture either from works which
treat on this subject or from conversation. Knowledge thus
acquired often misleads, and is at all times insufficient in a
country where agriculture is well understood; yet it is
preferable to mere practical knowledge, and a country
where a bad practice prevails, and where it is dangerous to
follow the routine, from which it is so difficult to depart.
Above all, much good may be expected, if a contemplative
mind like that of Mr. Jefferson, which takes the theory for
its guide, watches its application with discernment, and
rectifies it according to the peculiar circumstances and nature
of the country, climate, and soil, and conformably to the
experience which he daily acquires . . ." [7]

Two years before the Duc's visit to Monticello, Jefferson
wrote James Madison: "I find my mind totally absorbed in
my rural occupations. we are suffering much for want of
rain, tho' now at the 3d of April, you cannot distinguish the
wheat fields of the neighborhood yet from hence. fruit is
hitherto safe. we have at this time some prospect of rain.
asparagus is just come to table. the lilac in bloom, and the
first whip-poor-will heard last night. no martins yet . . ." [8]

When it came to his flower and vegetable gardens, the

records indicate that peas were his favorite vegetable. As for flowers, Jefferson liked iris and acacia or mimosa, and grew several species. He makes appreciative references to carnations, several varieties of dianthus, and delphiniums. He brought feathered hyacinth from Shadwell to Monticello, and the descendants of these plants still grow in the fields on the mountain top. He planted rhododendron, often called "laurel" by the native mountain people. He remarked of the Mirabilis, a genus of American plant of the four-o'clock family, "just opened. very clever." [9]

The pleasant art quite naturally was turned to the advantage of his countrymen, particularly through Jefferson's attempts to introduce the cultivation of olive trees and dry rice into South Carolina and Georgia. His main purpose was to improve living conditions among the slaves and to save them from the ravages of disease to which the low countries were subjected. When Jefferson listed in his *Autobiography* what he considered his most important services to his country, he ranked the introduction of dry rice and the olive tree into South Carolina with writing the Declaration of Independence, with his proposals to disestablish the church and to establish freedom of religion; with the acts he drafted to prohibit the importation of slaves, end entail and primogeniture; to humanize the punishment of crime; to vindicate the "natural right of man to expatriate himself at will," and to effect a more general diffusion of knowledge. He concludes his note regarding his effort to introduce dry rice culture into South Carolina by saying: "The greatest service which can be rendered any country is, to add an useful plant to its culture; especially, a bread grain; next in value is oil." [10]

Conversant as he was with the ideas and preferences of the ancients, Jefferson could not but be aware of the importance they attached to the art of gardening. The Greeks, he observed, had palace gardens in the Mycaenaean age; Homer, whom Jefferson read with such fervor, eloquently describes the gardens of Alcinoüs. Philosophers frequented the quiet groves of public gardens; it is known that Jefferson's favorite, Epicurus, taught in a garden at Athens. The Epicurean school of philosophy—Jefferson: "I, too, am an Epicurean"—was known as the "Garden," just as the Platonic school was called "Academy" and the Stoic school was called the "Porch" according to the locale of their teaching.

The Romans, in gardening as in the other arts, were strongly under Greek and Asiatic influence. Cicero, as well as Pliny, described both the great city houses with their gardens (villa urbana) and the country houses with theirs (villa rustica). Lord Kames, in discussing the art of gardening, mentions that Pliny's epistles described evergreens cut in animal shapes.[11] The remains of Hadrian's villa at Tivoli and the murals at Pompeii attest unmistakably to the importance of gardening to Roman gentlemen. The Renaissance brought a resurgence of the art to Italy; the princely villas which renewed the classical spirit in both town and country were set in magnificent gardens.

With the reign of Louis XIV, France became the decisive influence in the art of garden design. The idea of the garden under the Grand Monarque received its fullest expression in the art of André Le Nôtre, the author of a spacious and formal style which may be said to symbolize the ideology of absolute monarchq. Le Nôtre's was a rigid,

geometric art, which, by combining a multiplicity of subordinate details with the grand line, aimed at a grandeur of
effect as attractive to the monarchical mind as it was repugnant to the democratic. Through Le Nôtre and his
pupils, the French grand style spread throughout the Continent. It is significant that England, whose gardens Jefferson
admired above those of all the other European countries
he visited, was the one stronghold that held out against the
Le Nôtrian influence. Despite the predilection of Charles II
and his nobiilty for Le Nôtre's pretentiousness, this style
remained basically uncongenial to the English tradition.

During the eighteenth century there occurred a profound
change of taste in landscape gardening. It was a change that
reflected the breakdown of the monarchical principle, and
presaged the dawn of a new age. The geometrical magnificence of Le Nôtre was supplanted by the more intimate,
subtly personalized curves of the Rococo; the Hogarthian
esthetic became the hallmark of the age of sensibility.

The new point of view finds expression in the writers on
gardening who most strongly influenced Jefferson. Kames
declares that in an embellished field "a straight walk has an
air of formality and confinement: and at any rate is less
agreeable than a winding or waving walk; for in surveying
the beauties of an ornamented field, we love to roam from
place to place at freedom. . . . Avoid a straight avenue
directed upon a dwelling-house: better far an oblique approach in a waving line, with single trees and other scattered
objects interposed. . . . An oblique approach contributes
also to variety: the house, seen successively in different directions, assumes at each step a new figure." [12]

William Shenstone, whom Jefferson read as early as

1765,[13] writes: "It is not easy to account for the fondness of former times for strait-lined avenues to their houses; strait-lined walks through their woods; and in short, every kind of strait-line." [14] Dodsley's description of "The Leasowes," Shenstone's estate in England which is thought by some to have provided a model for the landscaping of Monticello, and which Jefferson found so attractive on his garden tour, abounds in references to winding walks, paths "serpentinizing" and an immense variety of romantic scenes, and is included in the collection of Shenstone's works.[15] Shenstone himself reflects the Hogarthian view in his gardening thoughts: "Ruinated structures appear to derive their power of pleasing from the irregularity of surface, which is VARIETY." [16] In discussing the pleasures of the imagination he adds, as a footnote to his reference to Burke and others on the theory of agreeable sensations: "Garden scenes may perhaps be divided into the sublime, the beautiful, and the melancholy or pensive; to which last I know not but we may assign a middle place betwixt the former two, as being in some sort composed of both. See Burke's Sublime, &C." [17]

Jefferson's notes on English gardens directly echo these views. The reader may recall that he remarks of the garden at Caversham that "the straight walk has an ill effect." In the Marquis of Buckingham's garden at Stowe, two temples seen "the one from the other, the line of sight passing not through the garden, but through the country parallel to the line of the garden," give a "good effect." At Esher Place "the clumps on each hand balance finely—a most lovely mixture of concave and convex." In the mile-long approach to Stowe through a straight avenue "the straight effect is very ill." So too, in the Duke of Marlborough's estate at Blenheim, "The garden has no great beauties. . . . The gravelled walks are broad—art appears too much." [18]

It would appear that in Jefferson's comment about art appearing too much at Blenheim he was remembering Shenstone, who concerned himself with "lanskip or picturesque-gardening" which consisted in "pleasing the imagination by scenes of grandeur, beauty or variety." [19] Shenstone felt that "Art should never be allowed to set a foot in the province of nature, otherwise than clandestinely and by night. Whenever she is allowed to appear here and men begin to compromise the difference.—Night, gothicism, confusion and absolute chaos, are come again." [20]

Lord Kames pointed out that gardening, like architecture, began as a useful art but was now improved into a fine art. One could therefore consider gardens—like buildings—from two different views: they could be destined for use solely, for beauty solely, or for both. It was consequently difficult to form an accurate taste in gardening, as in architecture: hence that "difference and wavering of taste in these arts, greater than in any art that has but a single destination." [21]

Gardening, according to Kames, "besides the emotions of beauty from regularity, order, proportion, colour, and utility, can raise emotions of grandeur, of sweetness, of gaiety, of melancholy, of wildness, and even of surprise or wonder." As we have seen, he ranked architecture below gardening in regard to beauty of color. Gardening, Kames asserted, possessed one advantage never to be equalled in architecture: "in various scenes, it can successively raise all the different emotions. . . . But to produce that delicious effect, the garden must be extensive, so as to admit a slow succession (of effects) : for a small garden, comprehended at one view, ought to be confined to one expression." [22]

Kames expatiates also upon the advantages of gardening with respect to virtuous education. In the beginning of life when the deepest impressions are made "it is a sad truth, that the young student familiarized to the dirtiness and disorder of many colleges pent within narrow bounds in populous cities, is rendered in a measure insensible to the elegant beauties of art and nature." He feels that good professors are not more essential to a college than "a spacious garden sweetly ornamented . . . to inspire our youth with a taste not less for simplicity than for elegance. In that respect, the university of Oxford may justly be deemed a model." [23]

This view finds an interesting transposition in Jefferson's plans for the University of Virginia: "I consider the common plan (for colleges) followed in this country, but not in others, of making one large and expensive building, as unfortunately erroneous. It is infinitely better to erect a small and separate lodge for each professorship, with only a hall below for his class and two chambers above for himself; joining these lodges by barracks for a certain portion of the students, opening into a covered way to give a dry communication between all the schools. The whole of these arranged around an open square of grass and trees would make it, what it should be in fact, an academical village. . . . Much observation and reflection on these institutions have long convinced me that the large and crowded buildings in which youths are pent up are equally unfriendly to health, to study, to manners, morals, and order." [24]

In treating of gardening as an art, Kames draws atten-

tion to its social and psychological advantages, basing himself upon the Burkian concept of sympathy: ". . . gardening, which inspires the purest and most refined pleasures,
cannot fail to promote every good affection. The gaiety and
harmony of mind it produceth, inclining the spectator to
communicate his satisfaction to others and to make them
happy as he is himself, tend naturally to establish in him a
habit of humanity and benevolence." [25] It need hardly be
pointed out how closely this fits in with the Jeffersonian
philosophy on the beneficial effects of moderate physical
exercise and on the blessings of rural as opposed to city life.
In the *Notes on Virginia* Jefferson writes: "Those who labor
in the earth are the chosen people of God, if he ever had a
chosen people, whose breasts he has made his peculiar
deposit for substantial and genuine virtue. It is the focus in
which he keeps alive that sacred fire, which otherwise might
escape from the face of the earth. Corruption of morals in
the mass of cultivators is a phenomenon of which no age
nor nation has furnished an example." [26]

"Agriculture" Jefferson wrote to David Williams in 1803,
"is the first in utility, and ought to be the first in respect.
The same artificial means which have been used to produce
a competition in learning, may be equally successful in restor-
ing agriculture to its primary dignity in the eyes of men. It
is a science of the very first order. It counts among its hand-
maids the most respectable sciences, such as Chemistry,
Natural Philosophy, Mechanics, Mathematics generally,
Natural History, Botany. . . . Young men closing their
academical education with this, as the crown of all other
sciences, fascinated with its solid charms, and at a time
when they are to choose an occupation, instead of crowding

the other classes, would return to the farms of their fathers, their own, or those of others, and replenish and invigorate a calling, now languishing under contempt and oppression. The charitable schools, instead of storing their pupils with a lore which the present state of society does not call for, converted into schools of agriculture, might restore them to that branch qualified to enrich and honor themselves, and to increase the productions of the nation instead of consuming them." [27]

As for the comparative difficulty of farming and gardening, Jefferson thinks: "We all know that a farm, however large, is not more difficult to direct than a garden, and does not call for more attention or skill." [28]

In Kames' view, gardening, as well as architecture, calls for "simplicity" as "a ruling principle." Profuse ornament has no better effect than to confound the eye and prevent the object from making an impression as one entire whole. Only artists destitute of genius supplied the defect by crowding the plan "with slight embellishments: hence in a garden, triumphal arches, Chinese houses, temples, obelisks, cascades, fountains without end." [29] Kames turned in disgust from the overornateness of the gardens of Versailles, which he called "a lasting monument of a taste the most depraved." [30] It is noteworthy that the same gardens impressed Jefferson's chosen adviser in esthetics, the painter John Trumbull, as "so vast, so magnificent as to bear down all criticism." It goes without saying that Jefferson, in his love of simplicity, stood far closer to the Scottish progressive humanist than to the American reactionary.

As for ruins, that singular preoccupation both of classic and romantic landscape gardening, Kames considered that gardens ought to have ruins to inspire "a sort of melancholy pleasure." He felt that a ruin ought to be Gothic rather than Grecian, because the Gothic ruin "exhibits the triumph of time over strength, a melancholy but not unpleasant thought"; while a Grecian ruin "suggests rather the triumph of barbarity over taste, a gloomy and discouraging thought." [31] Here, certainly, is a man of the eighteenth century speaking. Since gardening represented "nature itself ornamented . . . everything unnatural ought to be rejected." [32] Kames drew a distinction between intrinsic and relative beauty: a garden intended solely for pleasure gave the impression of "intrinsic beauty"; one destined for use solely had "relative beauty." [33]

Jefferson was no less sensitive to ruins than Kames. On his tour through Germany he writes of the grounds of Williamsbath, near Hanau: "There is a ruin which is clever. It presents the remains of an old castle. . . . I like better, however, the form of the ruin at Hagley, in England, which was thus a sentry box here, covered over with bark, so as to look exactly like the trunk of an old tree. This is a good idea; and may be of much avail in a garden." [34] Of the gardens lying above the chateau at Heidelberg and climbing up the mountain in terraces: "The situation is romantic and pleasing beyond expression. It is on a great scale much like the situation of Petrarch's chateau, at Vaucluse, on a small one." [35]

In Germany Jefferson encountered a style of gardening in the Le Nôtre tradition, the influence of the Frenchman having been carried into that country via Holland. Of German taste he writes: "The gardens at Schwetzingen show how much money may be laid out to make an ugly thing." [36]

Here too, however, the new Hogarthian style was already disputing the supremacy of the old or Le Nôtrian; for he adds: "What is called the English quarter, however, relieves the eye from the straight rows of trees, round and square basins, which constitute the great mass of the garden. There are some tolerable morsels of Grecian architecture, and a good ruin." [37] It would appear here that Jefferson was remembering his impressions of his tour of English gardens and conveyed by letter to his intimate friend John Page on his return to Paris in 1786: "The gardening in that country (England) is the article in which it excels all the earth. I mean their pleasure-gardening. This, indeed, went far beyond my ideas." [38]

Jefferson had found in Thomas Whately's *Observations on Modern Gardening* a guide to his own studies of English gardens. This book was published in London in 1770. It is mentioned in Jefferson's lists of books on gardening to be found in his 1815 Catalogue and in Appendix VII of *Thomas Jefferson's Garden Book*.[39] In the 1815 Catalogue of his library, Jefferson classified Gardening with Painting and Sculpture in Chapter XXXI under the heading "Fine Arts" and included: Chambers's *View of Kew Gardens, Description of Stowe,* Heely on the *Gardens of Hagley,* James on *Gardening* and Whately's *Observations on Modern Gardening.*[40] Appendix VII of *Thomas Jefferson's Garden Book* contains the lists of pamphlets and books on Agriculture, Gardening and Botany taken from the Catalogue of the Library of Congress, 1830, the Catalogue of President Jefferson's Library sold at auction in February 1829, miscellaneous letters, and Jefferson's own manuscript of his library's contents in 1783, of which the original is in the

Massachusetts Historical Society and a photostatic copy at the University of Virginia Library. Of the one hundred and ninety items listed by Betts, all of the gardening books classified with Painting and Sculpture under "Fine Arts" in the 1815 Catalogue are included. Among the many interesting items is Lord Kames' *The Gentleman Farmer*, published in Edinburgh in 1779.[41] Jefferson begins his notes on his tour of English gardens with the following reference to Whately: "While his descriptions, in point of style, are models of perfect elegance and classical correctness, they are as remarkable for their exactness. I always walked over the gardens with his book in my hand, examined with attention the particular spots he described, found them so justly characterized by him as to be easily recognized, and saw with wonder, that his fine imagination had never been able to seduce him from the truth. My inquiries were directed chiefly to such practical things as might enable me to estimate the expense of making and maintaining a garden in that style. My journey was in the months of March and April, 1786."[42] That Whately had any particular philosophy of landscape gardening is not apparent, but such as is emphasized would conform to the ideas that governed the composition of the actual English gardens that Jefferson inspected.

Jefferson found the landscape of Italy romantic as compared with those of other countries. In Italy he admired landscape, as well as landscape painting. At the Chateau di Saorgio near Ciandola he found "the most singular and picturesque scene" he had ever beheld: "The castle and village seem hanging to a cloud in front. On the right is a mountain cloven through to let pass a gurgling stream; on the left, a river, over which is thrown a magnificent bridge. The whole forms a basin, the sides of which are shagged with rocks, olive trees, vines, herds, &c." [43] This scene was closer to Burke's notion of the "sublime," which built the sense of it out of terror or fear, the instinct for self-preservation, and the pleasure of being close enough to danger to suffer its menace yet sufficiently safe from it to keep it an outer view rather than an inner condition. It is a sentiment appropriate to the flow of the Potomac through the Blue Ridge, as Jefferson describes it in *Notes on Virginia*, a scene which is "perhaps, one of the most stupendous in nature . . . worth a voyage across the Atlantic" to see, with the "riot and tumult roaring around . . . the evident marks of their disrupture and avulsion from their beds by the most powerful agents of nature . . . monuments of a war between rivers and mountains which must have shaken the earth itself to its centre." [44] In similar vein is our author's description of the Natural Bridge, which has already been partly quoted.

Jefferson, following Kames, seems to lean towards the Hogarthian rococo. This preference is as obvious as his preference in architecture is for the Palladian antique. The Hogarthian idea involves even his landscaping of the family graveyard which he plans in the area of Monticello described in the *Garden Book* as "The Open Ground on the West—A Shrubbery." [45] As the various gardening plans by Jefferson show, he is thinking definitely according to the Hogarthian prescription. Although the word "serpentine" seemed not to appear in any of the available remarks and plans of Jefferson for a garden, "spiral" and its derivatives are frequent. Thus, in his plan for a garden dated

about 1804, Jefferson proposes to form a thicket and declares "the best way of forming thicket will be to plant it
in labryinth spirally." [47]

All in all, although Jefferson regards gardening as a very
important art, conspicuously able to fuse beauty with use,
he has far less to say about landscape gardening than about
vegetable gardening. In the practice of the art rather than
the business, the combination of the Palladian architecture
with Hogarthian landscape represents, it may be concluded,
another Jeffersonian adaptation—the softening or humanizing of the severe classical line by the winding paths and
serpentine curves of the surrounding grounds—what Dr.
Kallen has called "the orchestration of the Palladian building with the Hogarthian landscape." [48] The rejection of the
rigid formalism of Le Nôtre brought a breath of life into
what had otherwise become a too austere line; and brought
into being a fluid landscape style as harmonious with the
spirit of American democracy as Le Nôtre's had been to
the hierarchical structure with the absolute monarchy.

CHAPTER EIGHT

1. To Charles W. Peale: Poplar Forest, Aug. 20, 1811, ME, XIII, pp.
78–79.

2. To Mrs. Angelica Church: Paris, Feb. 17, 1788, quoted on frontispiece
of Edwin M. Betts: *Thomas Jefferson's Garden Book*, Philadelphia (1944).

3. Travelling Notes for Messrs. Rutledge & Shippen: June 3, 1788, ME,
XVII, pp. 291–292.

4. To Charles W. Peale: Poplar Forest, Aug. 20, 1811, ME, XIII, pp.
78–79.

5. Edwin M. Betts: *Thomas Jefferson's Garden Book*, Preface, pp.
v–vii, Philadelphia, (1944).

6. Marquis de Chastellux: *Travels in North America*, I, pp. 40–46,
quoted in Sarah N. Randolph: *The Domestic Life of Jefferson*, pp. 58–61,
New York (1871).

7. Duc de la Rochefoucauld-Liancourt quoted in Sarah N. Randolph: *The Domestic Life of Jefferson,* pp. 235–239, New York (1871).

8. To James Madison: Monticello, April 3, 1794, from Jefferson Papers in Library of Congress, quoted by Edwin M. Betts: *Thomas Jefferson's Garden Book,* p. 216, Philadelphia (1944).

9. Edwin M. Betts: *Thomas Jefferson's Garden Book,* pp. 6–9, Philadelphia (1944).

10. *Autobiography (Note G):* ME, I, pp. 256–259.

11. Lord Kames: *Elements of Criticism,* II, p. 443, Edinburgh (Edition 1774).

12. *Ibid.,* pp. 445–446.

13. Marie Kimball: *Road to Glory,* p. 160, New York (1943).

14. William Shenstone: *Works* "Unconnected Thoughts on Gardening," II, p. 115, London (1775).

15. *Ibid.,* "A Description of Leasowes, the Seat of the late William Shenstone, Esquire," by R. Dodsley, II, pp. 285–320, London (1775).

16. *Ibid.,* p. 117, London (1775).

17. *Ibid.,* II, p. 111, London (1775).

18. *Memorandum made on a tour to some of the gardens in England:* ME, XVII, pp. 236–244.

19. William Shenstone: *Works,* II, p. 111, London (1775).

20. *Ibid.,* p. 121.

21. Lord Kames: *Elements of Criticism,* II, pp. 430–431, Edinburgh (Edition 1774).

22. *Ibid.,* pp. 431–432.

23. Lord Kames: *Ibid.,* p. 454, Edinburgh (Edition 1774).

24. To Hugh L. White and others: Monticello, May 6, 1810, ME, XII, pp. 387–388.

25. Lord Kames: *Elements of Criticism,* II, p. 453, Edinburgh (Edition 1774).

26. *Notes on Virginia:* ME, II, p. 229.

27. To David Williams: Washington, Nov. 14, 1803, ME, X, pp. 429–439.

28. To Dr. Josephus B. Stuart: Monticello, May 10, 1817, ME, XV, p. 112.

29. Lord Kames: *Elements of Criticism,* II, p. 434, Edinburgh (Edition 1774).

30. *Ibid.,* p. 444.

31. Lord Kames: *Ibid.,* pp. 446–447, Edinburgh (Edition 1774).

32. *Ibid.,* p. 442.

33. *Ibid.,* p. 447.

34. *Memorandums on a Tour From Paris to Amsterdam, Strasburg, and back to Paris, 1788:* ME, XVII, pp. 260–261.

35. *Ibid.,* p. 272.

36. *Ibid.,* p. 273.

37. *Ibid.*, p. 273.

38. To John Page: Paris, May 4, 1786, ME, V, pp. 304–305.

39. Edwin M. Betts: *Thomas Jefferson's Garden Book,* pp. 655–662, Philadelphia (1944).

40. *Catalogue of 1815 Library:* Jonathan Elliott, Washington (1815).

41. Edwin M. Betts: *Thomas Jefferson's Garden Book,* pp. 655–662, Philadelphia (1944).

42. *Memorandums made on a tour to some of the gardens of England:* ME, XVII, pp. 236–237.

43. *Memorandum of Travels in Italy:* ME, XVII, p. 185.

44. *Notes on Virginia:* ME, II, pp. 24–25.

45. Edwin M. Betts: *Thomas Jefferson's Garden Book,* pp. 25–27, Philadelphia (1944). "Here are Jefferson's plans as they appear in the *Account Book:* choose out for a Burying place some unfrequented vale in the park, where is, 'no sound to break the stilness but a brook, that bubbling winds among the weeds; no mark of any human shape that had been there, unless the skeleton of some poor wretch, Who sought that place out to despair and die in.' let it be among antient and venerable oaks; intersperse some gloomy evergreens, the area circular, abt. 60 f. diameter, encircled with an untrimmed hedge of cedar, or of stone wall with a holly hedge on it in the form below. (The form below is a spiral which Jefferson has drawn in the margin.) in the center of it erect a small Gothic temple of antique appearance. appropriate one half to the use of my own family, the other of strangers, servants, etc. erect pedestals with urns, etc., and proper inscriptions. the passage between the walls, 4 f. wide. on the grave of a favorite and faithful servant might be a pyramid erected of the rough rock-stone; the pedestal made plain to receive an inscription. let the exit of the spiral at (a) (this *a* refers to spiral diagram) look on a small and distant part of the blue mountains. in the middle of the temple an altar, the sides of turf, the top of plain stone. very little light, perhaps none at all, save only the feeble ray of an half extinguished lamp.

JANE JEFFERSON

'Ah! Joanna, puellarum optima!
Ah! aevi virentis flore praerepta!
Sit tibi terra laevis!
Longe, longeque valeto!

at the spring on the North side of the park.
a few feet below the spring level the ground 40 or 50 f. sq. let the water fall from the spring in the upper level over a terrace in the form of a cascade. then conduct it along the foot of the terrace to the Western side

of the level, where it may fall into a cistern under a temple, from which it may go off by the western border till it falls over another terrace at the Northern or lower side. let the temple be raised 2. f. for the first floor of stone. under this is the cistern, which may be a bath or anything else. the 1st story arches on three sides; the back or western side being close because the hill there comes down, and also to carry up stairs on the outside. the 2d story to have a door on one side, a spacious window in each of the other sides, the rooms each 8. f. cube; with a small table and a couple of chairs. the roof may be Chinese, Grecian, or in the taste of the Lantern of Demosthenes at Athens.

the ground just about the spring smoothed and turfed; close to the spring a sleeping figure reclined on a plain marble slab, surrounded with turf; on the slab this inscription:

> Hujus nympha loci, sacri custodia fontis
> Dormio, dum blandae sentio murmur aquae
> Parce meum, quisquis tangis cava marmora, sommum
> Rumpere; si bibas, sive lavere, tace.

near the spring also inscribe on stone, or a metal plate fastened to a tree, these lines: 'Beatus ille qui procul negotiis, Ut prisca gens mortalium, Paterna rura bobus exercet suis, solutus omni foenore; Forumque vitat et superba civium Potentiorum limina. Liget jacere modo sub antiqua ilice, modo in tenaci gramine: Labuntur altis interim ripis aquae: Queruntur in silvis aves; Fontesque lymphis obstrepunt manantibus, somnos quod invitet leves.' plant trees of Beech and Aspen about it. open a vista to the millpond, river, road, etc. qu, if a view to the neighboring town would have a good effect? intersperse in this and every other part of the ground (except the environs of the Burying ground) abundance of Jesamine, Honeysuckle, sweet briar, etc. under the temple, an Aeolian harp, where it may be concealed as well as covered from the weather.

This would be better.

the ground above the spring being very steep, dig into the hill and form a cave or grotto. build up the sides and arch with stiff clay. cover this with moss. spangle it with translucent pebbles from Hanovertown, and beautiful shells from the shore at Burwell's ferry. pave the floor with pebbles. let the spring enter at a corner of the grotto, pretty high up the side, and trickle down, or fall by a spout into a basin, from which it may pass off through the grotto. the figure will be better placed in this. form a couch of moss. the English inscription will then be proper.

Nymph of the grot, these sacred springs I keep,
And to the murmur of these waters sleep;
Ah! spare my slumbers! gently tread the cave!
And drink in silence, or in silence lave!"

46. Mr. Fiske Kimball reproduces a plate from manuscript in possession of the Massachusetts Historical Society in his *Thomas Jefferson, Architect,* Boston (1916), p. 168, which contains this passage. Jefferson's remarks are as follows:

"Garden or pleasure grounds

The canvas at large must be Grove, of the largest trees, (poplar, oak, elm, maple, ash, hiccory, chestnut, Linden, Weymouth pine, sycamore) trimmed very high so as to give it the appearance of open ground, yet not so far apart but that they may cover the ground with close shade.

this must be broken by clumps of thicket, as the open grounds of the English are broken by clumps of trees. plants for thickets are broom, calycanthus, altheas, gelder rose, magnolia, glauca, oralea, fringe tree, dogwood, redbud, wild crab, Kalmia merereon eunonymous, haletia, quamodid, rhododendron, oleander, serviutin, lilac, honeysuckle, bramble.

the best way of forming thicket will be to plant it in labryinth spirally putting the tallest plants in the center & lowering gradation to the external termination, a temple for seat may be in the center thus [The figure starts with a square in the center and goes in a *spiral* three full times and breaks off on the fourth mark of the line on a level with the center square.—E. D. B.] leaving space enough between the rows to walk & to trim up, replant the shrubs

Vistas to very interesting objects may be permitted, but in general, it is better so as to arrange thickets as that they may have the effect of vista in various directions.

Dells or ravines should be close in trees & undergrowths

Glens, or hollows should be opened downwards, being embraced by forest.

Temples or seats at those spots on the walks most interesting either for prospect or the immediate scenery.

The Broom wilderness on the South side to be improved for winter walking or riding, conducting a variety of roads through it, forming chambers with seats, well sheltered from winds, & spread before the sun. a temple with yellow glass panes would suit these as it would give the illusion of sunshine in cloudy weather.

a thicket may be of Cedar, topped into a bush, for the winter, surrounded by Kalomia. or it may be of Scotch broom alone."

47. H. M. Kallen: "Jefferson's Garden Wall," p. 82.

"THE FAVORITE PASSION OF HIS SOUL"

THE ART of music was closer to Jefferson's heart than painting or sculpture, and more personal than architecture. Here also he was a performer as well as an interested listener. He studied the violin with Francesco Alberti; played string quartets at Governor Fauquier's; invented an ingenious violin stand which, when folded, could serve as an end table. From his student days on, Jefferson considered music "the favorite passion of my soul."

Most biographers are fond of telling the story of Jefferson's deal for a magnificent violin which is thought to have been an Amati. Oscar Sonneck, writing of the musical side of America's early Presidents, thought it is possible that Jefferson owned one of the first instruments of that make to be found in America: "At least it is certain that John Randolph, the son of the King's Attorney-General, had bought a costly violin in Italy. Once Thomas Jefferson laid his eyes on his friend's coveted treasure and listened to its tones, it became the ambition of his life to possess it. He rested not until the owner agreed to part with it under certain conditions. The contract—for it was a contract, duly signed, sealed, witnessed and recorded in the general court of Williamsburg—reads (in part) 'It is agreed between John Randolph and Thomas Jefferson, that in case the said

John shall survive the said Thomas, the executors of the said Thomas shall deliver to the said John the value of 80 £ sterling of the books of the said Thomas, the same to be chosen by the said John, and in case the said Thomas shall survive the said John, the executors of the said John shall deliver to the said Thomas the violin which the said John brought with him into Virginia, together with all his music composed for the violin.' If others considered this agreement a joke, not so Thomas Jefferson . . . he added a codicil to his will, which he wrote as soon as he became of age, providing for the fulfilment of the compact by the executors. But the Revolutionary War interfered with the stipulations of the contract and will. Said John returned to England in 1775 and sold his precious instrument to said Thomas for the paltry sum of 13 £." [1]

These minutes of the General Court of Williamsburg for October 11, 1771, are quoted in full by Randall, and indicate the amount to have been 800 £ sterling "of the books of the said Thomas." [2] Is it conceivable, in view of the market for violins in those days, that Sonneck dropped a figure or Randall added one? But the price is not the important fact of the record. The important fact of the record is that Jefferson was very eager to own a good fiddle.

Jefferson, the young man-about-town of Williamsburg, refers frequently to the gentle art. From the items in his account book it is seen that he was an assiduous concert goer and that he "paid Dr. Pasteur for violin £ 5"; "paid at Hornsby's for fiddle-strings 3/"; "paid women at Staunton for singing 3d 3/4." [3]

Although most of the biographers of Jefferson hold the opinion that he was an able musician,[4] Sonneck does not.

He avers: "Especially his skilful violin playing has become traditional. But grandmothers in Virginia, who heard the truth from the preceding generation, quote an early authority as saying that Patrick Henry was the worst fiddler in the colony with the exception of Thomas Jefferson." [5]

In describing the charms of Miss Jenny Taliaferro to a fellow student Jefferson remarks: "I was vastly pleased with her playing on the spinnette and singing, but could not help calling to mind those sublime verses of the Cumberland genius. 'Oh! I was charmed to see Orpheus' music all in thee.'" [6] During his infatuation with Rebecca Burwell he writes his friend Page: "As soon as the Rebecca (the name I intend to give the vessel above mentioned) is completely finished, I intend to hoist sail and away. I shall visit particularly England, Holland, France, Spain, Italy, (where I would buy me a good fiddle,) and Egypt." [7]

Writing to Page of his mishaps at Fairfield on Christmas, 1762, one of the things he tells is "how the cursed rats, probably at the instigation of the Devil," ate up his pocket-book, which was in his pocket within a foot of his head, and "carried away my jemmy-worked silk garters and half a dozen new minuets I had just got, to serve, I suppose, as provision for the winter." [8]

Jefferson's account of the intimate gatherings in the Governor's palace at Williamsburg, during his stay at William and Mary—he was brought to Fauquier by his teacher Dr. Small and the latter's friend George Wythe—give a good idea of the most advanced intellectual and artistic level in Virginia at that time: "At these dinners I have heard more good sense, more rational and philosophical conversations, than in all my life besides. They were truly Attic

Fig. No. 13.

CAPITOL OF VIRGINIA AT RICHMOND. DESIGNED BY THOMAS JEFFERSON

Fig. No. 14.

University of Virginia at Charlottesville. Designed by Thomas Jefferson

societies. The Governor was musical also, and a good performer, and associated me with two or three other amateurs
in his weekly concerts." [9]

Legend has it that the favorite passion of Jefferson's soul
accounted for his successful courtship of Martha Skelton.
It is significant that a piano from London was to be the
young squire's musical gift for his bride. He wrote to his
agent there: "I must alter one article in the invoice. I wrote
therein for a clavichord. I have since seen a forte-piano and
am charmed with it. Send me this instrument then instead
of the clavichord: let the case be of fine mahogany, solid,
not veneered, the compass from double G to F in alt, a
plenty of spare strings; and the workmanship of the whole
very handsome and worthy of the acceptance of a lady for
whom I intend it." [10]

His plans for his home at Monticello include the formation of a small orchestra. Perhaps he felt about the relation
of the musical arts to the economy of his growing young
country as he felt about painting and sculpture; a country is
not yet sufficiently developed economically to bear the expense of orchestras for their own sake. Music must be
joined to business. For himself he makes a characteristic
arrangement in a letter to a correspondent in France whose
address has been lost: "If there is a gratification, which I
envy any people in this world, it is to your country its music.
This is the favorite passion of my soul, and fortune has cast
my lot in a country where it is in a state of deplorable barbarism. . . . The bounds of an American fortune will not
admit the indulgence of a domestic band of musicians, yet
I have thought that a passon for music might be reconciled
with that economy which we are obliged to observe. I retain

among my domestic servants a gardener, a weaver, a cabinet-maker, and a stone-cutter, to which I would add a *vigneron*. In a country where, like yours, music is cultivated and practiced by every class of men, I suppose there might be found persons of these trades who could perform on the French horn, clarinet, or hautboy, and bassoon, so that one might have a band of two French horns, two clarinets, two hautboys, and a bassoon, without enlarging their domestic expenses. A certainty of employment for a half dozen years, and at the end of that time, to find them, if they chose a conveyance to their own country, might induce them to come here on reasonable wages." [11] The productive craftsman maker is to double as a non-productive artist.

Five years later, in drawing a daily schedule for the guidance of his motherless daughter Martha—a schedule, incidentally, which omitted to allow time for eating—Jefferson directs her "from 8 to 10, practice music. . . . From 4 to 5, exercise yourself in music." Writing to her from Paris in 1787, he advises her that "music, drawing, books, inventions and exercise will be so many resources to you against ennui." There has already been occasion to point out, in another context, this typical argument of the Enlightenment in favor of learning.

Paris was a revelation to Jefferson of music even more than of the other arts. Recall his appreciation of its culture, as he had told it to Charles Bellini: "Were I to proceed to tell you how much I enjoy their [French] architecture, sculpture, painting, music, I should want words. It is in these arts they shine. The last of them, particularly, is an enjoyment the deprivation of which with us cannot be calculated. I am almost ready to say it is the only thing which from my heart I envy them, and which, in spite of all the authority of the Decalogue, I do covet." [12]

Hitherto Jefferson's taste in music had been determined by the state of the art in America—a robust, folksy and extremely catholic taste. He was familiar with Gay's perennially popular *Beggar's Opera*; with such examples of the classical operatic repertoire as the *Artaxerxes* of Johann Adolph Hasse, with its two airs that had been sung every evening for ten years by Carlo Broschi to soothe King Philip V of Spain; and with less formal works like *Thomas and Sally, or The Sailor's Return* and *Maid of the Mill.* Jefferson seems to have preferred psalms to hymns "as more suitable to the dignity of religious worship" [13]—a view showing an extremely sound musical judgment; and during one of his lovelorn interludes busied himself with copying out *The Charms of Lovely Peggy.* The chamber music he played at Governor Fauquier's would include a liberal sprinkling of Handel, the classical Italian masters— Corelli, Tartini, Vivaldi—perhaps some Boccherini, and the new masters of the rococo, headed by the sons of Bach, Karl Phillip Emmanuel and Johann Christophe.[14]

Now, in Paris, Jefferson came in contact with great European tradition. He attended the Opera, where the works of Lully, Rameau and Gluck upheld that tradition at its purest; he heard the *Concerts Spirituels* at the Tuileries, where the new symphonic style of Stamitz, Wagenseil, Haydn and Mozart was presented along with the works of the older masters of the Baroque. Especially he came in contact with the new Italian opera, and with its leading representative in Paris, the composer Piccini. "A new theatre is established," Jefferson writes to Madame de Brehan, "that of the Opera Buffons, where Italian operas are given, and good music . . ." [15] This was the informal popular opera which represented a revolt against the stately measures of Lully and Gluck. Since the majority of the Encyclopedists whom Jefferson knew in Paris were interested in the Opera Buffons, it was inevitable that he, too, should come under its spell.

The "War of the Buffons" had been a musical *cause célèbre* three decades earlier, when the first Italian troupe had brought Pergolese's *La Serva Padrone* to Paris. Rousseau headed the revolt against the inviolate hegemony of the classic French opera in his famous *Lettre sur la Musique Française*, in which he violently attacked the classical art of Lully, then the model for all French opera, as a dessicated, formalised art without humanity or spontaneity. Against it he held up as example the scintillating, humanly intimate style of the "Buffons," and added to it his own opera-comique *Le Devin du Village*. These two works were the French and Italian equivalents of *The Beggar's Opera*; they represented an attempt to introduce the *sensibilité* of the rococo into the formal, one might say, Palladian, architecture of classic opera. Since music drama was the favorite art form of the Court, and enormously popular all through Europe, the dispute between the adherents of the classic style and the "Buffonistes" represented a crucial cleavage of taste between the formalised classical art and the new, humanistic rococo. Diderot, Rousseau, Baron Grimm and D'Alembert ranged themselves on the side of the new, against the conservatives who looked to the great Rameau, heir of Lully's noble tradition, for leadership. The bitter dispute, which shook French drama and music to its founda-

tions, was exacerbated by the piquant circumstance that the
Queen ranged herself on the side of the opera, while
Mme. de Pompadour became the protectress of the radi-
cals.

Jefferson's casual reference, therefore, to the new theatre
of the Opera Buffons was a notice of one of the most
momentous chapters in French dramatic and musical art.
By the time of his arrival, the new opera-comique had firmly
established itself. Opera-comique violated the unities of
time, place and action which were adhered to in the older
form; it used music to enhance the emotions of servants,
peasants and plain people, instead of the kings and queens
who were the correct figures of classical opera; it brought
music down to personal, everyday emotions, instead of keeping it to the expression of the lofty conflict between honor
and love which was the chief theme of the older style; it
represented the popular, the romantic, the democratic elements in art as against the classic, aristocratic style. Soon
the comique immortalized the two revolutionary satires of
Beaumarchais in Mozart's *Marriage of Figaro* and Ros-
sini's *Barber of Seville*. The conflict between the two styles
during Jefferson's stay in Paris was exemplified in the
rivalry between Gluck and Piccini, a rivalry in which the
Buffonistes came off considerably the worse, since the Italian
was no match for the great Chevalier. Indeed, it was not
until Mozart that an artist of the highest rank gave his
genius to the new form. In any event, Jefferson's friendship
with Piccini must have flowed naturally enough from his
rapport with the revolutionary group with whose members
he was most friendly. Indeed, any close association with
Gluck would have been rendered almost impossible by

Jefferson's extreme aversion to Marie Antoinette, the pupil and protectress of the German composer.

It is during this period that Jefferson is concerned with improvements in the manner of quilling the harpsichord, a subject on which he corresponds with his friend Francis Hopkinson, the first known American composer: "I do not altogether despair, of making something of your method of quilling, though, as yet, the prospect is not favorable. I applaud much your perseverance in improving this instrument, and benefiting mankind almost in spite of their teeth. I mentioned to Piccini the improvement with which I am entrusted. He plays on the pianoforte, and therefore did not feel himself personally interested. I hope some better opportunity will yet fall in my way of doing it justice. I had almost decided, on his advice, to get a piano-forte for my daughter; but your last letter may pause me, till I see its effect." [16]

It must be remembered that the last quarter of the eighteenth century was the period of transition from the clavichord of Bach and the Baroque masters, and from the harpsichord favored by his sons and the musicians of the rococo, to the newly developed piano, which became the instrument of Mozart and Haydn, and of the great romantic school which followed them. Jefferson, as has been noted, changed his gift to his bride from a clavichord to a piano. Piccini, whose advice he respected, was for the new instrument; Hopkinson, his friend, was for the old. Jefferson was torn, in this issue, between his loyalty to his friend and his own interest in all that was new. But he missed no opportunity to encourage Hopkinson: "Houdon only stopped a moment, to deliver me your letter, so that I have not yet had an opportunity of asking his opinion of the improvement [of the last invented tongue for the harpsichord]." [17]

Despite Hopkinson's improvements, the march of musical history was with the piano as against its older sisters. By the end of Jefferson's life the issue was decided. From Monticello he writes his grand-daughter Ellen in 1826: "The piano-forte is also in place, and Mrs. Carey *happening* here has exhibited to us its full powers, which are indeed great. Nobody slept the first night, nor is the tumult yet over on this the third day of its emplacement." [18]

Several decades earlier, Jefferson had had an opportunity to play a favorable role in the development of the upright piano. John Isaac Hawkins, a young English liberal who was both inventor and musician, settled in Philadelphia at the end of the eighteenth century. Through the painter Charles Willson Peale he came to the notice of Jefferson when the latter was President. Jefferson, holding the highest office in the land, countersigned Hawkins' patents and ordered one of the upright pianos Hawkins invented for installation at Monticello, not only because of its mechanical virtues but also because he desired to help "a very ingenious, modest, poor young man." [19] This is not the only time where Jefferson used his personal influence in behalf of an enlightened patronage of the arts and of artists. One may readily recall, among many such attempts, his offers of aid to the painter Trumbull, the composer Hopkinson and the poet Barlow. The grateful Hawkins wrote a number of excellent marches and other pieces in Jefferson's honor. Also, he and other leading musicians of the period wrote marches and pieces for the Marine Band of the United States which Jefferson founded, and which began its career with nine instruments—two oboes, two clarinets, two French horns, two bassoons and drums.

Just as music had played a part in his youthful flirtations and in his courtship of his wife, so it was not absent from the romantic interlude in Paris with Maria Cosway. She was a talented musician as well as painter. In the "Dialogue between my Head and my Heart" which reveals under a pseudo-philosophic calm his suffering at her departure, he writes: *"Head* . . . I often told you, during its course, that you were imprudently engaging your affections, under circumstances that must have cost you a great deal of pain; that the persons, indeed, were of the greatest merit, possessing good sense, good humor, honest hearts, honest manners, and eminence in a lovely art; that the lady had, moreover, qualities and accomplishments belonging to her sex, which might form a chapter apart for her; such as music, modesty, beauty, and that softness of disposition, which is the ornament of her sex and the charm of ours." [20] In the postscript to the *Dialogue* Jefferson says: "I send you the song I promised. Bring me in return the subject, *Jours heureux!* Were I a songster, I should sing it all to these words '*Dans ces lieux qu'elle tarde a se rendre!*' Learn it, I pray you, and sing it with feeling." [21]

Maria Cosway had presented him with the duet *Tacit Ombre*, one of a number of Italian songs and duets with harp accompaniment which she had composed. When Jefferson received the collection—the title page carried an engraving she made after a drawing by her husband Richard Cosway, a vignette of a Cupid charming a savage lion with his piping—he wrote to John Trumbull: "Kneel to Mrs. Cosway for me and lay my soul in her lap." [22]

In Paris, too, Jefferson evinced his usual preoccupation with several other technical innovations in the instruments of the art. To Hopkinson he writes about the foot-bass newly invented by the "celebrated Krumfoltz": "It is precisely a piano-forte, about ten feet long, eighteen inches broad, and nine inches deep. It is of one octave only, from fa to fa. The part where the keys are, projects at the side in order to lengthen the levers of the keys. It is placed on the floor, and the harpsichord or other piano-forte is set over it, the foot acting in concert on that, while the fingers play on this. There are three unison chords to every note, of strong brass wire, and the lowest have wire wrapped on them as the lowest in the piano-forte. The chords give a fine, clear, deep tone, almost like the pipe of an organ." [23] Also, he displays interest in the indefatigable Hopkinson's attempt to improve the harmonica: "I am very much pleased with your project on the Harmonica, and the prospect of your succeeding in the application of keys to it. It will be the greatest present which has been made to the musical world this century, not excepting the Piano-forte." [24]

Jefferson reports similarly in detail upon Renaudin's invention of a new type of metronome: "I went to see it. He showed me his first invention; the price of the machine was twenty-five guineas; then his second, which he had been able to make for about half that sum. . . . This instrument has been examined by the Academy of Music here, who are so well satisfied of its utility, that they have ordered all music which shall be printed here, in future, to have the movements numbered in correspondence with this plexi-chronometer. . . . The instrument is useful, but still it may be greatly simplified. I got him to make me one, and

having fixed a pendulum vibrating seconds, I tried by that
the vibrations of his pendulum, according to the several
movements. I find the pendulum regulated to

Largo	50
Adagio	60
Andante vibrates	70 times in
Allegro	95 a
Presto	135 minute." [25]

It is interesting to notice that just as Jefferson observed
the aptitude of the Indians in painting and sculpture, so he
remarks upon the musical ability of the Negro: "In music
they [the blacks] are more generally gifted than the whites
with accurate ears for tune and time, and they have been
found capable of imagining a small catch. The instrument
proper to them is the Banjar [corrupted by the negroes
into 'banjo'] which they brought hither from Africa, which
is the original of the guitar, its chords being precisely the
four lower chords of the guitar. Whether they will be equal
to the composition of a more extensive run of melody, or of
complicated harmony, is yet to be proved." [26]

He also, with great astuteness, felt the necessity for musical talent in one who would aspire to be a performer. To
Burwell he writes in 1818: "Music is invaluable where a
person has an ear. Where they have not, it should not be
attempted. It furnishes a delightful recreation for the
hours of respite from the cares of the day, and lasts us
through life." [27]

He no more indicated his preferences among composers
than he did among the great masters in painting and sculp-

ture. There, however, one may judge of his predilections from the lists of desiderata he left. Unfortunately, Jefferson's extensive musical library was destroyed by fire; and the listing he made of his instrumental music, classifying them as sonatas, concertos and duets, has not yet been made completely available.[28]

From the passages quoted, it is apparent that Jefferson appears as much interested in the technical processes of music as he was in those of engraving. It was this preoccupation which has led Dr. Kallen to remark that "musician Thomas Jefferson was much more articulate about the processes of musical production . . . than the enjoyment of the musical product; his delight was more in the how than in the what of music." [29] It is indeed true that as far as the available material goes, Jefferson appears to have been completely silent on the "what" of music. Nowhere does he seem to have discussed the nature or the role of the art. This omission becomes less startling when it is remembered that his attitudes towards literature, painting, sculpture, architecture and gardening were all heavily tinged by the utilitarian bent of his mind, as well as by the functional qualities inherent in these arts. An eighteenth century musical instrument, the sticcado, which was a kind of xylophone and derived from the Italian *steccato* meaning "a palisade," was Jefferson's inspiration for a mold board. In a letter to John Taylor in 1794, Jefferson wrote: "I have imagined and executed a mould-board which may be mathematically demonstrated to be perfect, as far as perfection depends on mathematical principles, and one great circumstance in it's favor is that it may be made by the most bungling carpenter, & cannot possibly vary a hair's breath in it's form, but by gross negligence. You have seen the musical instrument called a sticcado. Suppose all it's sticks of equal length, hold the fore-end horizontally on the floor to receive the turf which presents itself horizontally, and with the right hand twist the hind-end to the perpendicular, or rather as much beyond the perpendicular as will be necessary to cast over the turf completely. This gives an idea (tho not absolutely exact) of my mould-board." [30] Jefferson's view of the fine arts was dominated by the role that they could play in the social life of the new republic. Did he not remark to Burwell that "the taste of this country . . . calls for this accomplishment [music] more strongly than for either of the others [drawing or dancing] ?" [31]

But music is the most abstract, the least representational —better, the most non-representational—among the arts. Its realm was that of emotion, mood, sentiment; not that of idea or ideology. The Baroque had discovered in music a means for projecting the loftiest spiritual experiences of man: had not Bach declared that the function of music was to purify the soul and ennoble its Maker? But this point of view was quite foreign to the man of the Enlightenment. Romanticism, again, discovered in music a perfect medium for the intense subjectivity, the passion, the sense of man striving against fate, which belonged to the children of the eighteenth century temper. The classical period saw in music the projection of an ideal of beauty, the ennoblement of personal sentiment in impersonal, perfect abstract forms. And the rococo tempered this abstract ideal by personalizing it, humanizing it through patterns of infinite grace and delight. In his appreciation of "the favorite passion" of his soul, Jefferson was a voice of the rococo.[32] True, he died one year before Beethoven and two before Schubert. But Monticello was a long way from Vienna.

CHAPTER NINE

1. Oscar Sonneck: *Suum Cuique: Essays in Music*, pp. 37–59, New York (1916).

2. Henry Randall: *Life of Thomas Jefferson*, I, p. 131, New York (1858).

3. Excerpts from MS. account books for 1768 and 1769, Library of Congress: in Bernard Mayo: *Jefferson Himself*, p. 19. New York (1942).

4. Henry Randall: *Ibid.*, Footnote 3, pp. 132–133:

"Capt. Bibby, an aid-de-camp of General Frasier, taken prisoner at Saratoga, and remained with the other Saratoga prisoners for several years at Charlottesville, Virginia, and who subsequently settled in New York, informed a friend of ours (Gen. J. A. Dix) that in the frequent visits of the British officers at Mr. Jefferson's house, music was often introduced—all who could, playing on some instrument, or singing with their host and hostess. He said he (Bibby) often played duets on the violin with Mr. Jefferson, and he considered him the finest unprofessional player he ever heard on the instrument. Bibby himself was a fine player."

5. Oscar Sonneck: *Ibid.*, p. 49.

6. To William Fleming: Richmond, 1763, ME, IV, p. 223.

7. To John Page: Shadwell, Jan. 20, 1763, ME, IV, pp. 7–8.

8. To John Page: Fairfield, Dec. 25, 1762, ME, IV, pp. 1–5.

9. To L. H. Girardin: Monticello, Jan. 15, 1815, ME, XIV, pp. 231–232.

10. To Thomas Adams: Monticello, June 1, 1771, ME, IV, pp. 235–236.

11. To ——, Williamsburg, June 28, 1778, ME, IV, p. 41.

12. To Charles Bellini: Paris, Sept. 30, 1785, ME, V, pp. 152–154.

13. Helen Duprey Bullock: Program Notes for Founder's Concert at University of Virginia, April 13, 1943.

14. A detailed account of musical life in America in earlier times can be gleaned from Oscar Sonneck: *Concert-Life in America, 1731–1800*. Leipzig (1907).

15. To Madame de Brehan: Paris, Aug. 14, 1789, ME, VII, pp. 307–308.

16. To Francis Hopkinson: Paris, Sept. 25, 1785, ME, V, p. 147.

17. *Ibid.*, Paris, Jan. 3, 1786, ME, V, p. 239.

18. To Ellen W. Coolidge: Monticello, March 19, 1826, ME, XVIII, pp. 352–353.

19. Helen Duprey Bullock: Program Notes for Founder's Concert at University of Virginia, April 13, 1943.

20. To Maria Cosway: Paris, Oct. 12, 1786, ME, V, p. 435.

21. *Ibid.*, pp. 448–449.

22. Helen Duprey Bullock: *Ibid.*

23. To Francis Hopkinson: Paris, Dec. 23, 1786, ME, VI, p. 22.

24. *Ibid.,* pp. 21–22.

25. *Ibid.,* Paris, Jan. 3, 1786, ME, V, pp. 238–241.

26. *Notes on Virginia:* ME, II, p. 195.

27. To Nathaniel Burwell: Monticello, March 14, 1818, ME, XV, p. 167.

28. The definitive study of Thomas Jefferson's musical interests is in preparation by Dr. Carleton Sprague Smith, Chief of Division of Music of New York Public Library, and Mrs. Helen Duprey Bullock.

29. H. M. Kallen: "The Arts and Thomas Jefferson," p. 273.

30. To John Taylor: Monticello, Dec. 29, 1794, from *Jefferson Papers* in Massachusetts Historical Collection, I: pp. 49–55, quoted by Edwin Morris Betts: *Thomas Jefferson's Garden Book,* Philadelphia (1944), pp. 222–223.

31. To Nathaniel Burwell: *Ibid.*

32. In Jefferson's 1815 Catalogue of his library, published at Washington by Jonathan Elliott, the following books on *Music* are listed in Chapter XXXII under *Fine Arts:*
   "Brennver's Rudiments of music
   Burney's present state of Music in Italy, &c.
   Burney's present state of Music in Germany, &c.
   Complete tutor for the Harpsichord
   Geminiani's Art of Playing the Violin
   Geminiani's Rules for playing in taste
   Holden's Essay towards a rational System of Music
   Jackson's Scheme of Sounds, with a preliminary Discourse
   Pasquali's Art of fingering the Harpsichord
   Pasquali's Thorough-Bass made easy
   Zuccari's Method of playing Adagios
   Revoluzioni del Teatro Musicale Italiano dal Arteaga"

CHAPTER TEN

JEFFERSON AND THE ART OF RHETORIC

To UNDERSTAND Jefferson's attitudes towards the arts of speaking and writing, we must bear in mind first, that he had, in a large measure, the fundamental attitudes and points of view of the American frontier; second, that he was also a man of the eighteenth century whose climate of opinion was the Enlightenment and whose education was in the classics; and third, that though he was by vocation a farmer, by profession a lawyer, and by fate a revolutionary statesman, he himself was essentially a "wordman." These matters affect his theory and practice of the rhetorical arts, both as speaker and writer.

The sources of Jefferson's knowledge of rhetoric are what he learned from his teachers Mr. Douglas,[1] Rev. James Maury,[2] Dr. William Small, George Wythe;[3] his frequent host Governor Fauquier;[4] and his early familiarity with the works and ways of the Indians of his native state.

The correctness of Jefferson's knowledge about rhetoric is shown by the books he possessed on the subject. The Catalogue of Jefferson's library which he made in 1815— books there listed became the nucleus of our Library of Congress—contains three subdivisions under Fine Arts, Chapter 40. They are "Logic, Rhetoric, Orations";

"Rhetoric"; and "Orations." The first subdivision lists Aristotle's *Logic*, Condillac's *Logic* (2 vols.), as well as works on logic by Aldrich, Crackenthorpe, Wallis and Watts. The second subdivision lists Aristotle's *Logic*, Cicero's *Orator*, as translated by Guthrie, two volumes of Cicero *On Oratory*, Quintilian's *Institutiones Oratoriae*, Demetrius Phalereus' *de Elocutione*, Vosii's *Rhetorica*, Adams' *Lectures on Rhetoric and Oratory*, Blair's *Lectures on Rhetoric*, Cambray *On Eloquence*, Dugard's *Rhetorices Elementa*, Mason *On Poetical and Prosaic Numbers and Elocution*, Sheridan on *Elocution*, and Ward's *Oratory*. The third subdivision, "Orations," lists speeches by Aeschines, Deinarchus, Andocides, Lysias, Isaeus, Antiphon, Herodes, Antisthenes, Alcidamas, Lycurgus, Demades, Gorgias, Demosthenes, Isocrates, Quintilian, Cicero and Seneca among the ancients, while the eloquence of Jefferson's own time is represented by Birch's *Virginian Orator*, the *Boylston Prize Dissertations, Orations of the 4th of July* and on the *Boston Massacre of March 5, 1770*; by Curran's *Forensic Eloquence*, and by *Eulogiums on Washington*. Guthrie's version of Cicero's *Orations* appears again in this list, probably by mistake.[5] Of the orations of antiquity, Jefferson's collection lacked only Hyperides of the ten Attic orators recognized by the Alexandrine canon. Since the fragments of six of Hyperides' speeches were only recovered from papyri after 1847 [Hyperides is known to modern times as "the Sheridan of Athens"] this is not surprising. It is safe, however, to assume that Jefferson had some knowledge of Hyperides, since he and John Adams from time to time discussed Dionysius of Halicarnassus in their correspondence, and the second part of the treatise

"On Imitation" in the latter's *Scripta Rhetorica* considers fragments of Hyperides.[6]

But educated as Thomas Jefferson was in the works of the ancients, he was first a child of the frontier, and a master of its skills. He was born in a house erected in a small clearing in the forest. His father had only three or four white settlers for neighbors when he established "Shadwell," and there were on his lands still fresh trails used by unfriendly Indians.[7] Peter Jefferson was "regarded with peculiar respect and veneration by the Indians far and near" [8] and his son "always possessed a particular veneration for the memory of his father." [9] Thomas Jefferson's childhood memories of friendly chiefs and embassies who used his father's house as a favorite stopping place going or returning from the Colonial capitol probably account for his lasting curiosity about the life and culture of the American Indian.[10] Notably he was a close observer and admirer of the rhetorical art as the Indian practiced it. In his *Notes on Virginia,* Jefferson writes: "The Indians . . . astonish you with strokes of the most sublime oratory; such as prove their reason and sentiment strong, their imagination glowing and elevated. . . ."[11] I may challenge the whole orations of Demosthenes and Cicero and of any more eminent orator, if Europe has furnished more eminent, to produce a single passage superior to the speech of Logan, a Mingo chief, to Lord Dunmore, then governor of this state." [12]

In Jefferson's mind rhetorical or classical education would be useful not only to lawyers but to nearly every variety of citizen. Thus he wrote to John Brazier that "the utilities we derive from the remains of the Greek and Latin languages" are not only "models of pure taste in writing" but the "luxury of reading . . . Greek and Roman authors in all the beauties of their originals" plus the power of classic pages to fill up the "vacuum of ennui" in old age from the "stores of real science deposited and transmitted us." Since these things are not useful to all men nor in all epochs of life "their acquisition should be the occupation of our early years only," but their utilities apply to the moralist for ethical writings; to the divine for a translation of "his primary code" before the "simple precepts of the Founder . . . became frittered into subtleties and mysteries and hidden under jargons incomprehensible to the human mind"; to the lawyer for "the system of civil law [in the Latin language] most conformable to the principles of justice . . . yet established among men"; to the physician "as good a code of his art as has been given us to this day"; to the statesman "history, politics, mathematics, eloquence, love of country, to which he must add the sciences of his own day"; to the sciences "the etymon and sound understanding of their fundamental terms." The businesses of the merchant, agriculturist, and mechanic do not need the classical languages. To them can they be "but ornament and comfort." Knowledge of the classics may not be indispensable to greatness, but it is a notable help. Though "there have been shining examples of men of great abilities . . . without any science . . . who can say what these men would not have been, had they started . . . on the shoulders of a Demosthenes or Cicero, of a Locke, or Bacon, or a Newton?" [13]

Rhetoric and oratory belonged in Jefferson's mind with belles-lettres, criticism, and ethics. This way of regarding rhetoric is that of the Enlightenment, and continuous, as the education of the time made inevitable, with the classical tradition. It underlay, quite as much as did the lack of personnel and the poverty of the institutions of higher learning, the fact that instructors were called upon to teach such a diversity of subjects. Jefferson's own beloved teacher, Dr. William Small, "a man profound in the most useful branches of science, with a happy talent of communicating correct and gentlemanly manners, and an enlarged and liberal mind," [14] had been first called to profess mathematics at William and Mary College. "Fortunately the philosophical chair became vacant soon after my arrival at College and he was appointed to fill it per interim: and he was the first who ever gave in that college regular lectures in Ethics, Rhetoric & Belles lettres." [15]

In the ancient world, it must be remembered, the study of rhetoric was to a great degree synonymous with what we call today a liberal education. Authorities on writing and speaking, such as Aristotle, Isocrates, Horace and Quintilian, not only taught *how* to write and speak, they also taught *what* to write and speak. As Dr. Kallen points out in his *Art and Freedom,* the rhetor was the master educator of antiquity, and the ancient world thought of rhetoric as "the universal art practiced by everybody who was anybody and addressed to all. Young free men were trained in oratory, and the skill of the spoken word came in the course of time to be the same as the cultivation and self-realization of personality and the integration of all wisdom. . . . Aristotle appreciated . . . how dynamic in the life of the state was this function of the art of persuasion. . . . Oratory alone of all the arts save war was held to be proper to the dignity and worth of a man well-born and thus 'free'.

. . . It could have been called the art of war with words.
. . . In studying oratory (under rhetors) every youth of
good family studied not only the technique of speaking but
the matter to be spoken . . . and came into the form and
substance of both a liberal and professional education." [16]

Jefferson's feeling for the ancient content of rhetorical
education—we call it "the classics"—retained much of this
attitude.[17]

Since Jefferson classified rhetoric with logic under Oratory and assigned them to the faculty of reason and the field
of philosophy, he made philosophy a necessary discipline in
the education of the lawyer. This again shows how little he
deviated from the tradition which Greek and Roman education embodied. It explains, too, why he gave the place he
did to rhetoric and oratory in his scheme of public education.
When he sketched such a scheme in a letter to Peter Carr,
he divided the citizenry into two classes, the laboring and
the learned. He further subdivided the learned as those
who must earn their livings by the practice of their profes-
sions, and as the wealthy who may aspire to "share in conducting the affairs of the nation or to live with usefulness
and respect in the private ranks of life." [18] For the proper
attainment of these goals, belles-lettres, including criticism,
poetry and composition as branches of rhetoric and oratory,
are to be taught by whatever competent teachers can be
engaged.

In the August 1818 *Report of Commissioners for the
University of Virginia to the Legislature of the State* which
Jefferson wrote, he defined the purposes and curriculum of
"the higher branches of education." They are the development of "the reasoning faculty of our youth"; the "forma-

tion of statesmen, judges and legislators on which the public prosperity and individual happiness are to depend" in
addition to the "training of able counsellors to administer
our country's affairs in all its departments, legislative, execu-
tive and judiciary" who shall "bear their proper share in the
councils of our national government." He thought that not
only the technique of speaking but the matter to be spoken
should be taught under "Ideology: General Grammar,
Ethics, Rhetoric, Belles Lettres and the Fine Arts." Jefferson said "Ideology is the doctrine of thought." [19] This integration, or as Dr. Kallen insists on saying, this "orchestration" of rhetoric with ethics, belles-lettres, the fine arts and
general grammar, under "ideology" is characteristic of
Jefferson.

Rhetoric, moreover, is a subject he wants universally
taught. This is shown by his *Bill for the Establishment of
District Colleges and University* where he counts rhetoric,
belles-lettres and the fine arts generally to be as necessary
to a knowledge of the state as language, ethics, history,
geography, philosophy and the sciences.[20] Here again we
may see how much, as Dr. Kallen keeps reminding us, the
how of expression is involved with the *what*.[21]

Indeed, what Jefferson preferred in the ancients was what
perhaps was closest to his own theory and practice of expression: it was logical form, clear and distinct conception
and compact statement.[22]

From all this may be inferred what value Jefferson set
on the arts of communication as against mere study or scholarship, which without the arts of communication is pedantry. But there is additional evidence. For example, Jefferson
wanted to engage the historian Robertson for the University

of Virginia (though he was not optimistic about obtaining his services) not because he was a man "of the first eminence established in reputation and office"; not merely because he wrote *Charles V, History of Scotland* and *History of America*; but because he was of "first merit" of the "eloquence of the pen" in English. Again, Jefferson despised David Hume for his content or "ideology." But he held Hume's *History of England* "in style equal to any . . . which if it were faithful" would be "the finest piece of history . . . ever . . . written by man . . . So bewitching was (Hume's) style and manner, (although he) suppressed truths, advanced falsehoods, forged authorities, and falsified records . . . his readers were unwilling to doubt anything, swallowed everything and all England became Tories by the magic of his art. His pen revolutionized the public sentiment of that country more completely than the standing armies could ever have done which were so much dreaded and deprecated by the patriots of that day." [23]

The "facts" become thus, willy nilly, that which the writer by his art makes them become, and the "wordman's" craft is the first instrument of the statesman's policy. Such writing, in Jefferson's mind, often overrules that which is written. And this is a subversion which Jefferson hated in writers.

To Jefferson the lasting cause which all speaking and writing should serve are the liberties of the citizens of a state. For the upkeep of such liberties he felt that there is needed an art of writing and speaking which should keep communication simple, flexible, lively, clear and distinct. He deprecated to John Waldo the Edinburgh reviewers who "set their faces against the introduction of new words in the English language" and who "feared that the writers of the United States would adulterate it." [24] He looked forward to an American style in English, and as a base for it he counted not only on Shakespeare and other English classics, but on a knowledge of Anglo-Saxon origins and Greek and Latin roots. In his *Report of Commissioners for the University of Virginia to the Legislature of the State* he indicated the advantages to be derived from the study of Anglo-Saxon: ". . . Anglo-Saxon is of peculiar value. . . . It has this value, too, above the Greek and Latin, that while it gives the radix of the mass of our language, they explain its innovations only. . . . It will form the first link in the chain of an historical review of our language . . . a language already fraught with all the eminent science of our parent country, the future vehicle of whatever we may ourselves achieve, and destined to occupy so much space on the globe, claims distinguished attention in American education." [25] And to J. Evelyn Denison he confessed: "I set equal value on the beautiful engraftments we have borrowed from Greece and Rome. . . . I am equally a friend to the encouragement of a judicious neology; a language cannot be too rich. The more copious the more susceptible of embellishment it will become." [26]

At one time or another, Jefferson discussed the arts of expressive speech, especially literary composition in prose. He remarks upon the art of writing and speaking correctly; upon the ways of using language so as to produce a desired or calculated impression upon the hearer. The remarks occur in his letters. His letters are where most of Jefferson's ideas are to be found.

It is worth while reflecting a moment upon the role of

the letter-form in Jefferson's practice of rhetoric. The form seems to have been Jefferson's characteristic vehicle of expression, and he may well be counted one of the world's greatest letter-writers. The contents of his letters embrace all knowledge, and some indeed strike one as very carefully composed encyclopedic expositions of obscure subjects. "The letters of a person" Jefferson told Robert Walsh, "form the only genuine journal of his life." He employed the letter consciously as his instrument. Letters on education went forth not only to the masculine and feminine members of his family in whose training he had a personal concern, but to the children of his friends, and to strangers. Randall [28] tells us a letter he wrote his daughter Martha when she had just turned eleven years of age is in the possession of the British royal family. The manes of Jefferson must be gratified that a Queen of England should have taken note of his suggestions for the proper education of a "female."

Jefferson kept copies of practically every manuscript that left his hands, and he could dig a letter up again fifty years after its inclusion in his files. He could tell John Minor in 1814: "I have found the paper of which you requested a copy. It was written near 50. years ago." [29] He could tell the young college students Summers and Garland: "Searching among my papers I find a letter written to him (Peter Carr) and conveying such advice as I thought suitable. . . . I enclose you a copy therefore." [30] He could write Abraham Small that he was able to inform him regarding the speech of Eugene Aram: "It has been upwards of 50 years since I read it, when the receipt of your letter induced me to look up a Ms. copy I had preserved. . . . I send you this copy which was taken for me by a school-boy, replete with errors of punctuation, orthography, and sometimes substitutions of one word for another." [31]

Instances of this conscious employment of the letter occur when Jefferson told Mons. de Chastellux: "I determined to give you my thoughts on it (English Prosody) in the form of a letter." [32] He told the Hon. J. Evelyn Denison at the end of an essay-letter on Anglo-Saxon: "I owe apology for this long letter . . . its subject having made an interesting part in the tenor of your letter and my attachment to it. It is a hobby which too often runs away with me where I meant not to give up the rein." [33] He concluded his long letter of self-defense to Martin Van Buren with ". . . although I decline all newspaper controversy, yet when falsehoods have been advanced, within the knowledge of no one so much as myself, I have sometimes deposited a contradiction in the hands of a friend, which, if worth preservation, may, when I am no more, nor those whom I might offend, throw light on history, and recall that into the path of truth; . . . if of no other value, the present communication may amuse you with anecdotes not known to every one. . . . But my letter is already too unmercifully long." [34]

Jefferson's letters affected national policy long after he had retired from public life. Both Madison and Monroe had benefited in their law studies from Jefferson's advice. There was a continuing epistolary as well as personal friendship between them and the mentor of their youth. Each, when he held the office of President of the United States, consulted Jefferson. Even the philosophy of the "Monroe Doctrine" is formulated in letters from Jefferson. There is the letter to William Short under date of August

4, 1820 [35] and the letter to President Monroe, dated October 24, 1823,[36] written six weeks before the "Monroe Doctrine" was officially promulgated.

Jefferson's correspondence with John Adams is legend, and it is full of complaints about the burdens which writing to strangers laid on his time and energy. The most recent public calculation is that Jefferson has written some 18,000 letters,[37] besides some 600,000 words of documents, although guesses range between an out-put of 50,000 and 75,-000 letters. Yet Jefferson did not regard letter-writing as the practice of a literary art, and did not count his letters as genuine art-forms. He told Horatio Spafford: "Except the *Notes on Virginia,* I never wrote anything but acts of office, of which I rarely kept a copy." [38]

Jefferson's interest in the style of discourse never lapsed. He was a conscious stylist and took great pains with his text. What he did as a "precisian" [39] with the various versions of the Declaration of Independence was a fair sample of what he did with all his texts. He deplored in his own work the quality he called "much hasty writing." In the letter he wrote young Bannister Jefferson urges that eloquence of the pen and tongue ensure distinctions in a free country. "What is called style in writing or speaking," he said, "is formed very early in life, while the imagination is warm and impressions are permanent." [40] And he therefore called young Bannister to literary diligence.

But this was not to be directed to the classics alone. Firm as was Jefferson's conviction of the importance of "the classics" it was neither fanatical nor lacking insight into their deficiencies. Thus he wrote to John Brazier: "To these (Latin and Greek) we are . . . indebted for the rational and chaste style of modern composition which . . . distinguishes the nations to whom these models are familiar. Without the models we should probably have continued the inflated style of our northern ancestors, or the hyperbolical and vague one of the east." [41] Then he also wrote to Robert Skipwith "Wherein is 'the utility of the entertainments of fiction' asks the learned sage big with the notion that nothing can be useful but the learned lumber of Greek and Roman reading with which his head is stored?" [42]

In poetry he deprecated rhyme and preferred the measured beat of blank verse. He thought rhyme was a childish thing: "When young, any composition pleases which unites a little sense, some imagination, and some rhythm, in doses however small. But as we advance in life these things fall off one by one, and I suspect we are left at last with only Homer and Virgil, perhaps with Homer alone. He like 'Hope travels on nor quits us when we die.' " [43]

We have seen how Jefferson's feeling for words and their uses led him into philology as well as rhetoric, logic, history and belles-lettres. His touchstone was always the social uses of expression and communication. Perhaps in the back of his mind was that sentence of Sallust's, whom he so often holds up to admiration: "It is glorious to serve one's country by deeds; even to serve her by words is a thing not to be despised. . . ." [44] Jefferson's expression about Sallust was more controlled than his praise of Ossian and his life-long approval of Homer. Sallust, the wealthy Roman who took to writing history after he had retired from public life and married Cicero's divorced wife Terentia, was, according to the learned, preoccupied with what was then a comparatively new branch of historiography—the historical monograph. Significantly, Cicero did not mention him as one of the great speakers of the day and Quintilian expressly warned orators against taking him for a model. In addition, Mr. Rolfe says: "Judged by modern standards the *Jugurtha* is rather like a historical novel of the better class than sober history." [45] Now, judged by modern standards of poetry, Ossian is not even poetry of the better class and says nothing to the modern temper. Jefferson, however, thought otherwise. In his letter to Charles Mac-Pherson requesting a copy of the Gaelic original of Ossian, he said: "I am not ashamed to own that I think this rude bard of the North the greatest poet that has ever existed. Merely for the pleasure of reading his works, I am become desirous of learning the language in which he sung, and of possessing his songs in their original form." [46]

The authenticity of much that is claimed to be the work of Sallust has been subject to a challenge similar to that which Dr. Samuel Johnson instigated about Ossian. It is a matter of some interest that Jefferson should have been so responsive to two such writers, one ancient, the other modern. Did he regard them both as "classic, chaste and pure models," or was he impressed by bits, such as the speeches which Sallust put in the mouths of Cato and Caesar? These, providing remarkable contrasts in patriotism, had always been regarded as meritorious. Sallust, in his account of *The War with Catiline*, has Caesar make a speech in the Senate in favor of appeasing the participants in the conspiracy of Catiline. He has Cato reject any kind of appeasement or temporizing. Cato's ringing words affirmed an ideal that to Jefferson was the lasting cause which all speaking and writing should serve—the liberties of the citizens of a state.

Mr. Roland Morris, President of the American Philosophical Society from 1932 to 1942, who wrote a paper on Jefferson's own eminence in the law as a part of his Society's celebration of its third president's bicentennial, calls attention to the fact that Randall and Parton, Jefferson's early biographers, despite the limitations of material available to them, were very cognizant of their subject's power as a lawyer, whereas later writers generally "ignore the right of Mr. Jefferson to be called a lawyer." [47] Mr. Morris points out that Jefferson spent almost fifteen years of devoted service with outstanding success in the practice of the law, despite the paucity of "legal" matters for study as they are understood in present-day law schools. He stresses certain "tenacious facts . . . set in Jefferson's mind by his study and his experience in the law" which are illustrated by his reforms in the law.

Yet Jefferson was well aware of the "drudgery of the bar" as he indicated to Monroe.[48] And to Isaac McPherson he wrote of the "lubberly volumes of the law." [49] But, lawyer as he was, and thoroughly appreciative of the social value of the law, Jefferson hated legal language. His deep concern about clear and distinct writing is perhaps most dramatically expressed in his view of the dialect of lawyers, both written and spoken. Always he pleaded for accuracy, brevity, and simplicity, instead of the tautologies, redundancies, and circumlocutions that characterize the "barbarous" style of the law.[50] What he conceived to be good examples of legal style is indicated in his reply to Abraham Small who had sent him a copy of *The American Speaker,* which Small appears to have been revising for the students of the time. The *Speaker* had been a textbook in Jefferson's own day and Jefferson himself had used it and had recommended its use to his advisees. In acknowledging Small's letter he wrote that among the added suggestions were the following: "To the speeches of Lord Chatham might be added his reply to Horace Walpole, on the Seamen's bill, in the House of Commons, in 1740, one of the severest which history has recorded. Indeed, the subsequent speeches in order, to which that reply gave rise, being few, short and pithy, well merit insertion in such a collection as this. They are in the twelfth volume of Chandler's Debates of the House of Commons. But the finest thing, in my opinion, which the English language has produced, is the defence of Eugene Aram, spoken by himself at the bar of the York assizes, in 1759, on a charge of murder, and to be found in the Annual Register of that date, or a little after. It has been upwards of fifty years since I had read it, when the receipt of your letter induced me to look up a Ms. copy I had preserved, and on re-perusal at this age and distance of time, it loses nothing of its high station in my mind for classical style, close logic, and strong representation. . . . To these I would add the short, the nervous, the unanswerable speech of Carnot, in 1803, on the proposition to declare Bonaparte consul for life. This creed of republicanism should be well translated, and placed in the hands and heart of every friend to the rights of self government. I consider these speeches of Aram and Carnot, and that of Logan, inserted in your collection, as worthily standing in a line with those of Scipio and Hannibal in Livy, and of Cato and Caesar in Sallust. On examining the Indian speeches in my possession, I find none which are not already in your collection, except that my copy of Cornplanter's has much in it which yours has not.

But observing that the omissions relate to special subjects only, I presume they are made purposely and indeed properly." [51]

Indications of Jefferson's views of style and of the function of rhetoric may be found in his comments on various writers and orators. Among his pen portraits he wrote of James Madison that he had "consummate powers" as an orator, that Samuel Adams was a "bulwark in debate," that John Adams was a "colossus in that debate" on the Declaration of Independence, that "all in all" Edmund Pendleton was "the ablest man" he had ever met with in debate. George Mason, George Wythe and Peyton Randolph also ranked high in his estimation of their oratory. George Washington he thought "unready, short and embarrassed when asked for a sudden opinion in public" but "he wrote steadily, rather diffusely, in an easy and correct style." He regarded Patrick Henry as a fiery orator who left one mystified about what he said, who lacked "sober reasoning and solid argumentations" who yet captivated all by his "bold and splendid eloquence." The discussions which the Marquis de La Fayette and his Patriot friends conducted in Jefferson's presence in Paris he felt "worthy of being placed in parallel with the finest dialogues of antiquity." And Jefferson considered Andrew Jackson "a dangerous man" unfit for high public office because of his "terrible passions," a man who was unable to speak when a Senator "on account of the rashness of his feelings."

Cicero, whose study Jefferson repeatedly recommended to students, and from whom he transcribed twenty-one passages in his *Literary Bible*,[52] was nevertheless not altogether a favorite of Jefferson's. He wrote of him to William

Short as "diffuse, vapid, rhetorical, but enchanting." He
wrote that "his prototype, Plato, eloquent as himself, dealing out mysticisms incomprehensible to the human mind,
has been deified by certain sects." [53] To John Wayles Eppes
he declared: "The models for that oratory which is to produce the greatest effect by securing the attention of hearers
and readers are to be found in Livy, Tacitus, Sallust, and
most assuredly not in Cicero. I doubt if there is a man in
the world who can now read one of his orations through
but as a piece of task work." [54]

When it came to the profession of the law, its connection
with rhetoric was in Jefferson's mind all the more impera-
tive. Rhetoric, he believed, had to be part of the education
of a "lawyer who is at the same time a lover of science."
Its mastery would enhance the usefulness of a young man
who wished to be a participant in the public life of his
country. In 1814 Jefferson sent John Minor a copy of a
letter he had written to Bernard Moore some time between
1764 and 1766 and brought up to date.[55] This letter, he
said, had formed "a basis for the studies of others subsequently placed under my direction, but curtailed for each in
proportion to his previous acquirements and future views
. . . without change, except as to the books recommended
to be read." Bernard Moore had been a fellow law student
asking advice. And Jefferson, then in his early twenties,
advised him. "This foundation being laid, you may enter
regularly on the study of the laws . . . with such kindred
sciences as will contribute to eminence in it's attainment."

What, then, was Lawyer Jefferson's design for the preliminary training of a lawyer, and what role had rhetoric
and oratory therein? I quote from his "basic" letter to

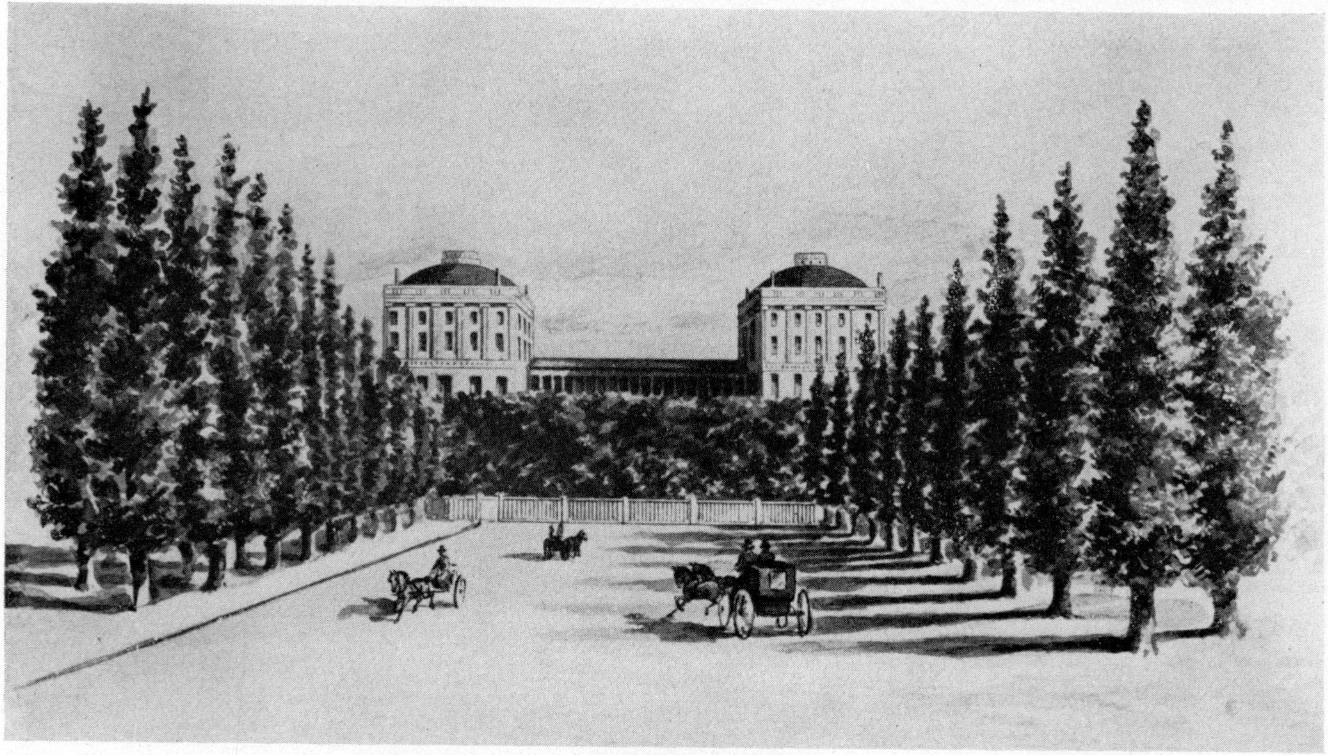

Fig. No. 15.
The Capitol of the United States — 1814

Ruynerne af Capitolen i Washington aar 1819

Fig. No. 16.

RUINS OF THE CAPITOL OF THE UNITED STATES AFTER BEING BURNT BY THE BRITISH — 1819

Courtesy of the Library of Congress

Bernard Moore: "The principal of these [subjects of study] are Physics, Ethics, Religion, Natural law, Belles lettres, Criticism, Rhetoric and Oratory. The carrying on several studies at a time is attended with advantage. Variety relieves the mind, as well as the eye, palled with too long attention to a single object . . .

From Dark to Bed-time. (Read) Belles lettres, criticism, Rhetoric, Oratory, to wit.

Belles lettres. Read the best of the poets, epic, didactic, dramatic, pastoral, lyric &c. But among these Shake-speare must be singled out by one who wishes to learn the full powers of the English language . . .

Criticism. Ld. Kaim's Elements of criticism. Tooke's Diversions of Purley. Of Bibliographical criticism the Edinbg Review furnishes the finest models extant.

Rhetoric. Blair's lectures on Rhetoric. Sheridan on Elocution. Mason on Poetic and Prosaic numbers.

Oratory. This portion of time (borrowing some of the afternoon when the days are long and the nights short) is to be applied to acquiring the art of writing & speaking correctly by the following exercises. Criticise the style of any books whatever, committing your criticisms to writing. Translate into the different styles, to wit, the elevated, the middling and the familiar. Orators and poets will furnish subjects of the first, historians of the second, & epistolary and Comic writers of the third— Undertake, at first, short compositions, as themes, letters &c., paying great attention to the correctness and elegance of your language. Read the Orations of Demosthenes & Cicero. Analyse these orations and examine the correctness of the disposition, language, figures, states of the cases, arguments &c. Read good samples of English eloquence, some of these may be found in Small's American speaker, and some in Carey's Criminal Recorder, in which last the defence of Eugene Aram is distinguishable as a model of logic, condensation of matter, & classical purity of style. Exercise yourself afterwards in preparing orations on feigned cases. In these observe rigorously the disposition of Blair into Introduction, Narration &c. Adapt your language & figures to the several parts of the oration, and suit your arguments to the audience before whom it is supposed to be spoken. This is your last and most important exercise. No trouble should therefore be spared. If you have any person in your neighborhood engaged in the same study, take each of you different sides of the same cause, and prepare pleadings, according to the custom of the bar, where the pl. opens, the def. answers and the pl. replies. It would farther be of great service to pronounce your orations (having only before you only short notes to assist the memory) in the presence of some person who may be considered as your judge." [56]

Nor was Jefferson unmindful of the social and personal value of the study of the law. He not only told his kinsman and son-in-law Thomas Mann Randolph that farming and the study of law was a wise combination since one would relieve the other, but that the latter qualified a man to be "useful to himself, to his neighbors, & to the public" and was the "most certain stepping stone to preferment in the political line." [57] He told his kinsman John Garland Jefferson that all a law student needed was "access to a library" and guidance in the order books are to be read. He wrote that any spare time not occupied by law reading should be filled up with "Lowthe's grammar, Blair's lectures on rhetoric, Mason on poetic & prosaic numbers, Bolingbroke's works for the sake of the stile . . . the English poets for the sake of style alone." [58] Almost three years later he advised the young man to supplement his readings in law and history by a thorough-going study of Blair, Mason and Quintilian and to "endeavor to catch the oratorical style of Bolingbroke." [59] Often, in volunteering or responding to requests for advice from young men regarding their studies, Jefferson mentioned the treatises of Blair, Mason or Sheridan. He detailed to Dr. Thomas Cooper [60] a conspectus for the study of the law which he supplemented by another letter to him the next month in which he wrote: "When I was a student of the law, now half a century ago, after getting through Coke-Littleton, whose matter cannot be abridged, I was in the habit of abridging and common-placing what I read meriting it, and of sometimes mixing my own reflections on the subject. I now enclose you the extract from those entries. They were written at a time of life when I was bold in the pursuit of knowledge, never fearing to follow truth and reason to whatever results they lead and bearding every authority which stood in their way." [61] Nor was there any change in his mind about being a "thorough lawyer" when he advised Dabney Terrell seven years later to read "history, ethics, physics, oratory, poetry, criticism, etc., as necessary as law to form an accomplished lawyer." [62]

In the 1820's, when young people were forming debating

societies in schools and colleges, a good many seemed to
have named their society for Jefferson and to have advised
him of this fact. With his usual courtesy the Sage of Monticello replied to each. Thus he wrote to David Harding,
president of the Jefferson Debating Society of Hingham,
Massachusetts: "I am justly sensible of the honor done my
name by associating it with the title of the society. The object of the society is laudable, and in a republican nation,
whose citizens are to be led by reason and persuasion, and
not by force, the art of reasoning becomes of first importance. In this line antiquity has left us the finest models
for imitation; and he who studies and imitates them most
nearly, will nearest approach the perfection of the art.
Among these I should consider the speeches of Livy, Sallust,
and Tacitus, as preeminent specimens of logic, taste, and
that sententious brevity which, using not a word to spare,
leaves not a moment for inattention to the hearer. Amplification is the vice of modern oratory. It is an insult to an
assembly of reasonable men, disgusting and revolting, instead of persuading. Speeches measured by the hour, die
with the hour. I will not, however, further indulge the disposition of the age to sermonize, and especially to those
surrounded by so much better advice." [63]

To George Summers and John Garland, college students,
Jefferson wrote: "I have received your favor of the 18th,
and am duly sensible of the honor done my name by its
association with the institution formed in your college for
improvement in the art of speaking. The efforts of the
members will, I trust, give a just reputation to the society
and reflect on its name the honor which it cannot derive
from it. In a country and government like ours, eloquence is

a powerful instrument, well worthy of the special pursuit of our youth. Models, indeed, of chaste and classical oratory are truly too rare with us; nor do I recollect any remarkable in England. Among the ancients the most perfect specimens are perhaps to be found in Livy, Sallust and Tacitus. Their pith and brevity constitute perfection itself for an audience of sages, on whom froth and fancy would be lost in air. But in ordinary cases, and with us particularly, more development is necessary. For senatorial eloquence, Demosthenes is the finest model; for the bar, Cicero. The former had more logic, the latter more imagination. Of the eloquence of the pen we have fine samples in English. Robertson, Sterne, Addison, are of the first merit in the different characters of composition. Hume, in the circumstances of style, is equal to any; but his tory principles spread a cloud over his many great excellencies. The charms of his style and matter have made tories of all England and doubtful republicans here." [64]

From these letters and others cited, a list of speeches may be assembled which Jefferson felt were worthy of study for one reason or another. Thus, he considered speeches by Logan, the Mingo chief, Carnot, Aram and Lord Chatham as deserving of close attention as those by Livy, Sallust, Tacitus, Demosthenes and Cicero. This illustrates Jefferson's mastery of the orator's art resting on what he learned and observed of rhetoric as used by the Indians; what he experienced through the practice of law; and what he knew of the theory and practice of classical antiquity.

Any speaker or writer can be helped by heeding Jefferson's advice on the "wordman's" art. As his letter to David Harding indicated, he would like a speech to have classical shortness, taste, condensation of matter; classical purity of style, logic, pith. He wanted it to be short, rational and chaste; plain but perspicuous; yet having elegance and rich sentiment. Other letters show he wanted whatever is uttered to be uttered with the "honest heart" and the "knowing head." The vices of oratory were for him not only the conventional eulogy, inflation, vagueness, hyperbole, amplification, but elaborate philippic and diatribe done with "passions vehement and viperous . . . catching at every gossiping story . . . supplying by suspicions what could (be found) nowhere else . . . arguing on . . . motley farrago as if established on gospel evidence." [65]

Jefferson's fundamental requirement was recognizable proof, which "is the duty of the affirmative side. A negative cannot be positively proved." [66] He also wrote "The proof of a negative can only be presumptive" [67] and in his *Bill for the Proportioning Crimes and Punishments in Cases Heretofore Capital*" he discussed types of proof as positive or circumstantial, contrary, conclusive and equivocal.[68] No honest orator or writer should let himself be "a very weak man . . . very prone to antipathies, boiling with party passions and under the dominion of those readily welcoming fancies for facts." [69] He confesses to Van Buren that "My rule of life has never been to harrass the public with fendings and provings of personal slanders" [70] such as churchmen often employ.

Out of the plethora of comments, admonitions, instructions, asides, analyses and direct expositions concerning the art of writing and speaking that appear in Jefferson's letters and other works, a summary of Jefferson's theory and practice in writing and speaking can be made up. It is clear that he wanted every form of composition—the oration, the essay, the letter, to be brief, clear and distinct, diversified, yet forceful and sympathetic. He favored the use of new words where it seemed desirable, and he deprecated rigid adherence to rules. He felt that the speaker must think of his audience and suit his arguments to them. In order to achieve this, he advised frequent presentation of speeches and the like before capable judges. He deprecated the use of notes. He deprecated pedantic adherence to grammar, purisms, wire-drawn expressions and barbarisms. He deprecated technicalities, especially such as are so conspicuous in the law. He deprecated straining for effect or originality. He urged in the dealing with any subject the boldness of an honest heart and a knowing head. He urged the development of an argument on the basis of exhaustive research and as nearly as possible, perfect knowledge employed with a strict logic. He was averse to overstatement and philippics, even on issues where his passions were strong. He forbade gossip, innuendo, intrigue, chicanery and dissimulation. Vehemence of any kind was anathema to him. To achieve the positive qualities of writing and speaking that he desired, and to escape the negative, he urged the study and imitation of the finest models in the art of reasoning.

I think it could be said that Jefferson in his own writing—and judging by his addresses to Congress and to the nation—in his speeches, practiced what he preached. The model he set is worthy of imitation. His precepts still form a corpus of rules which can be well employed in educating young men and young women into free citizens of a free land. They are the more important in view of the fact clearly established by Randall [71] and Bowers: [72] that Jefferson himself was a reluctant public speaker, and where he could, left the statement of his views to others. However, as Marie Kimball indicates by her quotation from Edmund Randolph's *Essay on the Revolutionary History of Virginia*,[83] when pressed to speak, Jefferson gave a good account of himself. Obviously this made it the more necessary that what he thought should be stated in such a way that nobody could be mistaken about it. And for him this was the whole aim of the rhetorical art.

CHAPTER TEN

1. Henry S. Randall: *Life of Thomas Jefferson*, I, pp. 17–18, New York (1858):

"Thomas Jefferson at nine . . . went to the school of Mr. Douglass, a Scotch clergyman, who taught him Latin, Greek and French . . . During his fourth year here his father died, leaving directions that his oldest son receive a thorough classical education. Mr. Jefferson often spoke of this dying direction with deep feeling. 'I have often heard him say (Col. Thomas J. Randolph, his grandson writes us) that if he had to decide between the pleasure derived from the classical education which his father had given him and the estate left him, he would decide in favor of the former.' "

2. *Autobiography:* ME, I, p. 3.

3. *Ibid.,* p. 4.

4. *Ibid.,* p. 4.

5. *Catalogue of the Library of Congress:* Jonathan Eliot, Washington (1815).

6. *The Roman Antiquities of Dionysius of Halicarnassus:* I, Introd. pp. xxv–xxvi, translated by Earnest Cary, based on Edward Spelman, London (1927).

Note: See also Sir Richard Jebb: *The Attic Orators from Antiphon to Isaeos*, 2 Volumes, London, (1876).

7. Henry S. Randall: *Life of Thomas Jefferson*, I, pp. 10–11.

8 *Ibid.,* I, p. 12.

9. *Ibid.,* I, p. 15.

10. To John Adams: Monticello, June 11, 1812, Ford, Fed. Ed., XI, p. 254.

"So much in answer to your inquiries concerning Indians, a people with whom in the early part of my life, I was very familiar, and acquired impressions of attachment and commiseration for them which have never been obliterated. Before the Revolution, they were in the habit of coming often and in great numbers to the seat of government, where I was very much with them. I knew much of the great Ontasseté, the warrior and orator of the Cherokees; he was always the guest of my father, on his journeys to and from Williamsburg. I was in his camp when he made his great farewell oration to his people, the evening before his departure for England. The moon was in full splendour, and to her he seemed to address himself in his prayers for his own safety on the voyage, and that of his people during his absence; his sound voice, distinct articulation, animated action, and the solemn silence of his people at their several fires, filled me with awe and veneration, although I did not understand a word he uttered."

11. *Notes on Virginia:* ME, II, p. 195.

12. *Ibid.,* pp. 87–88.

13. To John Brazier: Poplar Forest, Aug. 24, 1819, ME, XV, pp. 207–211.

14. *Autobiography:* ME, I, p. 3.

15. *Ibid.,* p. 3.

16. H. M. Kallen: *Art and Freedom,* I, pp. 52–66, New York (1942).

17. Perhaps the finest tribute paid to the force and influence of writers of classical antiquity by Jefferson is contained in his long essay-letter to Mons. Coray (Monticello, Oct. 31, 1823, ME, XV, pp. 480–490) in response to the Greek patriot-scholar's request for "some thoughts on the subject of national government." Jefferson tells Coray his thoughts "are the rest of the observations and reflections of an octogenary, who has passed fifty years of trial and trouble in the various grades of his country's service. They are yet but outlines which you will better fill up, and accommodate to the habits and circumstances of your countrymen. Should they furnish a single idea which may be useful to them, I shall fancy it a tribute rendered to the manes of your Homer, your Demosthenes, and the splendid constellation of sages and heroes . . . whose merits are still resting, as a heavy debt, on the shoulders of the living and the future races of men."

18. To Peter Carr: Monticello, Sept. 7, 1814, ME, XIX, pp. 211–221.

19. S. K. Padover: *The Complete Jefferson,* pp. 1098; 1100, New York (1943).

20. Bill dated October 25, 1817, Sec. 34; N. F. Cabell: *Early History of the University of Virginia,* pp. 417–427 (1856).

21. H. M. Kallen: *Art and Freedom, ibid.*

22. H. M. Kallen: "The Arts and Thomas Jefferson," pp. 269–283.

23. To an as yet unidentified correspondent: Monticello, Oct. 25, 1825, ME, XIV, pp. 124–128.

24. To John Waldo: Monticello, Aug. 16, 1813, ME, XIII ,pp. 339–347.

25. S. K. Padover: *The Complete Jefferson,* p. 1103.

26. To J. Evelyn Denison: Monticello, Nov. 9, 1825, ME, XVI, pp. 129–138.

27. To Robert Walsh: Monticello, April 5, 1823, MSS, University of Virginia, cited by Bernard Mayo in *Jefferson Himself,* p. 330.

28. Henry S. Randall: *Life of Thomas Jefferson,* I, pp. 390–391: "A copy of this letter (To Martha Jefferson, Annapolis, Nov. 28th, 1783) has appeared in Griswold's 'Republican Court' since it was transcribed for these pages. The original is in the possession of the Queen of England. When Mr. Aaron Vail was Charge d'Affaires of the United States at London, he was requested by the Princess Victoria to procure for her an autograph of Mr. Jefferson. Mr. Vail applied to a member of Mr. Jefferson's family, and the letter was transmitted to him for the Princess."

29. To John Minor: Monticello, Aug. 30, 1814, Ford, Fed. Ed., XI, p. 420.

30. To Messrs. George W. Summers & John B. Garland: Monticello, Feb. 27, 1822, ME, XV, pp. 352–354.

31. To Abraham Small: Monticello, May 20, 1814, ME, XIV, pp. 136–138.

32. Undated letter to Mons. de Chastellux: ME, XVIII, p. 414.

33. To J. Evelyn Denison: Monticello, Nov. 9, 1825, ME, XVI, pp. 129–138.

34. To Martin Van Buren: Monticello, June 29, 1824, ME, XVI, pp. 52–69.

35. To William Short: Monticello, Aug. 4, 1820, ME, XV, pp. 262–263.

36. To James Monroe: Monticello, Oct. 24, 1823, Ford, Ed., XII, pp. 318–321.

37. *New York Times:* Aug. 27, 1944.

38. To Horatio Spafford: Monticello, May 11, 1819, ME, XV, p. 190.

39. Randall: *Life of Thomas Jefferson,* I, p. 167.

40. To J. Bannister, Jr.: Paris, Oct. 15, 1786, ME, V, p. 187.

41. To John Brazier: Poplar Forest, Aug. 24, 1819, ME, XV, pp 207–211.

42. To Robert Skipwith: Monticello, Aug. 3, 1771, ME, IV, pp. 237–240.

43. *Thoughts on English Prosody:* ME, XVIII, pp. 447–448.

44. Sallust: *The War with Catiline,* II, 9–111, 5.

45. J. C. Rolfe: Translator of Sallust, pp. ix–xviii, London (1931).

46. To Charles McPherson: Albemarle, Feb. 25, 1773, ME, IV, p. 22.

47. Roland Morris: "Jefferson as a Lawyer," Proceedings of the American Philosophical Society, Vol. 87, No. 3, pp. 211–215, July (1943).

48. To James Monroe: Paris, Dec. 18, 1786, ME, VI, p. 16.

49. To Isaac McPherson: Monticello, Aug. 13, 1813, ME, XIII, p. 326.

50. To George Wythe: Monticello, Nov. 1, 1778, ME, I, p. 216.

51. To Abraham Small: Monticello, May 20, 1814, ME, XIV, pp. 136–138.

52. Gilbert Chinard: *The Literary Bible of Thomas Jefferson,* Baltimore (1928).

53. To William Short: Monticello, Oct. 31, 1819, Ford, Fed. Ed., XII, p. 140.

54. To John Wayles Eppes: Monticello, Jan. 17, 1810, ME, XII, p. 343.

55. To Bernard Moore: approx. 1764, Ford, Fed. Ed., XI, pp. 420–426.

56. *Ibid.*

57. To Thomas Mann Randolph: New York, May 20, 1790, Ford, Fed. Ed., VI, p. 62.

58. To John Garland Jefferson: Philadelphia, June 11, 1790, Ford, Fed. Ed., VI, p. 62.

59. To John Garland Jefferson: Philadelphia, April 14, 1793, ME, XIX, p. 104.

60. To Dr. Thomas Cooper: Monticello, Jan. 16, 1814, ME, XIV, pp. 54-63.

61. To Dr. Thomas Cooper: Monticello, Feb. 10, 1814, ME, XIV, p. 85.

62. To Dabney Terrell: Monticello, Feb. 26, 1821, ME, XV, p. 322.

63. To David Harding: Monticello, April 20, 1824, ME, XVI, p. 30.

64. To Messrs. George W. Summers & John B. Garland: Monticello, Feb. 27, 1822, ME, XV, pp. 352-354.

65. To Martin Van Buren: Monticello, June 29, 1824, ME, XVI, pp. 52-69.

66. Ibid.

67. To John Adams: Monticello, July 9, 1819, ME, XV, pp. 204-207.

68. Bill for Proportioning Crimes and Punishments in cases heretofore Capital: ME, I, p. 218.

69. To Martin Van Buren: Ibid.

70. To Martin Van Buren: Ibid.

71. Randall: Life of Thomas Jefferson, I, p. 50: "He (Jefferson) was disqualified from being a very successful advocate by a peculiarity in his articulation. His voice, if raised much above the loudness of ordinary conversation, began after a few moment's effort to 'sink in his throat'—in other words to become husky and inarticulate. Such was the reason assigned for his never speaking (beyond a few sentences at a time) before legislative and popular bodies, by Mr. Madison and Mr. Wirt.* . . . this natural impediment may have increased a natural distaste or incapacity, for addressing public bodies.

*We have this from those who heard the declarations from their own lips."

72. Claude G. Bowers: Jefferson in Power, p. 87, Boston (1936). Mr. Bowers tells of Jefferson's "personal horror of speech-making" and its part in his decision not to deliver Messages to Congress in person.

73. Marie Kimball: The Road to Glory, p. 84, New York (1943).

"Indefatigable and methodical, Jefferson spoke with ease, perspicuity and elegance. His style in writing was more impassioned, and although often incorrect, was too glowing not to be acquitted as venial departures from rigid rules. Without being an overwhelming orator, he was an impressive speaker who fixed the attention. On two signal arguments before the general court, in which Mr. Henry and himself were coadjutors, each characterized himself. Mr. Jefferson drew copiously from the depths of the law, Mr. Henry from the recesses of the human heart."

JEFFERSON AS LITTERATEUR AND CRITIC

A DISCUSSION of Jefferson's basic attitudes towards literature may very well begin with an examination of his literary Commonplace Book which has been published by Professor Gilbert Chinard as *The Literary Bible of Thomas Jefferson.* The Greek authors represented in this collection of quotations are Homer, Herodotus, Euripides, Anacreon and Quintus Smyrnaeus.[1] Jefferson's feeling for Homer is attested to, not only by the quotations, which we find strewn throughout his writings, from "that first of poets, as he must ever remain, until a language equally ductile and copious shall again be spoken" but by the fact that in the most tragic event of his life he turned for solace to the ancient poet, and inscribed two lines from the *Iliad* upon the tomb of his wife:

"If in the house of Hades men forget their dead,
Yet will I even there remember my dear companion."

Of the works of Euripides Jefferson made abstracts from *Hecuba, Orestes, Phoenissae, Medea* and *Hippolytus.* Significantly, there is no mention of Plato in the *Literary Bible.* Jefferson was consistent and outspoken in his dislike of Plato; the aristocratic, mystical elements in the philosopher's thinking were most uncongenial both to his rationalism and his egalitarianism. "While wading through the whimsies, the puerilities and unintelligible jargon of this work (Plato's Republic)" he writes John Adams "I laid it down often to ask myself how it could have been that the world should have so long consented to give reputation to such nonsense as this." [2] Of the Latin authors whom Jefferson quoted, the most important by far is Cicero. It was Cicero the philosopher, rather than the statesman or orator, whom Jefferson most appreciated. The quotations from the *Tusculanae Quaestiones*, regarding death and the existence of the soul come back with particular insistence half a century later in his correspondence with Adams. In a letter to William Short he sums up the influence of the classic authors upon his philosophy of life: "As you say of yourself, I too am an Epicurean. I consider the genuine (not the imputed) doctrines of Epicurus as containing everything rational in moral philosophy which Greece and Rome have left us. Epictetus indeed, has given us what was good of the stoics; all beyond, of their dogmas, being hypocrisy and grimace." [3]

Noteworthy, in respect to what we have observed again and again in Jefferson as an attempt to transplant an older tradition on to a new soil, is his treatment of the ancient poets. Prof. Chinard points out how, in Jefferson's transcription of Horace's second epode, without changing a word "simply by omitting every detail that was purely Roman he succeeded in lifting out of time this picture of Roman farm life and in changing it into a description fitting exactly America of the colonial days." The sturdy Apulian ploughman and his wife "lost their local characteristics, the Roman farm became similar to a Southern plantation and the slaves of the household could be mistaken for American Negroes playing in the yard after the day's work is done." [4]

Jefferson's abiding interest in the *how* as well as the *what* obtained in this realm too, leading him into the most detailed investigations with regard to his beloved Latin and Greek, investigations in which he displayed an astonishing aptitude for practical linguistics. To Edward Everett in 1823 he sends a minute analysis of the Ablative case in Greek. In this letter, too, he gives vent to his dislike of abstract speculation: "I acknowledge myself at the same time not an adept in the metaphysical speculations of Grammar. By analyzing too minutely we often reduce our subject to atoms, of which the mind loses its hold." [5] In the same spirit he writes to John Adams on the subject of accent in Greek: "Against reading Greek by accent, instead of quantity, as Mr. Ciceitira proposes, I raise both my hands. What becomes of the sublime measure of Homer, the full sounding rhythm of Demosthenes, if, abandoning quantity, you chop it up by accent?" [6] Jefferson's extraordinary feeling for language and for its laws of development, which we shall have occasion to comment upon in connection with his studies in Anglo-Saxon, comes out in his letter to Adams in which he tells of his approach to the problem of Greek pronunciation: "Early in life, the idea occurred to me that the people now inhabiting the ancient seats of the Greeks and Romans, although their languages in the intermediate ages had suffered great changes, and especially in the declension of their nouns, and in the terminations of their words generally, yet having preserved the body of the word radically the same, so they would preserve more of its pronunciation." He then explains how, in a language "so remarkable for the euphony of its sounds" as the Greek, if that euphony is destroyed in the modern usage, "we may presume some degeneracy has taken place." [7] He therefore reaches the conclusion that, even though the modern Greeks might have been considered the best authorities on the pronunciation of the ancient tongue, there is greater likelihood that foreign nations, using the language solely as a literary tongue, would be less given to corruption than those using it in their daily living.

There is found here, then, abundant evidence of that workman's delight in the *how* upon which Dr. Kallen has commented, united in this instance with the preoccupations of the wordman. In this own style Jefferson was the bold experimenter, appealing for ultimate authority to usage rather than to tradition: "Mine has been a life of business, of that kind which appeals to a man's conscience, as well as his industry, not to let it suffer, and the few moments allowed me from labor have been devoted to more attractive studies, that of grammar having never been a favorite with me. The scanty foundation, laid in at school, has carried me through a life of much hasty writing, more indebted for style to reading and memory, than to rules of grammar. I have been pleased to see that in all cases you appeal to usage, as the arbiter of language; and justly consider that as giving law to grammar, and not grammar to usage." [8]

Jefferson's love for the classics did not blind him to the fact that too great a reverence for the past may act as a brake upon the creative fancy and that the boldness of the creative artist is to be preferred to the rigidity of the academician: "I concur entirely with you in opposition to Purists, who would destroy all strength and beauty of style, by subjecting it to a rigorous compliance with their rules. . . .[9a] To explain my meaning by an English example, I will quote the motto of one, I believe, of the regicides of Charles I [also the motto on Jefferson's seal ring], 'Rebellion *to* tyrants is obedience to God.' Correct its syntax, 'Rebellion *against* tyrants is obedience to God,' it has lost all the strength and beauty of the antithesis." [9b]

With genuine pride the literary spokesman of the emerging democracy upholds the cause of a freshly evolving American style free from the shackles of the older English. With his perception of the functional adaptations inherent in all life processes, it was natural that he should champion this new linguistic development which would both express and stimulate the intellectual and emotional patterns of life in the New World: "But whether will these [American dialects] adulterate or enrich the English language? Has the beautiful poetry of Burns, or his Scottish dialect, disfigured it? Did the Athenians consider the Doric, the Ionian, the Aeolic, and other dialects, as disfiguring or as beautifying their language?" [10]

Jefferson anticipated Henry L. Mencken's concern for the American Language and its development by at least a century and a half. The evidence suggests that Jefferson was familiar with the problem while a college student, if we go back only as far as the letter to Bernard Moore of approximately 1764–1766. Mencken's first version of *The American Language* appeared in 1919, and has gone successively through four editions. It was rewritten in 1933 after a third edition. Mencken says in his preface to the Fourth Edition: "Since 1923 the pull of American has become so powerful that it has begun to drag English with it. . . .

The American people now constitute by far the largest fraction of the English-speaking race, and since the World War they have shown an increasing inclination to throw off their old subservience to English precept and example." [11]

Mencken calls attention to several aspects of Jefferson's preoccupation with the problem of the American language, speaking of William B. Cairns' study "British Criticisms of American Writings, 1783–1815," [12] in which literary criticisms, rather than linguistic matters are considered. Cairns shows the nature of the attack by the *European Magazine and London Review* in 1787 on Jefferson's English in his *Notes on the State of Virginia.* The periodical chose to be scathing about Jefferson's use of "to belittle" which he is said by Thornton to have coined. Marshall, author of the five-volume *Life of Washington,* Barlow and Bancroft, were among the other American authors derided. Cairns says the most constantly anti-American of the English and Scottish reviews of the time were the *Anti-Jacobin* and the *Quarterly,* who combined scurrility with their hostility. Both, at different times, were edited by William Gifford. "The *Anti-Jacobin* specialized in reviling George Washington and the *Quarterly* in spreading scandal about Thomas Jefferson." [13]

Mencken cites John Bach McMaster's *History of the People of the United States from the Revolution to the Civil War* for the comment: "It was generally believed the worst calumniators of the United States were subsidized by the British government, apparently in an effort to discourage emigration." [14] Jefferson particularly came in for violent abuse of his moral character. The English writers of travel books were full of "moral horror" as well as "grammatical disgust" says Mencken, and Mrs. Frances Trollope's "Domestic Manners of the Americans" concluded that "the want of refinement" was the great American curse.[15] Mencken serves notice that "This war upon Americanisms is in progress all the time, but it naturally has its pitched battles and its rest-periods between." [16] He says further: "The English objection is not alone to the American vocabulary; it is also to the characteristic American style, which begins to differ appreciably from the normal English style." [17]

It is Mencken's belief that "The earliest Americanisms were probably words borrowed bodily from the Indian languages—words, in the main, indicating natural objects that had no counterparts in England," [18] and that "the literature on the subject is rather meager." [19]

Mencken, in discussing the period of growth in a new nation in the making, says: "The first sign of the dawn of a new national order came with the election of Thomas Jefferson to the Presidency in 1800. The issue in the campaign was a highly complex one, but under it lay a plain conflict between democratic independence on the one hand and subservience to English precept and example on the other. . . . His [Jefferson's] first acts after his inauguration were to abolish all ceremonial at the court of the Republic, and to abandon spoken discourses to Congress for written messages. That ceremonial, which grew up under Washington, was an imitation, he believed, of the formality of the abhorrent Court of St. James's; as for the speeches to Congress, they were palpably modelled upon the speeches from the throne of the English kings. Both reforms met with wide approval. . . ." [20]

Mencken notes some interesting differences of usage between the American and English language. When certain Biblical names transplanted to the New World were not used derisively for American comic characters in English novels or plays, "Jefferson" or "Washington" were.[21] Familiar given names in the United States, such as Washington, Jefferson, Lincoln, Lee, are quite unknown in England.[22] He cites Dr. Josiah Combs' study "The Language of the Southern Highlanders" as authority that diminutives of proper names are very widely used,[23] and thinks the same conclusion might be drawn for most parts of the United States. To Dr. Combs' list he would add, among others, *Lafe* for *Lafayette,* *Wash* for *Washington,* and *Jeff* for *Jefferson.*[24] In his examination of American geographical nomenclature, Mencken finds "the whole land bespattered with Washingtons, Lafayettes, Jeffersons and Jacksons," and calls attention to the study of American place-names which fall into eight general classes, of which the first consists of those embodying personal names "chiefly the surnames of pioneers or of national heroes." [25]

Mencken also discusses Jefferson's use of "to belittle" and the storm of abuse it aroused; [26] "to compromit"—now obsolete; "to americanize"—first used by John Jay in 1797 and Jefferson in 1801.[27] "Rather curiously," says Mencken, *"americanization* did not appear until the middle of the nineteenth century." [28] Mencken ascribes to Jefferson, among many, such new words as "monocrats" in 1792 and "breadstuffs" in 1793.[29]

Mencken notes the history of Noah Webster's efforts on behalf of his "American Dictionary of the English Language" which eventually appeared in 1828. It is Mencken's belief that ". . . at least some of Webster's ideas seem to have made some impression on Thomas Jefferson, who was to ratify them formally in 1813." [30] Jefferson denounced Noah Webster to James Madison in 1801 as "a mere pedagogue, of very limited understanding and very strong prejudices and party passion, yet as editor of a paper and as of the Newhaven association he may be worth striking." [31] Mencken gives the history of the organization in 1820, after many unsuccessful efforts, of an American Academy of Language and Belles Lettres, with John Quincy Adams as president. Among its avowed purposes were to promote literary intelligence, as well as the purity and uniformity of the English language. The Academy was quite willing to accept English authority, and was supported by a number of famous men of the time, including John Marshall. Noah Webster, because he thought the society would be of little use until there was a standard American dictionary, opposed it, although he reluctantly accepted election as a corresponding member. Others in opposition were Edward Everett and Thomas Jefferson. Jefferson refused the honorary presidency of the Academy, and when he was elected an honorary member in 1821 he wrote its secretary, William Cardell: "There are so many differences between us and England, of soil, climate, culture, productions, laws, religion and government, that we must be left far behind the march of circumstances, were we to hold ourselves rigorously to their standard. If, like the French Academicians, it were proposed to *fix* our language, it would be fortunate that the step were not taken in the days of our Saxon ancestors, whose vocabulary would illy express the science of this day. Judicious neology can alone give strength and copiousness to language, and enable it to be the vehicle of new ideas." [32]

In shaping his philosophy of language, Jefferson set himself squarely against the authoritarian tenets of Dr. Samuel Johnson, the arbiter of the age in these matters as far as Tory England was concerned, and violently anti-American on every count. Understandably, Jefferson leaned towards the rational empiricism of Locke, whose *Essay on Human Understanding* had been called by Locke's disciple, John Horne Tooke, "A Grammatical Essay, or a Treatise on Words." Tooke, the philologist, whose *Diversions* of *Purley* Jefferson repeatedly recommended to students, commanded the loyalty of the American on several counts. In the first place, he had suffered imprisonment and punishment in the Tower of London because of his avowed sympathies for the Colonies during the Revolution. In the second "he examined facts according to the Baconian *a posteriori* methods of reasoning, instead of pursuing, as most philosophic linguists have done, the Aristotelic or *a priori* method." [33] Inevitably Jefferson adhered to the progressive, dynamic conception of language as against the static: "Dictionaries are but the depositories of words already legitimated by usage. Society is the workshop in which new ones are elaborated. When an individual uses a new word, if ill formed, it is rejected in society; if well formed, adopted, and after due time, laid up in the depository of dictionaries. And if, in this process . . . our trans-Atlantic brethren shall not choose to accompany us, we may furnish, after the Ionians, a second example of a colonial dialect improving on its primitive." [34]

In his awareness of the possibilities of growth in the

English language, Jefferson lashes out at the constricting influence of Dr. Johnson. The language can develop "not indeed by holding fast to *Johnson's Dictionary*; not by raising a hue and cry against every word he has not licensed; but by encouraging and welcoming new compositions of its elements." [35] The real development of the American tongue will have to wait, in his estimation, until the development of a large group of writers in the new world: "But we have no distinct class of literati in our country. Every man is engaged in some industrious pursuit, and science is but a secondary occupation, always subordinate to the main business of his life. Few therefore of those who are qualified, have leisure to write. In time it will be otherwise. . . . And should the language of England continue stationary, we shall probably enlarge our employment of it, until its new character may separate it in name as well as in power, from the mother-tongue." [36]

Jefferson strenuously objected to that pontifical bias in Dr. Johnson which led the spokesman of the Augustan style to favor the Latin elements in the English language at the expense of the Anglo-Saxon: "Johnson, besides the want of precision in his definitions, and of accurate distinction in passing from one shade of meaning to another in the same word, is most objectionable in his derivations. From a want probably of intimacy with our own language while in the Anglo-Saxon form and type, and of its kindred languages of the North, he has a constant leaning towards Greek and Latin for English etymon." [37]

What, then, was this new American style which, nourished on the literary masters of antiquity and of our own literature, and laying itself open to all the influences and demands of the new way of life, developed as the peculiar expression of the American mind. Unquestionably its finest utterance is to be found in the momentous document which marked the high point of Jefferson's literary style, the Declaration of Independence, called by its author "the genuine effusion of the soul of the country at that time"—the document which marks Jefferson, in the eyes of posterity, as the penman of the Revolution.[38] Fifty years later Jefferson had to defend himself against the charges of inoriginality preferred against him by the "Anglomen" who opposed everything that the Declaration stood for. His letter to Henry Lee contains the famous phrase to the effect that the Declaration "was intended to be an expression of the American mind." [39]

Jefferson's atitude towards the art of writing must be seen—like his attitude towards the other arts—in the framework of his activity as a revolutionary and as the architect of a rising democracy. Writing and oratory were the two prime weapons for arousing men to action; and Jefferson's task, as a revolutionary leader, was precisely that. It has been observed that modern statesmen, unlike the ancients, have rarely been masters of both the written and spoken word. The Revolution needed orators to exhort the people, and writers to explain its ideological issues to them. Patrick Henry became the prototype of the masterful orator; Jefferson, preeminently the intellectual, that of the masterful writer. Actually, he was not at his best in oratory. He was the master of the chiselled phrase that lived on paper rather than in the momentary quivering of the air. He composed best in solitude. By every bent of his mind and heart he was suited for becoming the scribe of the Revolution. The function of literature he held, was like the function of every intellectual or artistic discipline, to advance the happiness and the freedom of man.

Of the English writers included in Jefferson's *Literary Bible,* by far the most important, in respect of the number and weightiness of the extracts, is Lord Bolingbroke.[40] As against the fifty quotations from Bolingbroke, there are only ten from Pope, not counting those from Pope's translation of Homer which show a devotion to the Greek poet, rather than to the English. Neither Pope's aristocratic point of view, his fairly parochial estheticism nor his concurrence in the *status quo* could endear him to the Virginian. Far more congenial to Jefferson, both for the nobility of his verse and the moral elevation of his subject matter, was Milton, whose *Paradise Lost,* according to Prof. Chinard, exerted a very powerful influence on him.[41]

Of the dramatists, the most important place is occupied by Shakespeare, for whom Jefferson had great reverence. "Shakespeare must be singled out by one who wishes to learn the full powers of the English language" he wrote Bernard Moore.[42] His fondness for the greatest of English poets is matched by a preoccupation which is far more difficult for us to understand. This was his exaggerated admiration for the works of Ossian, who is well represented in the *Literary Bible.* Even after the antiquity of the poems had been shown to be spurious, Jefferson doggedly maintained to Lafayette that Ossian's poetry "if not ancient . . . is equal to the best morsels of antiquity." [43] The Marquis de Chastellux recalls his visit to Monticello in 1782: "I recollect with pleasure," says the Marquis, "that as we were conversing over a bowl of punch, after Mrs. Jefferson had retired, our conversation turned on the poems of Ossian. It was a spark of electricity which passed rapidly from one to the other; we recollected the passages in those sublime poems which particularly struck us. . . . In our enthusiasm the book was sent for, and placed near the bowl, where, by their mutual aid, the night imperceptibly advanced upon us." [44] In this connection Dr. Kallen remarks: "But at the same time this classicist (Jefferson) shared with Goethe and Napoleon an enthusiasm for Macpherson's *Poems of Ossian,* for its vague, gigantesque scenery, its mighty and simple heroes whom no convention binds. But, then, are not Ossian and Ilion brothers under the skin? Also Homer can be savored romantically for its primitive passions, grandiose and grotesque, as well as for its hard, elemental wisdom of life. Ossian may have been synthetic, but he had his appeal to the mighty of brawn and brain." [45]

Among the dramatists quoted in the *Literary Bible* we find several whom Jefferson included in his book list to Robert Skipwith. Otway, Dryden, Congreve, Young, Rowe —these were authors with whom a young man of Jefferson's background might be expected to be familiar. Among the English poets are to be found Thompson, Akenside, Langhorne and the two leading members of the "graveyard" school—Young and Blair. It becomes clear from all this that, in literature, as in music, architecture, gardening, painting and sculpture, Jefferson shared the taste of his time. That he did so with such completeness would seem to be due, as we have already noted, to the fact that he was functioning in a frontier environment.

Despite his deep and continuing interest in literature, Jefferson thought himself lacking in creative imagination.

To William Short he declared: "I never had that sort of poetical fancy which qualifies for allegorical devices, mottoes, etc. Painters, poets, men of happy imagination can alone do these things with taste." [46] And to John Adams: "I send you a piece of homespun. . . . Not of the fine texture or delicate character of yours, or to drop our metaphor, not filled as that was with that display of imagination which constitutes excellence in Belles Lettres, but a mere sober, dry and formal piece of logic." [47]

It is perhaps these circumstances that led Prof. Chinard to conclude that Jefferson "was not a poetical mind. Even as a student he read more for profit than for pleasure." [48] The point to attend to here is that for the men of Jefferson's generation, profit was pleasure. Certainly Jefferson, who declared to John Adams that "I cannot live without books"; who was so sensitive to literary style that he never read a work in translation if he could do so in the original; and who was so responsive to the nuances of language that he advocated the publication of the county dialects of England because we would find in Shakespeare "new sublimities which we had not tasted before"—certainly such a man cannot with justice be described as having read for profit rather than pleasure. He read because books symbolized knowledge, power, the joy of contact with great spirits, the joy of meeting new ideas. Certainly his intention to learn Gaelic so that he could taste the "sublime" beauties of Ossian in the original bespeaks the passionate reader, not the purely acquisitive one.

Dr. Kallen has pointed out the workman in Thomas Jefferson was more concerned with the *how* in art than with the *what*. In literature Jefferson was unquestionably concerned with the "what"; but as a penman he could not but consider the technical problems of writing, of prosody and versification, of Anglo-Saxon and grammar, and of the influence of the classics in shaping style. In considering his literary esthetic it must be remembered that he stemmed out of a period in which meaning was still a basic component of creative writing, just as melody was a basic component of music, and representational content of painting. Form and content, style and message were no less indissolubly joined than profit and pleasure. Indeed, in analyzing Jefferson's attitudes in terms of the "how" and the "what," the "profit" and the "pleasure," there is some possibility that we are retroactively projecting upon Jefferson conceptions which neither he nor his age had any inkling of. He was interested in what Homer or Shakespeare had said; and— judging from his *Thoughts on English Prosody*—he was equally interested in how they had said it: could one pay attention to the soul without the body? Jefferson knew no "pure" poetry or "pure" music or "pure" painting, any more than he knew a "pure" science or "pure" mathematics. Everything was applied—to the welfare of man. Even in the sphere of artistic judgment he functioned—with Lord Kames—on the level of practical or applied esthetics, leaving the "pure" to the professional philosophers.

As has been indicated, Jefferson's sensitivity to literary style comes out clearly in his attitude towards translations. To F. A. Delacroix he remarked that "The best translation can render a sentiment but imperfectly, often falsely." [49] Two years later he wrote him: "I say nothing of style . . . conscious I am no judge of it in a foreign language. I believe it impossible, in any but our native tongue, to be so thoroughly sensible of the delicacy of style, which constitutes an essential merit in poetical composition, as to criticise them with correctness." [50] Even more strongly he expressed himself on the subject of trying to write well in a language not one's own. Counselling his old friend Dupont de Nemours on this matter he wrote: "Did you ever know an instance of one who could write in a foreign language with the elegance of a native? Cicero wrote Commentaries of his own Consulship in Greek; they perished unknown, while his native compositions have immortalized him with themselves." [51]

Jefferson had personal experience of the problems of the translator through his labors on Destutt de Tracy's *Treatise on Political Economy*, as well as *Les Ruines* by Count Volney, the "bold infidel," as Napoleon called him, who "attempted to prove Christ a myth." [52] In regard to this latter translation, Dr. Kallen remarks: "If, while president, he (Jefferson) translated twenty chapters of Volney's *Les Ruines, ou meditations sur les revolutions des empires*, it was as much for its Ossianic style as for its geopolitical ideas. Jefferson's taste for Ossian had its extension in his taste for Sterne." [53] As for the translation of Destutt de Tracy, Jefferson told Albert Gallatin, then in Europe: "I worked on it four or five hours a day for three months comparing word by word with the original, and although I have made it a strictly faithful translation, yet it is without style, *le premier jet* was such as to render that impossible." [54]

For Jefferson's preoccupation with the problems of technique and form, as distinct from content, one must turn to his *Thoughts on English Prosody*. Jefferson, like many intellectuals, discovered that as the years passed he lost the passionate interest of his youth in poetry and fiction. He attributed this process simply to time which "withers the fancy as the other faculties of the mind and body." None the less, the letter on English Prosody, about whose date of composition there is a conflict among the authorities,[55] betrays the same workman's delight in the technique of the art as was to be observed in Jefferson's notes on the process of engraving or on the improved metronome and harpsichord. To the Marquis de Chastellux he sends the reasons for writing this essay-letter: "Among the topics of conversation which stole off like so many minutes the few hours I had the happiness of possessing you at Monticello, the measures of English verse was one. I thought it depended like Greek and Latin verse, on long and short syllables arranged into regular feet. You were of a different opinion. . . . A daily habit of walking in the Bois de Boulogne gave me an opportunity of turning this subject in my mind and I determined to present you my thoughts on it in the form of a letter." Jefferson gracefully admitted he had been mistaken: "Error is the stuff of which the web of life is woven and he who lives longest and wisest is only able to weave out the more of it. I began with the design of converting you to my opinion that the arrangement of long and short syllables into regular feet constituted the harmony of English verse. I ended by discovering that you were right in denying that proposition." [56] Jefferson's approach to the problem is largely empirical. For his examples he draws liberally upon his favorites—Milton, Shakespeare, Homer, Theocritus, and among his contemporaries, upon Pope, whose craftsmanship he admired, Gray, Young and Shenstone.[57] He presents the view that accent is the basis of English verse, rather than quantity, as Dr. Johnson had taught, and develops his point with the same thoroughness and thoughtful consideration of all examples that may lead to an objective decision, that characterizes his investigations no matter what the field. What is of particular interest to the reader today, in view of the charge that has been made that Jefferson lacked emotional appreciation of poetry, is the facility with which he marshals parallelism between poetry and music. Thus, he speaks of the "modulation" in the tone of the accents, of which it is impossible to give a precise idea in writing. Nevertheless, he tries to do so through an ingenious system of dashes which indicate four shadings of accent among the stressed syllables. After marking several passages from Armstrong, Young and Shakespeare in this fashion, he remarks, with unusual perception of the infinite nuances of which English poetry is capable: "I am far from presuming to give this accentuation as perfect. No two persons will accent the same passage alike. No person but a real adept would accent it twice alike. . . . I suppose that in those passages of Shakespeare, for example, no man but Garrick ever drew their full tone out of them, if I may borrow an expression from music." [58]

Posing the question "what is a verse?" Jefferson points out that even if a passage from Homer should be printed as prose—which he proceeds to do—"it would still be verse; it would still immortalize its author were every other syllable of his compositions lost." There follows this unusual passage on the nature of verse: "The poet then does not depend on the printer to give a character to his work. He has studied the human ear. He has discovered that in any rhythmical composition the ear is pleased to find at certain regular intervals a pause where it may rest, by which it may divide the composition into parts, as a piece of music is divided into bars. . . . The interval then between these regular pauses constitutes a verse. In the morsel before cited this interval comprehends six feet, and though it is written in the manner of prose, yet he who can read it without pausing at every sixth foot, like him who is insensible to the charm of music, who is insensible of love or of gratitude, is an unfavored son of nature to whom she has given a faculty fewer than to others of her children, one source of pleasure the less in a world where there are none to spare." [59]

After demonstrating the influence of the character of the language upon the verse, Jefferson states that "the language of Homer enabled him to compose in verse of six feet; the English language cannot bear this." This statement recalls Lord Kames' dictum: "Many attempts have been made to introduce Hexameter verse into the living languages, but without success. The English language, I am inclined to think, is not susceptible of this melody." [60] In this connection it is interesting to point out that Jefferson sides with Lord Kames against Dr. Johnson, who had based his analysis of English prosody upon the system of quantity native to Latin verse. As Boswell tells, Dr. Johnson had a poor opinion of Kames, and styled his *Elements of Criticism* "a pretty essay . . . though much of it is chimerical." [61] Voltaire, in his "egregious sneer" at Lord Kames' *Elements of Criticism*, sided with Dr. Johnson. Said Voltaire of this book, which Mossner considers to be in reality a concealed eulogy of the Scottish Enlightenment: "It is an admirable result of the progress of the human spirit that at the present time it is from Scotland we receive rules of taste in all the arts—from the epic poem to gardening." [62]

Kames writes: "the melody of English verse must depend less upon quantity than upon other circumstances: in which it differs widely from Latin verse, where every syllable having but one sound, strikes the ear uniformly with its accustomed impression." [63] Jefferson agrees with Kames too, in his dislike of rhyme. The Scotsman states: *"blank verse . . . differs from rhyme in rejecting the jingle of similar sounds, which purifies it from a childish pleasure."* [64] Even more emphatically, Jefferson declares: "It (blank verse) constitutes, therefore, the most precious part of our poetry. The poet, unfettered by rhyme, is at liberty to prune his diction of those tautologies, those feeble nothings necessary to introtrude the rhyming word. With no other trammel than that of measure he is able to condense his thoughts and images and to leave nothing but what is truly poetical. When enveloped in all the pomp and majesty of his subject he sometimes even throws off the restraint of the regular pause." [65] Here follows, as an example of the "pomp and majesty," the opening stanzas of *Paradise Lost.* Then Jefferson amplifies his argument: "What proves the excellence of blank verse is that the taste lasts longer than that for rhyme. The fondness for the jingle leaves us with that for the rattles and baubles of childhood, and if we continue to read rhymed verse at a later period of life it is such only where the poet has had force enough to bring great beauties of thought and diction into this form." [66]

Jefferson's interest in the mechanics of English prosody was matched by a sustained absorption in the origin and development of the English language. The study of Anglo-

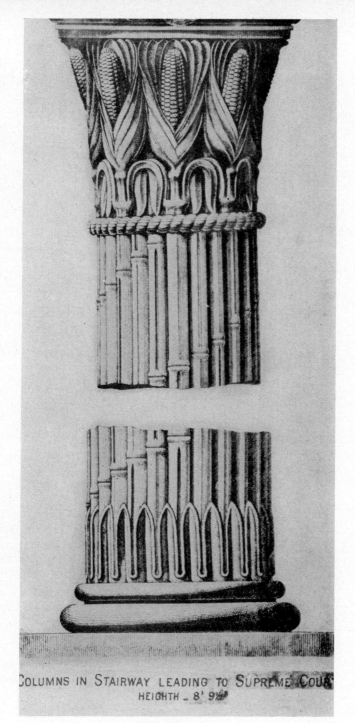

Columns in Stairway leading to Supreme Cou[rt]
Height _ 8' 9½"

Fig. No. 17.
Indian Corn Column and Capital — Latrobe. The
Capitol of the United States

Fig. No. 18.
INDIAN CORN CAPITAL AND COLUMN. THE CAPITOL OF THE UNITED STATES

Saxon was a hobby which, he confessed at the age of eighty-two, "too often runs away with me." This preoccupation culminated in the *Essay on Anglo-Saxon* written in 1798 and sent to the English etymologist Sir Herbert Croft, accompanied by a letter saying: "I was led to set a due value on the study of the Northern languages, and especially of our Anglo-Saxon, while I was a student of the law, by being obliged to recur to that source for explanation of a multitude of law-terms." [67] Twenty-two years later Jefferson wrote to John Adams: "In a letter which I had occasion to write to Mr. Crofts . . . I went into explanations with him of an easy process for simplifying the study of the Anglo-Saxon, and lessening the terrors and difficulties presented by its rude alphabet, and unformed orthography." [68] Just as in the matter of grammar and neology, Jefferson viewed language as a living organism adapting itself continuously to the functions of life: "The Anglo-Saxon is only the earliest we possess of the many shades of mutation by which the language has been tapered down to its modern form." [69]

As Jefferson had opposed the efforts of Dr. Johnson to base the analysis of English poetry on Greek and Latin verse forms, so he deprecated the efforts of the scholars, particularly Hickes and Bosworth, to superimpose the declension of Greek and Latin on the Anglo-Saxon nouns: "Dr. Hickes may certainly be considered as the father of this branch of modern learning. . . . In his time there was too exclusive a prejudice in favor of the Greek and Latin languages. . . . But nothing can be more radically unlike than the frames of the ancient languages, Southern and Northern, of the Greek and Latin languages, from those of

the Gothic family. Of this last are the Anglo-Saxon and
English." [70]

Since Jefferson was the first to suggest that Anglo-Saxon
be included in the curriculum of American colleges, the opening passage of the *Essay* is noteworthy: "The importance
of the Anglo-Saxon dialect toward a perfect understanding
of the English language seems not to have been duly esti-
mated by those charged with the education of youth; and
yet it is unquestionably the basis of our present tongue.
. . . Hence the necessity of making the Anglo-Saxon a
regular branch of academic education." [71]

The *Essay* is divided into four parts—alphabet, orthography, pronunciation and grammar. The last is the most
elaborate, Jefferson considering in turn the gender, cases,
numbers, verbs and moods, supines and gerunds of the
Anglo-Saxon, taking care throughout to indicate how these
must be distinguished from the Latin and Greek, with which
the scholars had consistently confused them. As an equali-
tarian, Jefferson was consistently against the mysterious
jargon in which the scholars wrapped their lore to mystify
and overawe the unlettered masses. The passionate advocate of free public education urged simplification, and ruthless excision of the needless complexities in which the problems of scholarship had become involved. This was the
"common-sense" approach, which believed in the ability of
the common man to understand what was properly explained to him—the same common-sense which rebelled
against the "whimsies, the puerilities and unintelligible
jargon" of Plato.

It is in this *Essay* that the passage appears which displays
Jefferson's sensitivity to what is perhaps the most subtle

element in the appreciation of language—the awareness of the overtones of the past in the forms of the present: "But if, as I believe, we may consider it [Anglo-Saxon] as merely an antiquated form of our present language, if we may throw aside the learned difficulties which mask its real character . . . and proceed to apply ourselves to it with little more preparation than to Piers Ploughman, Douglas, or Chaucer, then I am persuaded its acquisition will . . . richly repay us by the intimate insight it will give us into the genuine structure, powers and meanings of the language we now read and speak. We shall then read Shakespeare and Milton with a superior degree of intelligence and delight, heightened by the new and delicate shades of meaning developed to us by a knowledge of the original sense of the same words." [72]

Although writing twenty years before the establishment of the University of Virginia, it becomes apparent from the *Essay* what long range plans Jefferson had for his "bantling of forty years nursing": "As we are possessed in America of the printed editions of the Anglo-Saxon writings, they furnish a fit occasion for this country to make some return to the older nations for the science for which we are indebted to them; and in this task I hope an honorable part will in time be borne by our University." [73] His awareness of the limited resources of the United States, which came out in his dicta on painting and sculpture, are in evidence here, in regard to scholarly research. But in this instance, significantly enough, he feels that the young nation must play its part: "The publication of the inedited manuscripts which exist in the libraries of Great Britain only, must depend on the learned of that nation. Their means of science are great.

They have done much, and much is yet expected from them. Nor will they disappoint us. Our means are as yet small; but the widow's mite was piously given and kindly accepted." [74]

As a statesman, Jefferson is not unaware of the social and political implications of the study of the ancestral tongue, and of the role that it might play in cementing the friendship of England and America: "How much would contribute to the happiness of these two nations a brotherly emulation in doing good to each other, rather than the mutual vituperations so unwisely and unjustifiably sometimes indulged in both. . . . Let us then yoke ourselves jointly to the same car of human happiness, and vie in common efforts to do each other all the good we can—to reflect on each other the lights of mutual science particularly, and the kind affections of kindred blood." [75]

In the postscript to the *Essay* written twenty-seven years later, Jefferson triumphantly announces the fruition of his plan—the adoption of the study of Anglo-Saxon by the University of Virginia. The postscript ends with "A Specimen of the Form in Which the Anglo-Saxon Writings Still Extant Might Be Advantageously Published, for Facilitating to the English Student the Knowledge of the Anglo-Saxon Dialect." [76] Jefferson uses the first thirty-one verses of *Genesis* to illustrate his "form."

No discussion of Jefferson as litterateur would be complete without a consideration of some of his own poetic efforts. Like most young men with literary inclinations, Jefferson seems to have tried his hand at verse on a number of occasions. If, when we consider his response to poetry, we may question Prof. Chinard's assertion that his was not a poetic mind, that assertion stands indisputably when we consider Jefferson as a versifier. Like many distinguished writers of prose, he became constrained, inoriginal and "prosy" when he turned to verse. Of the four poems sometimes attributed to him, "Lovely Peggy" is not his, but was written by David Garrick and "addressed to the actress Peg Woffington. About 1749 it was set to music by James Oswald and again in 1760 by S. Howard. It became a popular street ballad during the latter part of the eighteenth century." [77] The verses were found in Jefferson's hand, and have been placed by many writers on Jefferson in the early 1760's; but while they are of the kind that appealed to the young man's fancy, they are not in the least characteristic of his style and diction. Far more likely from Jefferson's pen is the "Inscription for an African Slave" which was written in his copy of the *Virginia Almanack* for 1771, and is found nowhere else in print. Here is the elevated diction which he favored, and the conventional writing of one who was expressing himself in a medium not his own. The poem is dated 1771. Like the other three, it is in rhyme, not blank verse.

"Shores there are, bless'd shores for us remain,
And favor'd isles with golden fruitage crown's
Where tufted flow'rets paint the verdant plain,
Where ev'ry breeze shall med-cine every wound.
There the stern tyrant that embitters life,
Shall vainly suppliant, spread his asking hand;
There shall we view the billow's raging strife,
Aid the kind breast, and waft his boat to land." [78]

Prof. Chinard presents the third poem for the first time in the preface to the *Literary Bible* "as a curiosity and not for its literary value. . . . The fact that the last lines are incomplete, as if the young author had been unable to find the proper rhymes and bring his effort to a satisfactory completion, is at least an indication that Jefferson wrote the poem himself and did not copy it from an anthology.

> " 'Tis hope supports each noble flame,
> 'Tis hope inspires poetic lays,
> Our heroes fight in hopes of fame,
> And poets writes [sic] in hopes of praise
> She sings sweet songs of future years.
> And dries the tears of present sorrow;
> Bids doubting mortal cease their fears,
> And tells them of a bright to-morrow.
> And where true love a visit pays,
> The minstrell [sic] is always there,
> To soothe young Cupid with her lays
> And keep the lover from despair.
> Why fades the rose upon thy cheek;
> Why drop the lilies at the view?
> Thy cause of sorrow, Ellen speak,
> Why alter'd thus thy sprightly hue?
> Each day alas! with breaking heart,
> I see thy beautous form decline;
> Yet fear my anguish to impart;
> Lest it should add a pang to thine.
> I will not be afraid   wh.
> have to" [79]

Interesting for historical, rather than literary, reasons is the last of these poems "A Death-bed Adieu from Th. J. to M.R." (Martha Randolph, his daughter). These parting lines of the octogenarian quoted by his great-granddaughter,

Sarah Randolph, betray, too, the prose writer restricted within, for him, the artificial confines of verse. The two seraphs referred to in the poem are his wife and his daughter Maria:

"Life's visions are vanished, its dreams are no more;
Dear friends of my bosom, why bathed in tears?
I go to my fathers, I welcome the shore
Which crowns all my hopes or which buries my cares.
Then farewell, my dear, my lov'd daughter, adieu!
The last pang of life is in parting from you!
Two seraphs await me long shrouded in death;
I will bear them your love on my last parting breath." [80]

Much closer to authorship, in the modern sense, does Jefferson come in his descriptions of sketches of personages of the time. These were in the tradition of the "characters" of the eighteenth century, which have been resurrected as "profiles" in the twentieth. Here his sharpness of observation combines with a felicitous power of description to create memorable pen pictures. A few quotations will suffice to present the particular flavor of their style. Of George IV, at that time Prince of Wales: "He has not a single element of Mathematics, of Natural or Moral Philosophy, or of any other science on earth, nor has the society he has kept been such as to supply the void of education. It has been that of the lowest, the most illiterate and profligate persons of the kingdom, without choice of rank or mind, and with whom the subjects of conversation are only horses, drinking-matches, bawdy houses, and in terms the most vulgar. . . . He has not a single idea of justice, morality, religion, or of the rights of men, or any anxiety for the opinion of the world. He carries that indifference for fame so far, that he would probably not be hurt were he to lose his throne provided he could be assured of having always meat, drink, horses, and women. In the article of women, nevertheless, he is become more correct, since his connection with Mrs. Fitzherbert, who is an honest and worthy woman: he is even less crapulous than he was." [81] Of Napoleon: "The Attilla of the age dethroned, the ruthless destroyer of ten millions of the human race, whose thirst for blood appeared unquenchable, the great oppressor of the rights and liberties of the world, shut up within the circle of a little island of the Mediterranean, and dwindled to the condition of an humble and degraded pensioner on the bounty of those he had most injured. How miserably, how meanly, has he closed his inflated career! What a sample of the bathos will his history present! He should have perished on the swords of his enemies, under the walls of Paris." [82]

Of Necker: "Nature bestowed on Mr. Necker an ardent passion for glory, without at the same time, granting him those qualities required for its pursuit by direct means. The union of a fruitful imagination, with a limited talent, with which she has endowed him, is always incompatible with those faculties of the mind which qualify their possessor to penetrate, to combine, and to comprehend all the relations of objects." [83]

One of Jefferson's best portraits is of George Washington, showing real psychological perception and that ability to seize upon the salient points of character which, in the nineteenth century, became the perquisite of the novelist: "His mind was great and powerful, without being of the very first order; his penetration strong, though not as acute

as that of a Newton, Bacon, or Locke; and as far as he
saw, no judgment was ever sounder. It was slow in operation, being little aided by invention or imagination, but
sure in conclusion. . . . He was incapable of fear, meeting
personal dangers with the calmest unconcern. Perhaps the
strongest feature in his character was prudence, never acting
until every circumstance, every consideration, was maturely
weighed; refraining if he saw a doubt, but, when once decided, going through with his purpose, whatever obstacles
opposed. His integrity was most pure, his justice the most
inflexible I have ever known, no motives of interest or
consanguinity, of friendship or hatred, being able to bias
his decision. He was, indeed, in every sense of the words, a
wise, a good, and a great man. His temper was naturally
high toned; but reflection and resolution had obtained a
firm and habitual ascendency over it. If ever, however, it
broke its bonds, he was most tremendous in his wrath. . . .
Although in the circle of his friends, where he might be
unreserved with safety, he took a free share in conversation,
his colloquial talents were not above mediocrity, possessing
neither copiousness of ideas, nor fluency of words. . . .
His time was employed in action chiefly, reading little, and
that only in agriculture and history. . . . On the whole, his
character was, in its mass, perfect, in nothing bad, in few
points indifferent; and it may truly be said, that never did
nature and fortune combine more perfectly to make a man
great, and to place him in the same constellation with whatever worthies have merited from man an everlasting remembrance. . . . I felt on his death, with my countrymen,
that 'verily a great man hath fallen this day in Israel.' " [84]

Of Jefferson's sketches of literary men, the sharpest is

that of Grimm: "Did I know Baron Grimm while at Paris? Yes, most intimately. He was the pleasantest and most conversable member of the diplomatic corps while I was there; a man of good fancy, acuteness, irony, cunning and egoism. No heart, not much of any science, yet enough of every one to speak its language; his forte was belles-lettres, painting and sculpture. In these he was the oracle of society, and as such, was the Empress Catharine's private correspondent and factor, in all things not diplomatic. . . . It was in d'Holbach's conventicles that Rousseau imagined all the machinations against him were contrived; and he left, in his Confessions, the most biting anecdotes of Grimm. These appeared after I left France; but I have heard that poor Grimm was so much afflicted by them, that he kept his bed several weeks. I have never seen the Memoirs of Grimm." [85]

With his usual interest in the *how* as well as the *what* of art, we find Jefferson's interest in literature extending to such purely technical aspects as book making and book printing, the establishment of a free library and of the Library of Congress, the cataloguing of library books and the freedom of the press. His relationship with the poet Barlow paralleled that with Trumbull and Hopkinson. He encouraged Barlow to write a history of the United States to counter-act the "perversions of truth" in John Marshall's work, and hailed the poet's *Columbiad*. When Barlow was appointed Minister to France—the first of a long line of literary men whom an enlightened state policy rewarded with high diplomatic posts—Jefferson felicitated him, at the same time deploring that now the projected history would not be written. Jefferson took a leading part in the struggle to have the tariff on books rescinded, pointing out that "it makes a very serious addition to the price of the book and falls chiefly on a description of persons little able to meet it." [86] Always solicitous for the welfare of the artist, he helped in the establishment of copyright laws to protect authors, and wrote to Madison that he wished Congress had gone even farther than it had in its provisions. He followed with enthusiasm the growth of printing and bookmaking in the United States, preaching that the art of printing "secures us against the retrogradation of reason and information." [87] Should western civilization ever again be swamped by barbarians, as it had been during the Dark Ages, he looked to books to "maintain the mind where it is, and raise the conquering ruffians to the level of the conquered, instead of degrading these to that of their conquerors." [88]

Jefferson's *Bill for Establishing a Public Library*, drawn up in 1799, provided for the allocation of two thousand pounds annually for a public library at Richmond.[89] His own library, gathered by him over years, and containing whatever "was rare and valuable in every science" had a strong collection of works relating to America—"such a collection was made as probably can never again be effected, because it is hardly probable that the same opportunities, the same time, industry, perseverance and expense, with some knowledge of the bibliography of the subject, would again happen to be in concurrence" [90]—this library became the nucleus of the Congressional Library. Congress purchased it for $23,950 after the burning of the Capitol by the British. On the occasion of its sale Jefferson wrote to Samuel Smith: "It is the choicest collection of books in the

United States, and I hope it will not be without some general effect on the literature of our country." [91]

His love of books and of what they represent prescribes most minute details for their care. With characteristic foresight, he planned the transportation of his books from Monticello to Washington so that they would not be damaged; he did the packing himself. When the librarian of Congress, George Watterston, asked his advice in the cataloguing, Jefferson sent him a letter on library classification which became the basis for the plan adopted. So too, he guided the classification of books for the Library of the University of Virginia. He violently opposed censorship of books, coming to the defense of the Philadelphia bookseller Dufief when the latter was threatened with prosecution for selling De Becourt's *Sur la Creation du Monde,* stating that he was "really mortified to be told that, in the *United States of America* . . . a question about the sale of a book can be carried before the civil magistrate." [92] So, too, he uncompromisingly defended the freedom of the press, even though he himself was the victim of as unscrupulous, as venal and as mendacious a press as ever in our history assailed the character of a great public figure. "Where the press is free, and every man able to read, all is safe," he told Col. Yancey.[93] Abuses there might be on the part of powerful interests using the press for their own purpose. None the less, he had unwavering faith in the ultimate power of public opinion to beat back the lies of the unworthy part of the press. "The force of public opinion cannot be resisted, when permitted freely to be expressed.[94] . . . Were it left to me to decide whether we should have a government without newspapers or newspapers without a government, I should not hesitate a moment to prefer the latter." [95]

We have then, in Jefferson, a literary craftsman of high order, whose pen had the honor of producing the chief document of the American Revolution; a keen student of the laws of language, particularly in regard to the development of an American speech; a lover of literary style, a translator, and the author of essays on prosody and Anglo-Saxon which reveal both literary scholarship and linguistic attainments; a lover of books, who saw in their dissemination one of the bulwarks of democratic thought; a vigilant protector of the rights of authors and of the freedom of the press. He was above all an enlightened litterateur-statesman who, despite his intense Americanism, saw "the great republic of letters" as a "great fraternity spreading over the whole earth." [96] It need hardly be added to this, as in his attitudes towards each of the other arts, he was consistently the man of the Enlightenment, the revolutionary statesman, the humanist, utilitarian and progressive.

CHAPTER ELEVEN

1. Gilbert Chinard: *The Literary Bible of Thomas Jefferson,* pp. 5–6, Baltimore (1928).

2. To John Adams: Monticello, July 5, 1814, ME, XIV, pp. 147–150.

3. To William Short: Monticello, Oct. 31, 1819, Ford, Fed. Ed. XII, pp. 140–143.

4. Gilbert Chinard: *Ibid.,* pp. 32–33.

5. To Edward Everett: Monticello, 1823, in H. A. Washington: *Writings of Jefferson,* VII, p. 272.

6. To John Adams: Monticello, March 21, 1819, ME, XV, p. 184.

7. *Ibid.,* pp. 181–185.

8. To John Waldo: Monticello, Aug. 16, 1813, ME, XIII, p. 339.

9. Bernard Mayo: *Jefferson Himself,* pp. 301–302.

    a. To John Waldo: Monticello, Aug. 16, 1813, ME, XIII pp. 339–340.

b. To Edward Everett: Monticello, Feb. 24, 1823, ME, XV, p. 415.

10. To John Waldo: Monticello, Aug. 16, 1813, ME, XIII, pp. 340-341.

11. H. L. Mencken: *The American Language, Fourth Edition,* p. vi, New York (1945).

12. *Ibid.,* p. 14.

13. H. L. Mencken: *The American Language: Supplement I,* p. 36, New York (1945).

14. H. L. Mencken: *The American Language, Fourth Edition,* p. 20, New York (1945).

15. *Ibid.,* p. 25.

16. *Ibid.,* p. 30, (1945).

17. *Ibid.,* p. 42.

18. *Ibid.,* p. 104.

19. *Ibid.,* Footnote 2, p. 106.

20. *Ibid.,* p. 132.

21. *Ibid.,* p. 515.

22. *Ibid.,* p. 517.

23. *Ibid.,* Footnote 1, p. 519, (1945).

24. *Ibid.,* p. 519.

25. *Ibid.,* p. 529.

26. H. L. Mencken: *The American Language: Supplement I,* p. 84, New York (1945).

27. *Ibid.,* p. 89.

28. *Ibid.*

29. *Ibid.,* p. 369.

30. H. L. Mencken: *The American Language, Fourth Edition,* Footnote 2, p. 11, "In a letter from Monticello, August 16, to John Waldo, author of *Rudiments of English Grammar* . . . Jefferson adopted Webster's ideas categorically, and professed to believe that 'an American dialect will be formed.' "

31. To James Madison: Monticello, Aug. 12, 1801, Ford, Fed. Ed., IX, p. 285.

32. To William Cardell: Monticello, Jan. 27, 1821, quoted by H. L. Mencken: *The American Language: Supplement I,* p. 20, as taken from Allan Walker Read: "American Projects for an Academy to Regulate Speech," Publications of the Modern Language Association, December (1936) and Allan Walker Read: *American Literature,* May (1935).

33. John Horne Tooke: *Diversion of Purley,* p. xiii, revised by Richard Taylor, London (1860).

34. To John Adams: Monticello, Aug. 15, 1820, ME, XV, pp. 272-273.

35. To John Waldo: *Ibid.,* pp. 344-345.

36. *Ibid.,* p. 346.

37. To Herbert Croft: Monticello, Oct. 30, 1798, ME, XVIII, pp. 361-362.

38. Moses Coit Tyler: *The Literary History of the American Revolution*, I, pp. 495-496, Facsimile Library, New York (1941).

39. To Henry Lee: Monticello, May 8, 1825, Ford, Fed. Ed., XII, p. 409.

40. Gilbert Chinard: *Ibid.*, p. 20.

41. *Ibid.*, p. 21.

42. To Bernard Moore: approx. 1764, Ford, Fed. Ed., XI, pp. 420-426.

43. To Marquis de Lafayette: Monticello, Nov. 4, 1823, Ford, Fed. Ed., XII, p. 324.

44. Gilbert Chinard: *Ibid.*, pp. 25-26.

45. H. M. Kallen: "The Arts and Thomas Jefferson," pp. 270-271.

46. To William Short: Monticello, May 15, 1815, ME, XVIII, p. 286.

47. To John Adams: Monticello, April 20, ME, XIII, pp. 141-144.

48. Gilbert Chinard: *Ibid.*, p. 32.

49. To F. A. Delacroix: Washington, Dec. 21, 1807, ME, XIX, pp. 162-163.

50. To F. A. Delacroix: Washington, Feb. 3, 1809, ME, XII, pp. 244-245.

51. To Dupont de Nemours: Monticello, Dec. 31, 1815, ME, XIV, p. 372.

52. Henry S. Randall: *The Life of Thomas Jefferson,* II, p. 388, New York (1858).

53. H. M. Kallen: *The Arts and Thomas Jefferson,* p. 271.

54. To Albert Gallatin: Monticello, April 11, 1816, ME, XIX, pp. 234-235.

55. Note: The Editors of the Memorial Edition of Jefferson's Writings date its composition after Jefferson's return from Paris at the end of 1789. Prof. Chinard does not think so. In his footnote 2, pp. 27-28 of *The Literary Bible of Thomas Jefferson* he says: "The manuscript of the *Thoughts on English Prosody* written for Chastellux is undated. I cannot agree with the editor of the *Memorial Edition* that it was composed when Jefferson was Secretary of State. The letter which accompanies it shows clearly that it was written while Jefferson was in Paris and when the conversations he had with Chastellux at Monticello in 1782 were still fresh in his mind."

56. Introductory Notes: *Thoughts on English Prosody*, ME, XVIII, p. 414.

57. *Ibid.*, pp. 415-416.

58. *Ibid.*, p. 438.

59. *Ibid.*, pp. 441-442.

60. Lord Kames: *Elements of Criticism*, p. 337, New York (Edition 1855).

61. James Boswell: *Life of Johnson*, i. p. 393.

62. Ernest Campbell Mossner: *The Forgotten Hume, Le bon David*, New York (1943) p. 202.

63. Lord Kames: *Ibid.*, p. 318.

64. *Ibid.*, p. 333.

65. *Thoughts on English Prosody:* ME, XVIII, p. 446.

66. *Ibid.*, p. 447.

67. To Herbert Croft: *Ibid.*, p. 363.

68. To John Adams: Monticello, Aug. 15, 1820, ME, XV, p. 270.

69. To J. Evelyn Denison: Monticello, Nov. 9, 1825, ME, XVI, pp. 129–135.
70. *Essay on Anglo-Saxon:* ME, XVIII, pp. 375–376.
71. *Ibid.,* pp. 365–366.
72. *Ibid.,* p. 390.
73. *Ibid.,* p. 384.
74. *Ibid.,* pp. 384–385.
75. *Ibid.,* p. 385.
76. *Ibid.,* pp. 385–386.
77. Marie Kimball: *The Road to Glory,* p. 117, New York (1943). Mrs. Kimball's Footnote 36, p. 319, *Ibid.:* "Mr. W. H. Harding identified the poem which is to be found in Garrick's *Works,* II, p. 366, (1785)."
78. S. K. Padover: *The Complete Jefferson,* pp. 822–823, New York (1943).
79. Gilbert Chinard: *Ibid.,* pp. 26–27.
80. Sarah N. Randolph: *The Domestic Life of Thomas Jefferson,* p. 429, New York (1871).
81. To John Jay: Paris, Jan. 11, 1789, ME, VII, p. 262.
82. To John Adams: Monticello, July 5, 1814, ME, XVI, p. 145.
83. S. K. Padover: *Ibid.,* p. 919.
84. To Dr. Walter Jones: Monticello, Jan. 2, 1814, ME, XIV, pp. 48–52.
85. To John Adams: Monticello, April 8, 1816, ME, XIV, pp. 468–469.
86. To an unidentified correspondent: Monticello, 1821, p. 103, Sec. 913, *The Jefferson Cyclopedia,* edited by John P. Foley, New York (1900).
87. To M. Pierre Paganel: Monticello, April 15, 1811, ME, XIII, pp. 36–37.
88. To John Adams: Monticello, Sept. 12, 1821, ME, XV, p. 334.
89. *A Bill for Establishing a Public Library:* Ford, Fed. Ed., II, pp. 436–437.
90. To Samuel H. Smith: Monticello, Sept. 21, 1814, Ford, Fed. Ed., XI, pp. 427–429.
91. *Ibid.*
92. To N. G. Dufief: Monticello, April 19, 1814, ME, XIV, pp. 126–129.
93. To Col. Charles Yancey: Monticello, Jan. 6, 1816, Ford, Fed. Ed., XI, p. 497.
94. To Marquis de Lafayette: *Ibid.,* p. 322.
95. To Edward Carrington: Paris, Jan. 16, 1789, Ford, Fed. Ed., V, p. 253.
96. To John Hollis: Washington, Feb. 19, 1809, ME, XII, pp. 252–254.

CONCLUSION—LOOKING
BACKWARD

IF JEFFERSON speaks for America, then through Jefferson the young republic articulated its profoundest aspirations. In him the American mind attained a breadth of vision, a depth of toleration and compassion, an ideal and program giving a local habitation and a new name to the Good, the Beautiful and the True. In him they became both roads to Freedom and goals for Freedom initiating on the new continent a new culture that ever since his day continues to challenge and struggles to supersede the old.

That Jefferson had no philosophy of art, any more than he had a philosophy, in the professional sense, goes without saying. His writings do not contain a body of knowledge about art organized into a clearly constructed, formal system. His esthetic ideas express in effect a constellation of attitudes which are communicated via hundreds of observations occurring in all sorts of other connections throughout his voluminous writings. And these are heterogenous. Their formal inconsistencies cannot be counted as they change from one decade to the next in the context of the experiences of that long and active life. Yet they give one the feeling of a certain vital unity, of a continuity. Yet they are condensable into certain principles which may be considered fundamental to their author's personality. To Jefferson art was an integral part of life. He looked upon life's daily round with the eye of a humanist and an empiricist. He believed in reason, in utility, in the reality and significance of matter, in a deistic God who set this matter to his laws, and in a human liberty ordained according to these laws, which are the laws of nature and of nature's God.

I began by viewing Jefferson at the meeting point of several ways of life: the way of the frontier, the way of the tidewater aristocracy, the way of the gentleman farmer in a pre-industrial society, the way of the Parisian salons of the late Enlightenment. Jefferson, to use Dr. Kallen's expressive term, "orchestrated" these ways in terms of the sciences of man and nature stressed by the *philosophes* with their faith in reason and in matter and in man's mastery of matter through knowledge. He believed and acted on the belief that knowledge is power, and that the goal of power is the freedom of man.

These several ways, thus orchestrated, are at work also in Jefferson's reaction to the arts. His life spanned the change of taste from neo-classicism through rococo and sensibilité to romanticism. The book list that in 1771 he sent to his kinsman, Robert Skipwith, indicates not only his personal tastes and interests, but those of the typical English colonial gentleman. On the face of it, the difference from that of the contemporary English gentleman, alert and sensitive to the innovations of his times, is negligible. It is when we come to the matters which Jefferson selected out of the Greek and Roman classics and his own contemporaries—his *Literary Bible* and Commonplace books give them—that the difference becomes determinative. Then we realize that the artist in Jefferson is not to be separated from the philosopher-statesman and the revolutionary.

Reviewing the writers and thinkers from whom he drew most, we find the author of the Declaration of Independence at once an intuitionist *and* a utilitarian. We find him to have been nourished on Bacon and Newton and Locke; on Bolingbroke and Shaftesbury and Kames and on ·Hogarth and Burke; on Dugald Stewart and the French idéalogues, particularly on Cabanis and Destutt de Tracy. To these writers he owes his ideas of a moral sense and a sense of beauty, the equals and peers of the sense of sight and touch and hearing and taste and smell. Upon these ideas he formed his characteristic attitude toward the "sublime" and the "beautiful," he built his justifications for his predilections for the Palladian in architecture and the serpentine in landscape architecture, which he called gardening. Passage after passage shows the parallels between Jefferson and these writers, particularly Lord Kames. He drew upon them not only for the raw material of his ideas but also for the terms in which he expressed them.

But the use which Jefferson made of the ideas and the direction which he gave the terms of them were his own— his own and yet expressive of the wants and ways of the new people in the new land whose accepted voice he was; of the people who in their aspirations—preferred the pursuit of happiness to the acquisition of property, and in their practices were disposed to seek justification for "mere" beauty in personal and social utility. This preference is what led Jefferson to reject Burke as a tory in the field of politics and to draw upon him as a critic in the field of the arts.

It led to Jefferson's preference of the Hellenic over the Gothic and to his choice of form for American public buildings, including the school and the college. The "Oxford Collegiate Gothic" which has become a sign of so much of the academic in the national scene of our time, would to Jefferson's thought and taste be un-American.

The three writers who are central in the formation of Jefferson's esthetic are Kames, Burke, Hogarth. The works of all three were moments of the development of rococo in eighteenth-century art. All three gave to the new turn in taste the import of a principle. All three bear the marks of the heritage from Greece and Rome. Kames and Burke, as well as Jefferson, drew from Longinus whatever suited their times and occasions. All three have something to say of the connection between utility and beauty; Kames liked Ossian before Jefferson and told why. But in Jefferson's liking there was less of flight from the formality and ceremonialism of the eighteenth century and more of expression of the spontaneous naturalism of the American scene. It is in relation to this naturalism that Hogarth counts in Jefferson's thoughts on art. The "serpentine" is not only a compositional directive—it is a directive toward liberty. It goes with both the wilderness and the simple virtuous life of the American countryside which Jefferson contrasts so bitterly with that of Europe, country and city alike. Neither the gardens of England nor the salons of Paris could counterweigh his appreciation—"moral" of course, but with so obvious an esthetic component—of the abundances and liberties of America.

Hogarth, according to Dr. Kallen, the most original English painter of the age,[1] by his representations of both man and nature challenged the tradition of art whose capital was Paris and whose classical figures both revolutionaries and reactionaries employed to symbolize their antithetical ideologies. If Hogarth's representations of man were sardonic, his portrayals of nature were romantic. For both his theme and technique, particularly his technique, he had a justifying philosophy. Jefferson, who preferred Houdon and David for the imaging of men, as he preferred Palladio for the construction of buildings, felt with Hogarth regarding the shaping of landscape. In "gardening" the line of beauty is the serpentine line; the very walls of his gardens shall be serpentine.

When it came to painting, which is Hogarth's art, medium and method did not seem to have concerned Jefferson. That he preferred David seems to be due neither to David's workmanship nor his composition, but to what the painter said in his composition. And at the time Jefferson expressed his preference David was saying that which Jefferson himself had said, that which Condorcet was saying, that which Lafayette was saying. The meaning of a painter's work lay in the role it might play in promoting the freedom and happiness of man. It is this service which is envisaged in Jefferson's *Bill for a System of Public Education*, which included provision for a public art gallery and a Department of Fine Arts; it is this service which is Jefferson's prime interest throughout his life. Aside from commemorating the founders of the Republic and the great historic events in which they played the leading part; aside from ever keeping before the descendants of these worthies the ideals of republican virtue for which they had fought, paintings and sculptures could provide an innocent and useful commodity for the rich to buy and so save them from squandering their moneys on coarse and vulgar pleasures. Consistently with this attitude, Jefferson himself sat often for portraits as a matter of public duty; he insisted on a realistic and life-size image of Washington (though a generation later he found "our boots and regimentals have a very puny effect"); he befriended and protected artists, even such as became unfriendly, like Trumbull; he concerned himself patiently with the minutiae of engraving, the character of seals, and the wide distribution of prints of significant paintings, such as Trumbull's "Signing of the Declaration of Independence."

Jefferson seems to have responded to sculpture more readily and more intensely than to painting; the monumental qualities of the art endeared it strongly to him. Houdon meant more to him than David. His taste, not always above reproach, seems to have resulted from the fact that the tasks of his world were not those of a leisure class free to establish nice discriminations between this painter and that, or between this sculptor and that, but to think beauty in terms of use. In a new and undeveloped economy, an active interest in any kind of painting, sculpture, architecture or music was in itself a positive step forward. Where a Grimm or a Diderot, with the same general philosophy, could advise the gentlemen connoisseurs, a Jefferson had to make art as such meaningful to his countrymen. His judgment of sculpture, hence, is of a piece with his judgment of painting; it is a judgment of "social significance." And this is why his approach to these arts was literary and sociological. It was from that side, rather than the collector's, that he dealt with the casting of coins and medals, with modelling in wax. It was from that side that his appreciation came of the sculpture and painting of the American Indian.

The fissions of interest and possibilities of conflict inherent in the other arts disappear when Jefferson deals with architecture. Here he is a workman, an innovator and an expert instead of an interested bystander. In his letter of advice to Shippen and Rutledge he says that architecture is "among the most important arts." The art had been, until the close of the Revolution, a gentleman's avocation rather than a profession. Jefferson's concern with it, which gave it a powerful impulsion toward professional practice, got its direction from the study of Palladio, a study which contributed perhaps as much as his democratism and ethical vision to his aversion from "the Gothic." He was early condemnatory (see the *Notes on Virginia*) of the state of the art of building in the colonies; he urged the use of stone instead of wood as a material; he insisted on a style for public buildings which should express the democratic spirit and serve the ways of democracy. That the style was neoclassic was in keeping with his feeling for David and Houdon in the other arts. His esthetic of architecture, though not his taste, owed a good deal to Kames. But, functionalist as he was, he seems entirely to have disregarded the protest which Hogarth made against the indiscriminate use of the Palladian style precisely on the grounds of that style's functional failures. Authorities are far from agreed on the functional adequacy of Monticello—Jefferson's concern with function however is evinced, if not in the ground-plan, in the number and variety of the gadgets which he incorporated in this house he built on a mountain top which did become a model for the great houses of Virginia. Jefferson seems to have liked French architecture better than English. His interest in building ranged from garden walls to cities. His conception of what is right determined the national style and held the various architects of the Capitol to its line. Hamlin is on firm ground when he declares that Jefferson is largely responsible for the birth of American architecture. His last public building project—the University of Virginia, not uninfluenced by Kames' ideas—did not, many think unfortunately, exercise a corresponding influence upon academic construction. There the Gothic he deplored came to prevail.

Nor is there any greater continuity with his conceptions of the garden as the natural setting of the house. In the academic community Le Nôtre's straight line is still the shortest distance between two points. The "winding and wavy line" which Kames appreciated as much as Hogarth, might be nature's line and more beautiful, but it is not functional for students hastening between classrooms or for citizens finding their way in city or country. Here Jefferson sees perhaps with the gentleman's eye as well as the pioneer's. Consequently he prefers the English garden to the Continental, and at Monticello and in Charlottesville he achieves "the orchestration of the Palladian building with the Hogarthian landscape."

Music is another of the arts which, like architecture and gardening, Jefferson practiced at least as much as he contemplated. A violinist all his life, sensitive to the quality and make of his instrument, a player of quartets, concerned with orchestras and bands, even his love life was conditioned upon a musical interest, both Martha Skelton and Maria Cosway being musicians. The fullness of his musical experience came with his ambassadorship to Paris. He paid considerable attention to the musical education of his daughters. Paris revealed to him new glories of the art heard at the *Concerts Spirituels* and at the *Opera*, and he assisted at the quarrel between opera bouffe and the classic opera, with its musical, social, historical and political overtones. It was in Paris that he tried to aid in Hopkinson's efforts to improve the harpsichord, that he became intrigued by the possibilities of the newly invented piano-forte, and by such technical innovations as the metronome and the foot-bass. He made many friends among musicians and his concern for them was of a piece with his concern for painters, sculptors and architects. His attempts to encourage Hopkinson and Hawkins set a precedent for intelligent state-patronage of the arts. Jefferson was among the first, if not the first, to call attention to the musical talents of the Negroes. Yet, as Dr. Kallen pointed out, when it comes to any indication of his preferences among composers and compositions, there is not a word. Jefferson has plenty to say about instruments and techniques—nothing—so far at least —about the music they produce.

The one art which is peculiarly Jefferson's own is of course the art of words. Jefferson was a "wordman" par excellence; one of the greatest of letter writers in a great age of letter writing, and by general acclamation the scribe of the American Revolution. The rhetorical art was a function of all his passions, interests and activities. In a sense it provided the ground-plan of his classical education; it enters into his practice of writing legal briefs and legislative bills as well as the Declaration of Independence. He held it to be an art needful to the citizens of a free republic—

and he gave it a predominant place in the curriculum that he planned for the University of his Virginia. His emphasis fell on logical order, on simplicity, and on brevity. He recognized the power of the spoken and written word, and he demanded that it should be freely spoken and written, since this freedom is the safeguard against error as well as against tyranny. Freedom, moreover, was to Jefferson the life of speech. Language grows and changes; usage shifts, and as English altered from Chaucer to Shakespeare so it could well alter from British to American. For the sake of this alteration he wanted to go back to the Anglo-Saxon springs of English speech, retaining its ancient music in its new locutions and constructions.

Withal, Jefferson never forgot that language was first and last a vehicle of communication. It is this function that he insisted on alike for lawyers' briefs, for students' debates and for the advice of those who sought his guidance in their studies. That letter of his to Bernard Moore points up all that he thought and said on this subject.

Of course, they are ideas which suffuse and guide his ways as litterateur and critic. The beginnings are clear in his Literary Commonplace Book. The writers whom Jefferson quoted, the character and number of the quotations which he copied out in it, indicate both his emotional tone and his intellectual predilections. His admiration of Homer, his dislike of Plato, his savoring of certain phases of Cicero, and almost all of Epicurus, show us a man by no means unaware of the harsh realities of existence, yet ready to deal with them bravely and hopefully. In this context his philological studies in the ancient tongue, his readiness to coin phrases that shall convey the strength and feeling of thought; his hospitality to new words; his low opinion of Dr. Samuel Johnson; acquire a moral as well as a literary pertinence. Jefferson's views of the writer's medium and techniques are those of the social revolutionary to whom language must be a viable, a dynamic instrument for furthering the happiness and freedom of man. The mind of such a man, Prof. Chinard to the contrary notwithstanding, was truly "a poetical mind" in the classical, rather than the modern sense of "poetical"; i.e., it was a mind that, like the mind of Horace or of Cicero, felt form and content, pleasure and profit, indissolubly associated. Although Jefferson's "criticism" here rested on Kames and the classics, he gave it a personal turn by his own studies of English prosody, with their insights into the creative techniques, and their testimonies of his poetic preferences. Shakespeare and Homer were Jefferson's favorites! He chooses blank verse as against rhyme, and like every gentleman, he tries his hand at verse—and like most gentlemen, unsuccessfully. But his prose is rhythmic, and could be reprinted as free-verse. Mr. Padover has so recast the Declaration of Independence [2] with effects that give one to think. Jefferson's "Dialogue between my Heart and my Head" is a true elegiac prose-poem, and his pen portraits of his contemporaries could not be bettered by Edgar Lee Masters. Jefferson's concern that free letters should prosper extended to such practical undertakings as his encouragement of the poet Barlow, his attempt to rescind the tariff on books, the passage of copyright laws, the *Bill for Establishing a Public Library*, the installation of his own collection—the finest in the country—as the Library of Congress, and the encouragement and patronage of men of letters.

There have been many Americans whose interest in the arts and sciences matched Jefferson's; there have been those whose political eminence matched his. But I know of no other President of the United States who has been the recognized initiator and center of so many cultural and educational activities. It is characteristic that Jefferson considered his election as President of the American Philosophical Society "the most flattering incident of my life, and that to which I am the most sensible. I feel . . . an ardent desire to see knowledge so disseminated through the mass of mankind, that it may at length reach even the extremes of society, beggars and kings." [3] To Delaplaine, who had asked him for data on his membership in learned societies, he wrote: "I could not readily make a statement of the literary societies of which I am a member, they are many and would be long to enumerate and would savor too much of vanity and pedantry. Would it not be better to say merely that I am a member of many literary societies in Europe and America?" [4]

Spokesman for the vitality and courage that informed the Revolutionaries of his country and age, Jefferson desired to make man's life on this earth as abundant as possible—and from the very beginning saw clearly the role that art could play in this abundance, which he believed the right of the people in all things spiritual and material. During his whole life he voiced their needs and strove for their satisfaction, and his utterances and strivings received a form and strength as effective as they were natural. In the world of the arts, of esthetic, it was with Jefferson as in the world of politics. He had said of the Declaration of Independence it "was intended as an expression of the American mind" and so was all else he did—an initiation of something distinctively and originally American. Art, science, education and statecraft were to him all alike weapons in the struggle for the freedom and happiness of humanity. Jefferson's faith in the innate goodness and ultimate perfectibility of man never wavered. With the vision of an artist and the faith of a lover of people, he saw freedom as the first step towards happiness—and art as one of the first steps towards freedom.

CHAPTER TWELVE

1. H. M. Kallen: *Art and Freedom*, I, p. 171, New York (1942).

2. S. K. Padover: "Jefferson's Prose Poem: The Declaration of Independence," *American Mercury*, February, 1942.

3. To American Philosophical Society: Monticello, Jan. 28, 1797, printed in the TRANSACTIONS of American Philosophical Society, 4: xii–xiii, (1799).

4. To Joseph Delaplaine: Monticello, April 12, 1817, ME, XIX, p. 247.

A P P E N D I X   I.

This book list, dated August 3, 1771, contains one hundred and forty items recommended by Jefferson for Robert Skipwith's library and accompanied a letter, written by him to Skipwith on the same date. The original manuscript is in the possession of the Massachusetts Historical Society. Jefferson noted the cost of each book on the same line as its title and author. With his usual precision, he made a total at the conclusion of each of the eight headings under which the books are grouped. The final total on the second page is not distinct because a fragment of the paper is missing, although it appears to be 106. However, in the upper left hand column of the first page of the manuscript there is clearly written in Jefferson's handwriting:

> "Thos. Waller. Fleet Street. London
> for elegant gilt bindings marbled on edge. 20 pr. Cen.
> for (not clear)—garden's marbled bindings. 50. p. cent.
> in plain bindings they will cost £ 106.15"

The list is as follows:

> "Fine arts
> Observations on gardening. published by Payne
> Webb's essay on painting
> Pope's Homer's Iliad & Odyssey
> Dryden's Virgil
> Milton's works. 2 v. Donaldson Edinburgh 1762
> Hodle's Tasso
> Ossian. with Blair's criticisms. 2 v.

268

Telemachus by Dodsley
Capell's Shakespear
Dryden's plays. 6 v.
Addison's plays
Otway's plays. 3 v.
Rowe's works. 2 v.
Thompson's work. 2 v.
Young's works. 4 v.
Home's plays.
Mollet's works. 3 v.
Mason's poetical works.
Terence
Moliere. Engl.
Farquhar's plays. 2 v.
Vanbrugh's plays. 2 v.
Steele's plays.
Congreve's works. 3 v.
Garric's dramatic works. 2 v.
Foote's dramatic works. 2 v.
Rousseau's Eloisa. Eng. 4 v.
———— Emilius & Sophia. 4 v.
Marmontel's moral tales. 3 v.
Gil Blas by Smollet.
Don Quixote by Smollett. 4 v.
David Simple. 2 v.
Roderic Random. 2 v.
Peregrine Pickle. 4 v.   } these are
Launcelot Greaves   } by Smollett
Adventures of a guinea. 2 v. }
Pamela. 4 v.
Clarissa. 8 v.   } these are
Grandison. 7 v.   } by Richardson
Fool of quality. 3 v.   }
Fielding's works. 12 v.
Constantia. 2 v.   }
Solyman & Almena.   } by Langhorne

Belle Assemblea. 4 v.
Vicar of Wakefield. by Dr. Goldsmith. 2 v.
Sidney Bidulph. 5 v.

Lady Julia Mandeville. 2 v.
Almoran & Hamet. 2 v.
Tristram Shandy.
Sentimental journey. 2 v.
Chaucer.
Spencer. by Hughes. 6 v.
Waller's poems.
Dodsley's collection of poems. 6 v.
Pearch's collection of poems. 4 v.
Gray's works.
Ogilvie's poems.
Prior's poems. 2 v.
Gay's works.
Shenstone's works. 2 v.
Dryden's works. 4 v.
(b) Pope's works. by Warburton
(c) Swift's works. 21. v.
———— literary correspondence. 3 v.
Spectator. 9 v.—Tatler. 5 v.
Guardian. 2 v.—Freeholder.
(b) Churchill's poems. 4 v.
Ld. Lyttleton's Persian letters.
(c) Hudibrass
(a) "Percy's reliques of ant. Eng. poetry. 3 v.
Hau Kiou Chouan. by Percy. 4 v.
———— Chinese Pieces. 2 v. ————'s Runic poems.

Criticism on the fine arts

L. Kaim's elem. of critic. 2 v.
Burke on the sublime & beautiful.
Hogarth's analysis of beauty.
Reid on the human mind.
Smith's moral sentiments.
Johnson's dictionary. 2 v.
Capell's (not clear) -usions

Politics. Trade.

Montesquieu's spirit of laws. 2 v.
Locke on government.

TOBACCO CAPITAL IN SMALL ROTUNDA. NEAR SUPREME COURT.
SCALE ⅓ FULL SIZE . HEIGTH OF COLUMN 12 FEET.

Fig. No. 19.
TOBACCO CAPITAL — LATROBE. THE CAPITOL
OF THE UNITED STATES

Fig. No. 20.
TOBACCO CAPITAL AND COLUMN. THE CAPITOL OF THE
UNITED STATES

Sidney on government.
Marmontel's Belisarius
Ld. Bolingbroke's political works 5 v.
Montesq's rise & fall.
Shiert's political occonomy. 2 v.
Petty's political arithmetic.

Religion.

1. Locke's conduct of the mind.
9. Kaim's natural religion.
4. Antonius. by Collins.
3. Epictetus. by Mrs. Carter. 2 v.
5. Cicero's offices. by Guthrie.
7. Ld. Bolingbr. phil. works. 5 v.
8. Hume's (not clear). 4 v.
10. Philosophical (not clear) of nature.
11. Oeconomy of human life.
12. Sterne's sermons. 7 v.
13. Sherlock on death.
14. ———— on a future state.
6. Cicero's Tusculan questions.
2. Xenophon's memoirs of Socrates. by **Fielding.**

Law.

Ld. Kaim's principles of equity. last **edn.**
Blackstone's commentaries. 4 v.
Cunningham's Law. dict. 2 v.

Ancient history

Bible.
Rollin's ant. history. 13 v.
Stanyan's Graecian hist. 2 v.
Livy.
Gordon's Sallust
———— Tacitus.
Bladen's Caesar.
Josephus.
Vertot's revotns. of Rome. Eng.
Langhorne's Plutarch's lives. 6 v.

Jeffrey's hist. & chron. chart.
Bayle's dict.

Modern hist.
Robertson's history of Chas. V. 3 v.
Farnsworth's Davila.
Hume's hist. of Eng. 8 v.
Clarend's hist. revoltn. 6 v.
Robertson's hist. Scotld. 2 v.
Keith's hist. of Virga.
Stith's hist. of Virga.

Mathematics, Nat. phil. & c.
Nature displayed. 7 v.
Franklyn on electricity.
Home's princip. of Agric. & vegetn.
Tull's horse-hoeing husbandry
Duhamel's husbandry
Miller's gardener's dict. fol.
Buffon's nat. hist.
a compendium of Phys. & surgery
Addison's travels
Anson's voice.
Thompson's travels. 2 v.
Lady W. Montague's letters. 4 v.

Miscellania.
4. Locke educn.
5. Burn's dict. arts. (not clear), 2 v.
3. Voltaire's works.
1. Ld. Lyttleton's dialogues of th dead.
2. Fenelon's dialogues of the dead.

BIBLIOGRAPHY

The following books and articles have been consulted in the preparation of this work:

Abbott, Wilbur C.: *New York in the American Revolution*, New York (1929).

Adams, James Truslow, Ed.: *Album of American History*, Colonial Period, New York (1944).

Adams, Randolph G.: *Political Ideas of the American Revolution*, New York (1939).

Addison, Joseph: *The Spectator*, 6 Vols. New York (1854) Vol. 5.

Allen, Robert J.: *The Clubs of Augustan London*, Cambridge (1933).

Allen, B. Sprague: *Tides of English Taste (1619–1800)*, 2 Vol. Cambridge (1937).

Altick, Richard: "Humorous Hogarth—his Literary Associations," *Sewanee Review*, (April 1939) Sewanee 1939, pp. 255–267.

Beard, Charles Austin: *Economic Origins of Jeffersonian Democracy*, New York (1915).

Beard, Charles A. and Mary R.: *The American Spirit*, New York (1942).

Becker, Carl: *The Declaration of Independence, A Study in the History of Political Ideas*, 2nd Edn. New York (1942).

Betts, Edwin Morris: *Thomas Jefferson's Garden Book*, Philadelphia (1944).

Blum, André: *Hogarth*, Paris (1931).

Binyon, Lawrence: "Hogarth" *Catalogue of Drawings by British Artists in the British Museum*, London (1900).

Bosanquet, Bernard: *History of Aesthetic*, London (1910).

Boswell, James: *Life of Johnson,* Oxford (1934).

Bowen, Marjorie (pseud.): *William Hogarth, The Cockney's Mirror*, London (1935).

Bowers, Claude G.: "Architect of the All-American System," *The Virginia Quarterly Review*, Vol. 19 (Spring 1943) pp. 178–188.
——— "Jefferson and the Freedom of the Human Spirit," *Ethics*, LIII, (July 1943) pp. 237–245.
——— *Jefferson and Hamilton*, Boston (1925).
——— *Jefferson in Power*, Boston (1936).
——— *The Young Jefferson*, Boston (1945).
Boyd, Julian P.: *The Declaration of Independence*, Princeton (1945).
Bridenbaugh, Carl and Jessica: *Rebels and Gentlemen*, New York (1942).
Brooks, Van Wyck: *The Flowering of New England*, New York (1938).
Brown, Ralph H.: *Mirror for Americans*, New York (1943).
Bullock, Helen Duprey: "Program Notes for Founder's Concert at University of Virginia, April 13, 1943."
Burke, Edmund: *Essay on the Sublime and Beautiful*, Oxford (1925).
Burroughs, Alan: *Limners and Likenesses, Three Centuries of American Painting,* Cambridge, Mass. (1936).
Byrd, William: *Secret Diary of William Byrd of Westover 1709–1712*, Richmond (1941).
——— *Another Secret Diary of William Byrd of Westover 1739–1741*, Richmond (1942).

Cambridge History of American Literature, 4 Vols., Cambridge, Eng. (1927).
Channing, Edward: *The Jeffersonian System* (The American Nation Series, Vol. 12) New York (1906).
Chastellux, Francois Jean, Marquis de: *Travels in North America in 1780–1782*, New York (1827).
Clapiers, Luc de, Marquis of Vauvenargues: *Reflections and Maxims,* London (1940) trans. by F. C. Stevens.
The China Trade and its Influence: published by the Metropolitan Museum of Art (1941).
Chinard, Gilbert: "An American Philosopher in the World of Nations" *The Virginia Quarterly Review*, Vol. 19 (Spring 1943) pp. 189–203.
——— "Jefferson Among the Philosophers," *Ethics*, Vol. LIII, No. 4, (July 1943) pp. 255–268.

—— "Jefferson and the American Philosophical Society" *Proceedings of the American Philosophical Society*, Vol. 87, No. 3, (July 1943) pp. 263–276.

—— *Jefferson et Les Idéologues*, Baltimore (1925).

—— *Honest John Adams*, Boston (1933).

—— *Houdon in America*, Washington (1930).

—— *Sainte-Beuve, Thomas Jefferson et Tocqueville,* Washington (1943).

—— *The Literary Bible of Thomas Jefferson*, Baltimore (1928).

—— *Thomas Jefferson, Apostle of Americanism*, Boston (1939).

—— "Thomas Jefferson as a Classical Scholar" *The American Scholar*, I, pp. 133–143 (1932).

—— "Jefferson's Influence Abroad" *Mississippi Historical Review*, Vol. XXX, No. 2, (Sept. 1943) pp. 171–186.

Crévecoeur, Hector St. John: *Letters from an American Farmer*, London (1912).

Curti, Merle: *The Growth of American Thought*, New York (1943).

Dennis, John: *The Age of Pope*, London (1896) ed. by Prof. Hales.

Dewey, John: *Jefferson*, New York (1940).

Dictionary of American Biography: 21 Vols. Edited by Allen Johnson and Associates, New York (1935).

Dictionary of National Biography: 25 Vols. Edited by Sir Leslie Stephen and Sir Sidney Lee, Oxford (1938).

Diderot, Denis: *Oeuvres*, Vol. X, (1876).

Dobson, Austin: *William Hogarth*, London (1902).

Dorfman, Joseph: "Fulton and the Economics of Invention" *Political Science Quarterly*, LIX (December 1944) pp. 578–593.

—— "The Economic Philosophy of Thomas Jefferson" *Political Science Quarterly*, LV (March 1940) pp. 98–121.

—— "Joel Barlow: Trafficker in Trade and Letters" *Political Science Quarterly*, LIX (March 1944) pp. 83–100.

Dos Passos, John: *The Ground We Stand On*, New York (1941).

Downs, Joseph: *The Chinese Style in Europe*, New York (1941).

—— "The Greek Revival in the United States" New York (1943).

Dunlap, William: *History of the Rise and Progress of the Arts of Design in the United States*, 2 Vols. New York (1834).

Elliott, Jonathan: *Jefferson's Library Catalogue of 1815*, Washington (1815).

Elson, L. C.: *The History of American Music*, New York (1925).

Foley, John P.: *The Jeffersonian Cyclopedia*, Washington (1900).

Ford, Paul Leicester: *The Works of Thomas Jefferson*, 12 Vols. in Federal Edition, New York (1904).

Frary, I. T.: *They Built the Capitol*, Richmond (1940).

—— *Thomas Jefferson, Architect and Builder*, Richmond (1939).

Hamlin, Talbot: *Greek Revival Architecture in America*, New York (1944).

Hartley, Lodwick: *This Is Lorence*, Chapel Hill (1943).

Hawkins, Richmond L.: *Madame de Staël and the United States*, Cambridge (1930).

Haworth, P. A.: "Thomas Jefferson—Poet," *The Bookman*, Vol. XXXI, (1910) pp. 647–650.

Hazlitt, William: "Lectures on the English comic writers" (on the works of Hogarth) Philadelphia (1819).

Hogarth, William: *The Analysis of Beauty*, London (1753).

—— *The Analysis of Beauty*, Pittsfield (1909).

Hirst, Francis W.: *Life and Letters of Thomas Jefferson*, New York (1926).

Home, Henry, Lord Kames: *Elements of Criticism*, 5th Edition Edinburgh (1774).

—— *Elements of Criticism*, New York (1855, 1883).

Honeywell, Roy J.: *The Educational Work of Thomas Jefferson*, Cambridge (1931).

Howard, J. T.: *Our American Music; Three hundred years of it*, New York, 1939.

Howard, Leon: *The Connecticut Wits*, Chicago (1943).

Hutcheson, Francis: *An Inquiry into the Original of Our Ideas of Beauty and Virtue*, London (1753).

Jaffe, Bernard: *Men of Science*, New York (1944).

Jebb, Sir Richard: *The Attic Orators from Antiphon to Isaeos*, 2 Vols. London (1876).

Johnson, Gerald W.: *American Heroes and Hero Worship*, New York (1943).

—— "The Changelings" *The Virginia Quarterly Review*, Vol. 19 (Spring 1943) pp. 236–255.

Jones, Howard Mumford: *America and French Culture*, Chapel Hill (1927).

—— *Ideas in America*, Cambridge, (1944).

Kallen, Horace M.: *Art and Freedom*, 2 Vols. New York (1942).

—— "Jefferson's Garden Wall" *The American Bookman*, Vol. I, No. 1. (Winter 1944) pp. 78–82.

—— "The Arts and Thomas Jefferson," *Ethics*, Vol. LIII, No. 4 (July 1943) pp. 269–283.

Kames, Lord, see Home, Henry, above.

Kimball, Fiske: "Beginnings of Sculpture in Colonial America" *Art and Archaeology*, VIII (1919).

—— *Domestic Architecture of the American Colonies and of the Early Republic*, New York (1922).

—— "Jefferson and the Arts," Proceedings of the American Philosophical Society, Vol. 87, No. 3 (July 1943) pp. 238–246.

—— *Thomas Jefferson, Architect*, Cambridge (1916).

Kimball, Marie: "Jefferson's Four Freedoms" *The Virginia Quarterly Review*, Vol. 19, (Spring 1943) pp. 204–221.

—— *The Furnishings of Monticello*, Philadelphia (1940).

—— *The Road to Glory*, New York (1943).

—— *Thomas Jefferson's Cook Book*, Richmond (1941).

—— "Unpublished Correspondence of Mme de Staël with Thomas Jefferson" *North American Review*, Vol. 208 (July 1918) pp. 63–71.

Kirkwood, Kenneth P.: "Harunobu and Hogarth," *Cultural Nippon*, Vol. VI, No. 3 (November 1938) pp. 41–46.

Koch, Adrienne: *The Philosophy of Thomas Jefferson*, New York (1943).

Koch, Adrienne and Peden, William: *The Life and Selected Writings of Thomas Jefferson*, New York (1944).

Krout, John Allen and Fox, Dixon Ryan: *The Completion of Independence*, New York (1944).

Krutch, Joseph Wood: *Samuel Johnson*, New York (1944).

La Follette, Suzanne: *Art in America*, New York (1929).

Lambeth, William A.: *Thomas Jefferson as an Architect and Landscape Gardener*, Boston (1913).

Locke, John: *Of Civil Government, Two Treatises*, London (1924).
———— *An Essay Concerning Human Understanding*, Oxford (1934).
Longinus On the Sublime: translated by A. O. Prickard, Oxford (1930).
Lipscomb, Andrew A. and Bergh, Albert: *The Writings of Thomas Jefferson*, 20 Vols. Washington (1904).
———— Issued under the auspices of the Jefferson Memorial Association of the United States. Washington, D. C. (1903). This is referred to in my footnotes as the "Memorial Edition."

Mabee, Carleton: *American Leonardo, A Life of Samuel F. B. Morse*, New York (1943).
Malone, Dumas: "Mr. Jefferson to Mr. Roosevelt" *The Virginia Quarterly Review*, Vol. 19 (Spring 1943) pp. 161–177.
Manchée, William: "Hogarth and his friendship with the Huguenots" *Huguenot Society Proceedings*, Vol. 12, pp. 132–140.
Mayo, Bernard: "A Peppercorn for Mr. Jefferson" *The Virginia Quarterly Review*, Vol. 19 (Spring 1943) pp. 222–235.
———— *Jefferson Himself*, Boston (1942).
———— *Thomas Jefferson and his unknown brother Randolph*, Charlottesville (1942).
Mencken, Henry L.: *The American Language, Fourth Edition*, New York (1945).
———— *The American Language, Supplement I*, New York (1945).
Miller, John C.: *Origins of American Revolution*, Boston (1943).
Minnigerode, Meade: *Jefferson, Friend of France, 1793*, New York (1928).
Morley, John: *Diderot and the Encyclopaedists*, 2 Vols. London (1891).
———— *Burke*, London (1936).
———— *Voltaire*, London (1886).
Morris, Roland: "Jefferson as a Lawyer," *Proceedings of the American Philosophical Society*, Vol. 87, No. 3 (July 1943) pp. 211–215.
Mossner, Ernest Campbell: *The Forgotten Hume, Le bon David*, New York (1943).
Morison, Samuel Eliot and Commager, Henry Steele: *Growth of the American Republic*, 2 Vols. (1939).
Mott, Frank L.: *Jefferson and the Press*, Baton Rouge (1943).

Mumford, Lewis: *Sticks and Stones*, New York (1924).
—— *Technics and Civilization*, New York (1934).

Nettleton, George Henry: *English Drama of the Restoration and Eighteenth Century, 1642–1780*, New York (1914).
Nicolay, John G.: "Thomas Jefferson's Home," *The Century Magazine*, XXXIV (1887) pp. 643–653.
Nock, Albert Jay: *Jefferson*, New York (1926).

Ossian: translated by James Macpherson, Edinburgh (1886).
Otis, William Bradley: *American Verse, 1625–1807, A History*, New York (1909).

Gardner, Albert Ten Eyck: *Yankee Stonecutters*, New York (1945).
Gilbert, Katherine and Kuhn, Helmut: *A History of Esthetics*, New York (1939).
Gosse, Edmund: *A History of Eighteenth Century Literature, 1660–1780*, London (1906).
Greene, Evarts Boutell: *The Revolutionary Generation*, New York (1943).

Padover, S. K.: "Jefferson's Prose-Poem: The Declaration of Independence," *The American Mercury,* February (1942).
—— *The Complete Jefferson*, New York (1943).
—— *Jefferson*, New York (1942).
—— *Democracy by Thomas Jefferson*, edited by Saul K. Padover, New York (1939).
Page, Elizabeth: *The Tree of Liberty*, New York (1939).
Parker, Harold Talbot: *The Cult of Antiquity and the French Revolutionaries*, Chicago (1937).
Parrington, Vernon: *Main Currents in American Thought*, 3 Vols. New York (1930).
Parton, James: *Life of Jefferson*, Boston (1894).
Peebles, John Kevan: "Thomas Jefferson, Architect," *American Architect and Building News*, XLVII (1895) pp. 28–35.
Pope, Alexander: *Essay on Criticism*, London (1917).
—— *Essay on Man*, London (1913).

Randall, Henry S.: *Life of Thomas Jefferson*, 3 Vols. New York (1858).

Randolph, Sarah N.: *The Domestic Life of Thomas Jefferson*, New York (1871).

Riley, Woodbridge: *American Thought*, New York (1915).

Rourke, Constance: *Roots of American Culture*, New York (1942).

Read, Stanley E.: "Some Observations on Hogarth's Analysis of Beauty: A bibliographical study," *Huntington Library Quarterly*, Vol. 5 (San Marino 1942) pp. 360–373.

Sallust: *The War with Catiline; Jugurtha,* translated by J. C. Rolfe, London (1931).

Shaftesbury, Anthony Ashley Cooper, 3d Earl of: *Characteristics of Man, Manners, Opinions, Times*, 3 Vols. London (1900).

Schapiro, J. Salwyn: *Condorcet and the Rise of Liberalism*, New York (1934).

Scott, James Brown: *James Madison's Notes of the Debates in the Federal Convention of 1787* and their Relation to a more Perfect Society of Nations, New York (1918).

Shepperson, Archibald: *John Paradise and Lucy Ludwell*, Richmond (1942).

Shenstone, William: *The Works in Verse and Prose*, 2 Vols. 2nd Edition, London (1775).

Sonneck, Oscar: *Concert-life in America,* 1731–1800, Leipzig (1907).

———— *Suum Cuique: Essays in Music*, New York (1916).

Stephen, Leslie: *English Thought in the 18th Century*, 2 Vols. 3d Edition, New York (1902).

Stockton, Frank R.: "The Later Years of Monticello," *The Century*, Vol. 34 (1887) pp. 654–658.

Taft, Lorado: *The History of American Sculpture*, New York (1930).

Tooke, John Horne: *Diversions of Purley*, Philadelphia (1806). *Ibid.:* London (1860).

Trevelyan, G. O.: *The American Revolution,* 6 Vols., New York (1909).

Trumbull, John: *Autobiography, Reminiscences and Letters*, New York (1841).

Trusler, Rev. Dr.: *Hogarth Moralized*, London (1831).

Tyler, Moses Coit: *The Literary History of the American Revolution*, 2 Vols. New York (1941).

Tytler, Alexander Fraser, Lord Woodhouselee: *Memoirs of the Life and Writings of the Hon. Henry Home of Kames*, 2 Vols. (1807).

Walpole, Horace: *Anecdotes of Painting in England*, Vol. 5, New Haven (1937).

Washington, H. A., Editor: *The Writings of Jefferson*, 9 Vols. (1853).

Weitenkamp, Frank: "A bibliography of William Hogarth," Harvard University Library. Bibliographical Contributions. Vol. 2, No. 3. Cambridge (1890).

Wendell, Barrett: *A Literary History of America*, Boston (1900).

White, Andrew D.: *A History of Warfare of Science with Theology in Christendom*, 2 Vols. New York (1936).

Wilstach, Paul: *Jefferson and Monticello*, New York (1928 and 1938).

Woodward, W. E.: *The Way Our People Lived*, New York (1944).

Wright, Louis B.: "Jefferson and the Classics" *Proceedings of the American Philosophical Society*, Vol. 87, No. 3 (July 1943) pp. 223–234.

Zunder, Theodore Albert: *The Early Days of Joel Barlow, A Connecticut Wit*, New Haven (1934).

INDEX